D0225567

Universitas
BIBLIOTHECA
Ottaviensis

THREE
PHILOSOPHERS

MARIE-ANNE-PIERRETTE AND ANTOINE-LAURENT LAVOISIER.
From the portrait by David, 1788.

Reproduced by permission of the Rockefeller Institute, New York.

[Frontispiece.

THREE PHILOSOPHERS

(LAVOISIER, PRIESTLEY AND CAVENDISH)

BY

W. R. AYKROYD

GREENWOOD PRESS, PUBLISHERS
WESTPORT, CONNECTICUT

Universitas
BIBLIOTHECA
Ottaviensis

Originally published in 1935
by William Heinemann, London

First Greenwood Reprinting 1970

SBN 8371-2890-0

PRINTED IN UNITED STATES OF AMERICA

TO

SIR CHARLES J. MARTIN, F.R.S.

PREFATORY NOTE

THE principal character in this book, Antoine-Laurent Lavoisier, contributed largely to physics and chemistry ; he may also be regarded as the virtual founder of the science of nutrition, in the sense that he originated methods of enquiry in this field which were the basis of almost all later developments. There exists to-day a large and growing number of men and women professionally concerned with the science of nutrition in its various branches ; many of these, I felt, would be glad to learn more of a man who did remarkable pioneer work in their subject— a man who accomplished a great deal in a short lifetime and died tragically. Since it is not possible to discuss the achievements of any scientific worker without reference to those of his contemporaries whose work dovetails with his own, I have included two other major characters—Joseph Priestley and Henry Cavendish. The life-histories of these two men are comparatively familiar to the English reader, so that the main excuse for this book must be that it portrays an eighteenth-century French scientist who has been given relatively little attention by English writers.

I feel it necessary to apologise for having attempted to write a biography with an eighteenth-century background without possessing any special knowledge of the period. In extenuation of an amateur attempt to sketch an interesting and dramatic period of history, I can only plead an enthusiastic admiration for a figure who has never received justice from the professional historian.

CONTENTS

LIST OF ILLUSTRATIONS

THREE PHILOSOPHERS

CHAPTER I

THE YOUNG LAVOISIER

THE only son of Jean-Antoine and Jeanne Lavoisier was born in Paris on August 26th, 1743, in the 35th year of the reign of Louis XV. At his baptism, which took place on the same day, the infant was given the names Antoine and Laurent. In the year of Antoine-Laurent's birth Samuel Johnson attained the age of thirty-four, Voltaire the age of fifty, while Rousseau, the future prophet of the Revolution, was just past his thirtieth year.

Antoine-Laurent's father and mother both came of solid middle-class families, the latter's being the wealthier of the two. An appreciation of the value of money was in the Lavoisier blood, and Jean-Antoine had taken care to marry the daughter of a lawyer in very comfortable circumstances. The family originated in Villers-Cotterets, a town about fifty miles north-east of Paris in the Department of the Aisne, not far from Soissons. It could trace its descent back to a certain Antoine Lavoisier, who was a groom in the King's stables at the beginning of the seventeenth century. The groom's son attained a position in the postal service, and step by step, during the next hundred years, the family raised its social status. Antoine-Laurent's grandfather, a minor legal official in Villers-Cotterets, had been able to send his son to the Faculté de Droit in Paris, where the latter had so far succeeded in his profession as to be appointed, in 1741, *avocat au parlement*—one of the law officers of the Crown.

Jeanne Lavoisier, who gave birth to a daughter two years later, did not survive long to enjoy her placid bourgeois

existence. When her eldest child was five years old she
died. Lavoisier *père* thereupon sold his house and went
to live with his mother-in-law, Madame Punctis, whose
second daughter, Constance, devoted herself entirely to the
upbringing of the children. When the girl died at an early
age Aunt Constance's lavish affections were left with a
single object. Though well dowered, she never married ;
her purpose in life was to mother Antoine, and when she
died she left him her entire fortune. She was a voluble,
fussy, kindly creature, whose affection Antoine returned
with amusement and tolerance. Between father and son
there existed a close relation of familiarity and friendship. Jean Lavoisier, a man of ability, who had carved
out a considerable career for himself, had great ambitions
for his lively and intelligent son. If, as some hold, severe
parental discipline, or the struggle for existence in a large
family, provide the best training for after-life, Antoine was
handicapped from the start. Nothing was too good for the
boy, the darling of a household in which everything he
wanted was immediately supplied.

A legacy of 30,000 francs which the Lavoisiers received
from the father of Madame Punctis helped towards the
expenses of Antoine's education. At eleven years of age he
was sent as day boy to the College des Quatre Nations,
founded by Cardinal Mazarin, an institution which, though
primarily intended as a boarding-school for a limited
number of young noblemen, was open as a day school to the
sons of well-to-do Parisians. It was a fortunate choice, for
the College Mazarin had the distinction of giving the best
instruction in science of any college in France, and its staff
included a number of distinguished scientists. Among
these was the astronomer and mathematician, the Abbé La
Caille, who was said to have made more observations
and calculations than the entire body of contemporary
astronomers. This remarkable and attractive man had made
an astronomical expedition to the Cape of Good Hope, where
he measured an arc of the meridian, and, it is said, observed
10,000 new stars and named 14 new constellations. The

journey brought him fame, both because of the valuable scientific results to which it led, and because he calculated his expenses as 9,144 livres, 5 sous. No doubt the addition was mathematically correct, but the Parisians found the 5 sous, as part of the expenses of an expedition of four years' duration, uproariously funny. The Abbé had a small observatory at the College Mazarin, and during the later years of his educational career at school and at the Faculté de Droit, Lavoisier spent much time studying under his direction.

Another distinguished man who influenced Lavoisier's development was the chemist Rouelle, employed at the Jardin du Roi. Rouelle was also an enthusiast; it is reported of him that as an unknown young man he had conducted chemical experiments in the village smithy. He is remembered by chemists, Thorpe remarks, as " having just missed the discovery of the Law of Combination by Definite Proportions." In spite of a certain degree of eccentricity and bad temper, Rouelle was a fine teacher who inspired a number of young men, later to become famous, with an enthusiasm for chemistry. His habits of discarding wig, cravat, coat, and waistcoat in succession as he warmed up to his discourse cannot but have endeared him to his pupils. So must his habit of leaving the lecture room in search of forgotten apparatus, and continuing to deliver his lecture in a loud voice while looking for it, in spite of having left the class behind. One of the walls of his laboratory bore in large characters the inscription " *Nihil est in intellectu quod non prius fuerit in sensu.*" At the Jardin du Roi was also to be found Bernard de Jussieu, a botanist of note belonging to a family of botanists extending in an unbroken line from 1700 to 1850. Lavoisier was in the habit of accompanying him in country expeditions for purposes of research. His holidays were usually spent in expeditions of this nature.

He was a model schoolboy, quick to learn and understand, and a most conscientious worker. He took prizes in a variety of subjects, including rhetoric. One branch of study seems to have been neglected at the College Mazarin

—that of languages ; it was a period of French ascendency, and probably foreign languages were regarded as being unworthy of serious attention, as in Victorian England. Later in life he was to find himself handicapped by his ignorance of English and German.

Literature did not greatly attract him. In the first fervours of adolescence he dreamed, like nearly every other imaginative and intelligent youth, of vast literary successes, and actually began to compose a prose drama with the fashionable subject of " *la Nouvelle Heloïse*." But he soon threw off the contagion, for only the first three scenes were ever written. He had the type of mind which regards literature as waste of time, or, at best, a pretty parlour game for those with nothing better to do. He learned to write clearly and lucidly, but never, one imagines, to take any pleasure in writing for its own sake. He was not above occasional spelling mistakes. He enjoyed listening to music, and in later years became a keen patron of the opera, but painting and sculpture were not included among his livelier interests. Some notes of his made later in life during a visit to an exhibition of paintings are still in existence ; they display a conscientious attempt at appreciation, but no spontaneous pleasure. Still less was he drawn to the cultivation of the graces and extravagances of social life. Time flowed incessantly away ; the great ocean of scientific truth lay all undiscovered before him. Not a moment should be wasted in a drawing-room. As a handsome and promising young man of nineteen he found himself in considerable social demand, and, in order to be free to devote himself to scientific work without gaining a reputation for eccentricity, which would be abhorrent to a Lavoisier, he allowed the rumour of delicate health to circulate. His friends worried unnecessarily, for, as his enormous capacity for work shows, Lavoisier enjoyed abounding health all his life.

Early in his schooldays his scientific bent became obvious to the staff of the College Mazarin, and every effort was made to develop his interests in that direction. On leaving school, he studied law for a short time, and actually took a legal degree, but simultaneously he worked hard at various scientific subjects under the direction of his old instructors, now his personal friends. At the age of twenty he began his first research, which consisted in recording readings of the barometer three or four times daily. The chemist Dalton opened his scientific career in the same way. To the uninitiated research means wearing a white coat and playing with amusing toys in a laboratory, but indeed much scientific work consists of tedious activities such as taking barometric or other readings three or four times a day or rather more often. Lavoisier continued to make records of barometric pressure all his life. On the business trips which later occupied much of his time, he took a barometer with him, and the Paris records were never interrupted. When he was away Aunt Constance was pressed into the service of science ; whatever else was neglected in the Lavoisier home the barometer must receive attention. Later on in life he had a number of barometers constructed at his own expense and arranged for agents to take readings in several of the provinces ; he actually had an agent in Bagdad, in the person of de Beauchamp, a missionary. The underlying idea was the not unambitious one of reducing weather forecasting to an exact science. Unfortunately, death came on him before he was able to bring all his records together and subject them to critical analysis— otherwise the world might have learned of anti-cyclones and secondary depressions seventy years earlier.

In 1767, Lavoisier undertook to accompany the geologist Guettard, with whom he had already made several minor research expeditions, on a semi-official journey to the Vosges. He was now no longer an unknown young man. Two years before he had read an excellent paper to the Academy on the hardening of plaster of Paris, and he had achieved an unexpected success with an essay, which included original observations, on the best and most economical methods of lighting city streets. William Cole, who visited Paris in 1760, remarks that the streets " are most abominably lighted up ; perhaps three or four round

Lanthorns of Lead and greenish glass enlighten one street, being flung across a Rope which crosses the street, and so hang in the middle of the street from the Rope." On windy nights many of the lanterns were blown out. The murkiness of the streets provided cover for all kinds of villainy ; ordinary citizens, without servants to accompany them, were habitually obliged to employ professional lantern-bearers, of whom large numbers existed, to light them home and keep off robbers. There was much grumbling on the part of citizens, and the Academy of Science offered a prize of 3,000 francs for the best essay containing suggestions for improving the whole lighting system. Lavoisier's entry did not win first place, for the reward was divided equally between three engineers with more practical experience of the subject, but the judges were so struck with the originality of his paper that they gave him a special medal, presented by the King, as a consolation prize. His essay was later published at the Academy's expense. The newspapers expressed great surprise that so young a man should have gained so high a distinction—it was without precedent in the annals of the Academy.

Lavoisier himself looked forward with pleasure to the mild adventure of the expedition with Guettard, but his relations were filled with the most dismal forebodings. Good Parisians, they felt that civilisation ended, for practical purposes, not very far from the boundaries of their city, and here was Antoine proposing to penetrate into the wilds of Alsace to visit such remote and outlandish places as Belfort, Strasburg, and even Bâle. Three hundred miles was a very considerable journey in the eighteenth century. He was going to study mines, and Aunt Constance had a horror of mines, which she associated with floods and explosions. Possibly too, his elders looked a little askance at the companion of his travels. Guettard might be a distinguished scientist, but he was an exceedingly curious individual. He was very rude and very pious ; most of his conversation dealt with the iniquity of the expulsion of the Jesuits, to whom he owed his education. Socially, he seems to have been one of those impossible men who speak their mind freely on all occasions ; as a result, he quarrelled with most people he met. Strangely enough, the highly respectable, precise, and well-mannered young Lavoisier took great pleasure in Guettard's company, and remained on affectionate terms with him for many years. Guettard was an excellent geologist and a stimulating observer of nature, and, however important *comme-il-faut* behaviour might be, science came first with Lavoisier.

He took a servant with him on the journey, and his father saw to it that their mounts were excellent. His final words to his weeping family consisted of an exhortation not to forget to take barometer readings, while Aunt Constance sobbed that she would await the postman as she would the Messiah. That very evening, at their first halt, Lavoisier wrote that they were all *en joie et en santé* and that the horses had made an excellent supper. For the next three months letters between the wanderer and his admiring relations struggled backwards and forwards along the rugged roads of France. If a few days unexpected delay elapsed between the arrival of one letter and the next, Lavoisier *père's* anxiety grew feverish. " Do write more frequently," he begged, " even if it is only a line giving the place and date and saying you are in good health." He was afraid that all letters from Paris did not reach Antoine. Would it be in order for him, he wrote, to address them " To M. Lavoisier, on His Majesty's Service in the Vosges ? " The postal authorities might take greater care of letters so inscribed. Aunt Constance sent her nephew the news that the cat had kittens and told him to be careful with his firearms. They might be necessary to help the travellers to defend themselves against robbers and wild beasts—but she distrusted all firearms.

Antoine wrote frequently to allay his family's anxiety. He was horrified at the primitiveness and squalor of some of the villages in which they were forced to stay ; in one village the only lodging they could find was a draughty loft smelling of onions, containing two dirty feather mattresses and nothing else for their accommodation. It was necessary to scour the whole village before bed-coverings could be found. The interest and excitement of the journey quite outweighed incidental discomfort, but youthful impressions are lasting. His first-hand knowledge of the poverty of the French countryside was destined to influence Lavoisier all his life, and in particular, to influence his attitude towards reform and revolution. All could not be well with a country in which such wretchedness could be found. Later we shall have to tell of his efforts on behalf of French agriculture.

Throughout the journey he plied his aunt and father with commissions ; new thermometers must be sent to await them at Strasburg ; the aerometer was out of order and needed some spare parts ; would his aunt get the tailor to make him a grey or a green suit with a gold stripe ? Aunt Constance was informed by the tailor that grey had fallen out of fashion, so a green suit was made and sent on. At one request even the infatuated father was taken aback. He had arranged to meet the travellers on their return journey at Bourbonne-les-Bains, and a lady living in that town, with whom Antoine and Guettard had stayed, had expressed a longing for a bowl of gold fish to ornament her apartments. Antoine wrote to his father to bring some from Paris ; they could be obtained, he said, in the square of the Palais Royal. His father found the request a little outrageous. " It will be necessary," he protested, " to carry the bowl in our arms all the way, and even then it is doubtful whether the fish will survive the journey. It certainly seems rather an embarrassing parcel to travel with." He brought the gold fish, however.

Lavoisier found interest in almost everything he saw during the long rides of that sultry summer with Guettard and the man-servant Joseph. It was all recorded in his notebooks—the nature of the soil, the vegetation, the mines, the local industries. In the town they inspected the dusty collections of the local naturalists, and made an inventory of their contents. Everywhere he took temperature records and noted the density of river and lake water, and every night, true to the family tradition, he made a careful note of the day's expenses. Life must have seemed very delightful then to this enquiring and intelligent young man. With good prospects of wealth, with an admiring family ready to fulfil his slightest wish, with the fairyland of science opening out its gracious vistas before him, the cup of youthful happiness must have been full to overflowing.

The travellers arrived home at 11.30 on a night in mid-October, tired and dirty. Lavoisier, after a brief submission to the embraces of Aunt Constance, hurried off to take a reading of the barometer.

CHAPTER II

SCIENCE, FINANCE, AND MARRIAGE

LAVOISIER's study of the best methods of street illumination, awarded a special medal by the Academy, is really a remarkable piece of work for a young man of twenty-one. It is said, probably untruthfully, that in the course of this investigation he spent six weeks in a dark room with the object of sensitising the retina to minor differences in illumination. Every kind of lamp, whether oil or candle, is dealt with exhaustively in his memoir ; the area which each is capable of lighting up is carefully explained by means of diagrams, and whole sections are devoted to different varieties of wicks and lamp oil. He seems to take peculiar pleasure in elaborate calculations of the cost of maintaining this or that variety of lamp. Lavoisier was interested in artificial lighting all his life, and fifteen years later published an entertaining article on the lighting of theatres—a thorny problem in the eighteenth century. An elliptical reflector invented by himself, whose advantages are described in the prize essay, afterwards came into general use.

During the next two years Lavoisier published a paper on the composition of various waters, the material for which had been collected during his voyage with Guettard. The latter contained the tabulated analyses of 128 samples of water of different origin, giving the specific gravity of each, its content of certain mineral salts, and the nature of the soil from which it originated. These investigations, together with the earlier one on plaster of Paris, were sufficient, in a period when original research was a rare activity, to make Lavoisier a candidate for election to the Academy of Science.

The members of the Academy were, at that date, divided

into a number of grades.   First came the honorary members
of noble rank, some of scientific distinction and others
who might reasonably be suspected of interest in science ;
next in rank were 18 salaried members, then 12 associates,
and lastly 12 *adjoints*, membership of the latter two groups
being divided among the sciences of geometry, astronomy,
engineering, chemistry and botany.   Vacancies among the
pensionnaires were filled from the associates, and those
among the associates from the *adjoints*, who were junior
members without full privileges.   A few foreign scientists
of distinction were included as honorary associates.

As early as 1766 Lavoisier's name was included on the list
of possible *adjoints*, but it was not until two years later that
his chances of election became serious.   The vacancy to
be filled was that of *chimiste-adjoint*.   Lavoisier's chief
rival was the metallurgist Jars, a man of thirty-six, attached
to the Service des Mines, whose candidature was strongly
supported by Buffon and by a Minister of State, Saint-
Florentin.   Jars, who had done much valuable work for
France in the field of industrial technology, was a formidable
rival to a young worker of great promise but small achievement.   The Academy, however, was anxious to secure
Lavoisier young, and elected him, with Jars as second choice.
One of its most distinguished members, Lalande, asked why
he had voted for the younger and obscurer candidate,
explained that " a young man with knowledge, brains, and
energy, with sufficient private means to enable him to live
without practising a profession, would be extremely useful
to science."   But the Academy was not an autonomous
body ; it was supported by State funds and all its appointments had to be ratified by the King.   The authorities
decided that, in spite of the vote of the Academy, the claims
of Jars could not be passed over ; but, in order to avoid
offending the Academy, they created a new post of *chimiste-
adjoint* for Lavoisier.   The proviso was made that when the
next vacancy occurred among the chemists no new election
should be held, so that the membership of the Academy
would not be permanently increased.   Actually, such a

vacancy occurred very soon afterwards, for Jars died in the following year.

Lavoisier's early election to the Academy of Science filled his friends and relations with delight, and indeed it was no small honour. A friend of Aunt Constance wrote to her in the following strain : " I am sure that your eyes are dancing with delight now that your dear nephew has been elected to the Academy. How splendid that at so early an age, when other young men are occupied in amusing themselves, he should have made great contributions to the progress of science, and have obtained a position which is usually won, with great difficulty, by men past their fiftieth year ! " In actual fact, Lavoisier's record of scientific work at that date scarcely justified of itself election to the Academy, and that body was acting with an eye to his future—and its own, for the Academy, both individually and collectively, was chronically short of money.

The members of the Academy who had voted for Lavoisier received an unpleasant shock when, a few weeks after his election, he accepted a position in the powerful and wealthy company which collected the revenue, the executives of which were known as the *fermiers généraux*. Since his adherence to this body was a factor of momentous import-ance in Lavoisier's life, it is necessary to give at this point a description of its nature and purpose. The auctioning of taxes by the State to private individuals to make what they could out of them was a common practice in Roman times, a practice which led to fraud and extortion on a colossal scale. In seventeenth-century France what was called the " indirect revenue " had been collected by officials acting directly for the King or by semi-private agents who were entitled to a percentage of their takings. The difficulty of controlling an unco-ordinated multitude of agents scattered through the provinces led Colbert, in 1681, to entrust the collection of the entire " indirect revenue " in the majority of provinces to a single company of financiers—the *ferme générale*. The annual sum paid by the company at that date amounted to 56 million livres ; in return it had the right to collect taxes on salt, tobacco, certain beverages, and various customs duties at the ports and at the gates of Paris. The contract given to the company, which was of six years duration, was drawn up in the name of a " man of straw," the Farmers themselves remaining discreetly in the background.

This custom of anonymity was followed throughout the life of the company. Each six-year contract was known by the name of the dummy who appended his signature to it—receiving a pension of 4,000 livres a year for his pains—and the forty (later sixty) Farmers kept out of the public eye as much as possible, mysterious and ominous figures like the international financiers in Mr. Belloc's novels. The value of the taxes, and of the income enjoyed by the Farmers, mounted steadily during the eighteenth century. The original six-year contract, signed in 1681, had cost the Farmers 56 million livres ; in Julien Alaterre's contract from 1768-1774, during the course of which Lavoisier joined the Farm, the amount put down amounted to 90 millions. Of this each of the 60 Farmers contributed a million and a half. The transactions between the company and the Crown were on the best modern financial lines, for actual money changed hands as little as possible, each side paying debts by a credit entry in its books in favour of the other. But intricate as was the book-keeping involved, the results of the whole system were comparatively straightforward : the Crown was relieved of the responsibility and odium of tax collection and secured a regular revenue, the Farmers made princely fortunes, and the people paid.

The income of the individual Farmers has been reckoned as high as 200,000 livres per annum, and as low as 52,000.[1] The latter estimate was Lavoisier's, made at a moment when it was politic to minimise the company's taking as much as possible, and it is probable that the true figure lay some-

---

[1] In 1770 a livre was worth a little less than a franc (.95 franc, or about 1/26 of an English pound). The income of a Farmer General was therefore in the neighbourhood of £5,000 a year—or three or four times this figure in terms of modern money. It is sufficient to say that the farmers were extremely wealthy men by the standards of their age and country.

where between the two. Lavoisier, on joining the Farm, did not put down a sum of money which would entitle him to full membership and an income of this order. He bought a third share from an aged Farmer, Baudon, who was seventy years old and thinking of retiring. This cost 520,000 livres, of which Lavoisier himself supplied 340,000 livres, the bulk of the fortune left him by his mother, while his father lent him the balance. In the next six years' contract he was able to advance his share to a half, and finally, in 1779, on the death of Baudon, he became a full Farmer with a complete share in the company's income, subject to certain payments to Baudon's widow.

The Revenue Farm was highly unpopular; that goes without saying. Tax-collectors cannot expect the affection of their fellow-citizens—witness the jokes in our comic papers. The modern tax-payer, though aware that the money he disburses is scrupulously audited, that none of it is diverted to fill middlemen's pockets, has often difficulty in suppressing irrational spasms of dislike for those who collect his money. He feels vaguely that income tax officials enjoy their work overmuch. How much greater would be his irritation if his taxes had to be paid to a royally-chartered unaudited private company run by a few fat financiers who were rumoured to pocket most of the takings! The Farm was a huge company; its agents were every-where, and often carried out their duties in an insolent and high-handed manner. In some provinces the sale of salt was a monopoly of the company, and an enormous contraband traffic was in existence between these and other provinces in which its production and sale were freely per-mitted. To suppress this traffic the Farm employed over 20,000 men, and is said to have caused, in a single year, the arrest of over 1,000 smugglers, the majority of whom were sent to the galleys. Every year hundreds were condemned to the galleys for this venial crime (one third of the criminals at the galleys were convicted smugglers) and the agents of the Farm, swaggering across the countryside, with the right of entry into private houses, were feared and detested.

In 1766, the year before Lavoisier joined the Farm, a merchant named Monnerat was suspected of smuggling by an official in the employ of the company.   The official asked for a *lettre de cachet*, *i.e.*, a special royal order by means of which individuals could be imprisoned without trial or hope of legal assistance—and this was promptly granted.   Monnerat was thrown into a dark cell in the Bicêtre prison, where he was kept for three months, with a chain weighing 50 lbs. round his neck.   After this he was transferred to a slightly better cell, in which he spent seventeen months.   He would probably have remained in prison for the rest of his life, had not some friends interfered on his behalf.   It was then discovered that there had been a departmental error ; he had been mistaken for someone else ; the *lettre de cachet* had been intended for a man called La Feuillade.   Monnerat claimed damages from the Farm, damages which in the circumstances were scarcely excessive ; he wished, he said, to have money enough to cure himself of the scurvy which he had contracted in his filthy dungeon.   But the company flatly refused to pay anything at all, and Monnerat appealed to the *Cour des Aides*, which would in all probability have granted him a sympathetic hearing.   But the *fermiers généraux*, exerting their corrupt and boundless influence, had the case transferred to the royal council, which meant that Monnerat had no possible hope of redress.   Such incidents did not add to the popularity of the Farm.

The *Gabelle*, or salt tax, was peculiarly detested by the poor.   Even if a peasant was in a position to obtain contraband salt, he did not escape fleecing, for every commoner over seven years of age was registered as having bought 7 lbs. of government salt a year.   A peasant family of four persons paid each year a sum equal in value to nineteen days full labour for salt provided by the Government.   The annual 7 lbs. could be used only for human consumption and not given to animals ; if a pig was salted with such salt it was liable to confiscation, although poor peasants in general were unable to buy sufficient salt to preserve their meat. Further, it was forbidden, under pain of severe penalties, to use sea water for salt, or to graze animals on a salty marsh. In Provence, armed smugglers of salt, assembled to the number of five, were liable to a fine of 500 livres and nine years in the galleys; in all the rest of the kingdom, to death.

The money collected by the Farm enriched not only the Farmers themselves, but a number of outsiders who had bought or otherwise acquired shares in the company. The King himself held a whole share, and Mesdames du Barry and de Pompadour were both beneficiaries. A number of parasites, handed over to the Farm by the King as part of the price of contract, had also to be supported. In 1774 the Finance Minister, the Abbé Terray, sent a confidential request to the headquarters of the Farm demanding information about such pensions. Through a clerk's indiscretion the list was published, and Paris learnt, with due indignation, that 400,000 livres of public money were being paid annually to various protégés of the Court. These included the nurse of the Duke of Burgundy (10,000 livres), an opera singer (2,000 livres), and Madame du Barry's favourite physician (10,000 livres). Subsequently illegal payments of this nature were suppressed, and the incomes of the *fermiers généraux* thereby augmented.

Lavoisier, then, in joining the *fermiers généraux*, was connecting himself with a shady and highly unpopular concern. While the Farmers included business men of ability and integrity, they included also men who squandered their fortunes with vulgar ostentation. Saint James was said to have spent 400,000 livres in furnishing his salon; la Reynière's horses had the privilege of eating out of a silver manger. Two witticisms of Voltaire at the expense of the Farm are on record. "There are in Persopolis," he wrote, "40 plebeian Kings who hold the Empire of Perse to ransom, and hand over some of their takings to the monarch." Once when he was dining at some family party the guests were exchanging stories of robbers at whose hands they had suffered. When it came to Voltaire's turn, he began, "*Jadis, il y avait, un fermier-général—ma foi, Messieurs, j'ai oublié le reste!* " The average citizen or peasant probably expressed himself more bluntly and forcibly on the subject. To him the Farm was a malignant organisation, mysterious and invulnerable, which took his money and gave no return.

" Those who consider the blood of the people as nothing in comparison with the revenue of a prince," said Adam Smith, " may perhaps approve of this method of levying taxes."

An executive position in the Farm was no sinecure ; it demanded a large part of a man's time and energies. The Academy was justified in its forebodings that it had seen the last of Lavoisier as a genuine disciple of science. One of its members, Fontaine, remarked cynically that at least Lavoisier would now be able to give his colleagues good dinners, the implication being that he would give them nothing else. It would seem, however, that Lavoisier, though still in his early twenties, knew exactly what he was doing, and was determined, in his clear-headed way, to make the best of both worlds. Some of his biographers maintain that his motive in joining the Farm was to secure a large income which could be devoted to the service of science. This may be so ; more likely it was only one of his motives and not a very powerful one. His means and expectations were sufficient, unsupplemented, to enable him to keep clear of money-making altogether and spend his days un-interrupted in the laboratory. Scientific equipment was expensive then as now, but the Academy made grants towards its purchase, and Lavoisier without an income derived from the Farm would have been much richer than the majority of his colleagues. It seems more likely, remembering the existence of a certain quality in Lavoisier's nature which may be called " grabbiness," that he wanted money, and the power it brings, for himself and not for science, and the fact that only a fifth of his time would hence-forward be devoted to research did not deter him. But though fond of money, he was very far from being an ungenerous man ; again and again throughout his life he showed himself capable of spending money freely on unselfish ends.

Generally speaking, money-making and scientific research of high quality are incompatible activities. Both are full time jobs. The modern scientific worker, dissatisfied with suburban amenities, must as a rule abandon research entirely in favour of some more lucrative calling. In Lavoisier's case, the possession of enormous physical and intellectual energy enabled him to serve God and Mammon, or, as one might perhaps better express it, to do the work he liked and make money at the same time. His life was one long rush from the counting-house to the laboratory, and it is typical of him that he was equally at home in either. There is never any suggestion that he considered the profession of finance in any way derogatory to his position as philosopher, to use the eighteenth century term for scientist. He was prepared to undertake any task in the fields of administration, finance, and applied science, and carry it through with zest and with rather more efficiency than any other Frenchman of his time.

Whatever misgivings may have been felt by scientific friends, whatever future tragedy might be entailed, Lavoisier's admission to the *ferme générale* produced one unquestionably happy result. It secured him introduction to his wife. Among the more ambitious and able members of the organisation was Jacques Paulze, who became one of the privileged sixty in 1768. He had other business interests, being a director of the Compagnie des Indes, and he was allied by marriage to the Abbé Terray, Controller-General of Finance. Paulze, a man of education and intelligence, struck up a warm friendship with the latest recruit to the ranks of the Farmers.

He had a very young daughter, Marie-Anne-Pierrette, born in 1758, who at the date when Lavoisier joined the Farm was still captive behind the sheltering walls of a convent school. Marie was destined for an exciting career. At the early age of thirteen she received a most unsuitable proposal of marriage—the first of quite a number of

proposals. Her great-uncle, the Abbé Terray, acting under
the influence of the Baronne de la Garde, approached Paulze
with the suggestion that the Baronne's brother, d'Amerval,
would make an excellent husband for Marie. Marie, he
probably refrained from adding, would also make an
excellent wife for d'Amerval, since the latter was entirely
without the means to live as a gentleman should. His
claims were strongly backed by his sister, the Baronne, who
painted for Marie glowing pictures of the delights which
would be hers when she was married into the nobility and
actually presented at Court.

But neither Marie nor her father thought much of the
proposed husband. To the girl, d'Amerval, fifty years of
age and unattractive in person, was simply an ogre, while
Paulze, though chary of offending the powerful Abbé, had
more sensible plans for his only daughter. Writing to the
Abbé he protested that it was too early to consider the question
of her marriage. When the time came he would seek out
for her a husband suitable as regards age, character and
means. On all three accounts d'Amerval possessed no
advantages whatever. He was fifty, Marie was thirteen.
He could scarcely muster an income of 1,500 francs a year,
while Marie, though not exactly an heiress, would have a
dot of quite considerable proportions. As to character :
perhaps the Abbé was not acquainted with M. d'Amerval's
character ? He, Paulze, had heard stories. As an after-
thought he added that his daughter had a strong aversion to
her elderly suitor, and he would not force her against her
will into so dubious a contract.

M. Paulze's spirited objections got him into considerable
trouble with the Abbé, who threatened to do him financial
injury unless he capitulated over the match. Other members of the Farm came to Paulze's rescue, but the Abbé continued to press d'Amerval's claims. Finally, Paulze, wishing
to end an intolerable situation, offered his daughter's hand
to Lavoisier. Lavoisier was willing to oblige his friend, his
family had no serious objection, and thus, unromantically,
a highly successful and affectionate marriage partnership

originated. At the time of their marriage Marie was
fourteen and Antoine twenty-eight. She was exceptionally
mature for her age. " She is so well-developed, so reasonable," wrote one of her aunts, " that I am sure she will make
her husband happy." There were good looks on both sides.
Antoine was tall, auburn haired and blue-eyed, with a fine
profile and a ready smile ; Marie was smallish, with blue
eyes and brown hair and an admirable complexion. Study
of her portait by David,[1] painted some years later, leaves
no doubt of her sex appeal—to employ the American
expression which, born in Hollywood, has proved so useful
an addition to most languages of the world that it must soon
win academic recognition. The portrait, in fact, is that of a
very beautiful woman.

Lavoisier was a good-tempered and amiable man, who
carried his intellectual superiority lightly. He was fond
enough of company and conversation, but had little time to
spare for them. Marie, as she grew to womanhood, developed a rather sharper personality. At the time of their
marriage she was very fresh and charming, full of enthusiasm
to prove herself a worthy wife, and romantically stirred by
the young genius for whom all predicted a brilliant career.

Their wedding in December, 1771, was attended by
minor nobilities, ministers of State, by the dignitaries of
science and finance, and even by the Abbé Terray. Guettard, absent in Italy on scientific business, sent his warm
congratulations. Lavoisier's young wife brought him good
looks, brains and money. Actually, her fortune was less
than his own. His net income in 1771 was about
20,000 livres ; he had the prospect of rapid advancement in
the Revenue Farm and of being the legatee of several
wealthy relatives. Her dowry amounted to only 80,000
livres, of which 21,000 was paid down and the remainder
in six yearly instalments. By marrying her, however,
Lavoisier strengthened his connection with a man of financial
ability whose foot was firmly planted on the ladder. Paulze,

---

[1] Now in the library of the Rockefeller Institute for Medical Research,
New York.

who in 1771 was still feeling the effects of the heavy initial outlay occasioned by the purchase of a full share in the Farm, was destined to become a very wealthy man in the course of the next decade.

From the outset Marie Lavoisier threw herself heart and soul into her matrimonial career. Married as a child, with her education scarcely begun, she was able to direct her later studies into channels likely to be useful to her husband. She learned Latin and English so as to be able to translate scientific works for him. She polished up her considerable natural ability at drawing and painting, and later made the diagrams and illustrations for his books. David, from whom she took painting lessons, thought a great deal of her work. Two excellent drawings which she made of Lavoisier at work in his laboratory are well known to physiologists, and important records in the history of science ; they show Lavoisier conducting respiration experiments with herself at an adjacent table taking notes. She mastered what was then known of chemistry ; that in later years she was able to translate a chemical treatise by Kirwan, and actually to add a refutation of his conclusions, indicates her grasp of the subject. Sometimes, when experiments were on hand which necessitated the taking of a series of readings throughout the night, she would take her turn on watch in the laboratory. Altogether, a most admirable wife, who during their married life scarcely left her husband's side, who shared his successes and vindictively opposed his adversaries. Unquestionably her contribution to his career was invaluable ; without a trained assistant at his side, fully understanding the purpose of his experiments and capable of taking much secretarial and routine work off his hands, he would never have achieved what he did. David, in his portrait of Lavoisier and his wife (it was painted in 1788 and cost 7,000 livres), clearly wishes to emphasise the fact of their partnership. Marie is looking over her husband's shoulders as he writes, while he looks up at her as though to ask her opinion on what he has written. It is a pity that they had no children.

Lavoisier and his young bride took up residence in a house in the Rue Neuve des Bons Enfants, accompanied by Aunt Constance, who from the wedding day onward seems to disappear into the background. Probably she devoted herself to household affairs, leaving Marie free for more interesting pursuits. In 1775 Lavoisier was appointed *régisseur des poudres*, a position to which reference will be made later, which necessitated a move from the Rue Neuve des Bons Enfants to a suite of rooms in the Arsenal, where a laboratory was expensively constructed and equipped. Jean Lavoisier died in 1777 of apoplexy, in his sixty-first year. Shortly before his death, in a final effort on behalf of the son whose career had been the main interest of his life, he purchased (for some 65,000 livres) a title—*conseiller-secrétaire du roi, maison, finance et couronne de France*—which carried with it hereditary noble rank. Antoine Lavoisier made little use of his title, having, by the time he succeeded to it, more genuine claims to honour, but it was later to be mouthed ironically by his enemies. The legacy which the young couple received from Jean Lavoisier was supplemented in a few years by legacies from Madame Lalaure, Antoine's great-aunt, and from Constance Punctis, who died in 1781. Antoine and his wife both came of distinctly unfertile families, and, since heirs were few, money accumulated in their hands.

CHAPTER III

LAVOISIER'S BACKGROUND

During Lavoisier's first two years as a member of the Farm, much of his time was occupied in travelling on its business in the provinces, but subsequently he was able to settle down to a full and active life in Paris. His industry was prodigious. In spite of the exactions of finance, he gave six hours a day to scientific research, from six to nine o'clock in the morning and from seven to ten o'clock in the evening, and, in addition, a whole day a week was devoted to this activity. " It was a very happy day for him," wrote Madame Lavoisier long afterwards. " A number of instructed friends, and a number of young men proud to be allowed to assist in his experiments, would meet in his laboratory early in the morning. They would have their meals there, and discuss scientific subjects, and it was in this atmosphere that the theory which has immortalised its author was born."

All he wrote he wrote with extreme care. Rough drafts of letters would often be handed to a secretary, who would make a fair copy, which he would again examine sentence by sentence and correct. The pernicious habit of dictation had not yet arisen to darken counsel. Unhurried, easy mannered, Lavoisier polished off dull administrative work with method and precision, and turned unfatigued to more appealing activities.

The major discoveries on which Lavoisier's fame rests were made at intervals during the two decades following his marriage. All this time he was strenuously engaged not only with the business of the Farm, but with that of the Academy of Science. The latter institution occupied a more official position in France than did the Royal Society of London in

England. Both, it is true, were founded under royal patronage ; both carried out inquiries for their respective governments, and acted as a final court of appeal on scientific questions. But the official connections of the Academy were more binding than those of the Royal Society. Its head-quarters were in the Louvre, where it was allowed the use of a number of rooms, in which meetings were held, apparatus was kept, and a small museum of scientifically interesting objects, open to public view, was maintained. New associates were presented to the King in person, and a considerable number of the senior members were full-time Government servants in the sense that their membership involved a salary. Much more than privately conducted scientific research was expected from the Academy. Since the days when the Grand Monarch had set his academicians to devising ingenious fountains for Versailles, and working out the odds at various games of chance, the Academy of Science had been under the obligation to produce some fairly tangible return for the grants of money it received. Essentially it was a state endowed Scientific Research Institution rather than a free society of distinguished men of science, as the Royal Society has been since its foundation. The Royal Society, during the earlier centuries of its existence, was a club of gentlemen of independent means engaging in scientific research because scientific research is a most interesting activity, and even to-day, when most of its members make their living by research, some of the earlier spirit lingers. The amateur atmosphere still, to a consider-able extent, pervades English laboratories. The ambitious young research worker is not encouraged to take himself too seriously, to strike attitudes, or to spell science with a large " S."

Lavoisier's connection with the Academy brought him a great diversity of tasks. At one moment he would be writing a memoir on the possibility of improving the water supply of Paris—a most urgent practical problem not solved until more than a century later—and at another he would be assessing the merits of mechanical armchairs designed for the use of invalids. He wrote reports on gelatine soup for the sick, the construction of prisons and hospitals, divining rods, the great cold of 1776, and Mesmer's animal magnetism. All kinds of weird inventions, submitted to the Academy for its approval, he conscientiously investigated and reported on —would-be flying machines, repairing docks for ships, fire extinguishers, perpetual motion machines and other ingenious if useless contraptions. Meteors, Normandy cider, and the best way of provisioning ships for long voyages, were among the subjects which came under his purview. In spite, however, of his numerous public and business duties, and of his perilous scientific versatility, Lavoisier worked steadily at his chemical investigations for most of his life. There were two main interruptions. It appears, from study of his laboratory notebooks, that from 1777–1782 he could find no time to work in the laboratory at all, so that the highly productive years between thirty-four and thirty-nine were lost to science ; and during the last four years of his life he had little opportunity for pure scientific research. But the story of the achievements which made him famous is a connected story of steady advance from point to point ; except towards the end, the thread of his real life-work was never lost in a hurly-burly of secondary activities.

First-class scientific achievement in one's spare time was less impossible in the eighteenth than in the twentieth century for the obvious reason that a man could more easily make himself master of his chosen subject. That formidable thicket, the Literature, through which the modern worker so wearily hacks his way, had scarcely begun to sprout. It was not necessary to read fifty papers, in several languages, before learning, with some surprise, that nothing definite is known about a particular scientific subject. The progress of research had not yet led to problems so complicated that they can only be attacked with the help of organised teams of assistants who each add quotas of expert knowledge and special technique to the ensemble and who may individually be devoid of creative ability.

Lavoisier had fewer facts to grasp than the modern research worker in chemistry, physics or physiology ; so much the better for his chances of making original discoveries in the course of a crowded life. But, at the same time, we must remember that he had to deal with a disorganised subject which had become entangled in the meshes of a faulty generalisation. Whatever the state of development of a science, high gifts and strenuous purpose are required by those who contribute to its advance.

The Lavoisiers did not belong to the aristocracy of birth, but between that aristocracy and the *haute-bourgeoisie* of the capital there were many points of contact. The two classes were growing to resemble each other in appearance, manners, and social habits, as the wealthy manufacturers and the landed gentry in Victorian England grew to resemble each other. A gulf still existed ; even the most wealthy and cultivated financier might on occasion be courteously snubbed by his betters and reminded that he was only a *parvenu* whose daughter might be just worthy to marry an impoverished nobleman if her dowry were large enough. Vanity, said Talleyrand, made the French Revolution ; the remembrance of pinpricks in their self-esteem made the wealthy middle classes, in 1789, throw their powerful influence into the scale against the old *régime*. But even by the middle of the century the manners of the aristocracy were growing more tolerable. Such incidents as the beating of Voltaire by the servants of an offended seigneur were becoming rare. Social friction, nevertheless, persisted. Lavoisier himself, though he attained noble rank on the death of his father, belonged essentially to the *bourgeoisie* and not to the aristocracy. But, as a scientist, he was in a specially privileged position. In an era of rapid decline in religious faith, science was held in considerable respect, and with some reason. " More new truths concerning the external world," says Buckle, " were discovered in France during the latter half of the eighteenth century than during all preceding periods put together." It was particularly in mathematical and physical science that great successes had been achieved ; on the basis of the great work of Newton the scientists of France had built more successfully than Newton's own fellow-countrymen. Nothing succeeds like success, and science was fashionable ; lectures on chemistry and astronomy were attended by finely dressed and well-born dilettantes, as well as by serious students. Clever people, even if without scientific training, would try to win fame as discoverers : Voltaire had a chemical laboratory ; Marat was intensely eager to achieve recognition as a physicist. " I should pity the man," wrote Arthur Young in 1789, " who expected, without other advantages of a very different nature, to be well received in a brilliant circle at London, because he was a fellow of the Royal Society. But this would not be the case with a member of the Academy of Science at Paris ; he is sure of a good reception everywhere." Lavoisier, of course, did possess advantages of a very different nature which would have assured him respect in London or anywhere else ; namely, great possessions. But the passage is worth quoting because it helps us to understand the atmosphere in which he lived and worked.

A modern man, transported by a miracle to Paris in the year 1775, would find there a restless sceptical spirit whose kinship with the spirit of his own times he would readily recognise. He would feel quite at home at a meeting of the Academy of Science, or in a salon surrounded by witty conversationalists discussing not only the latest scandal, but also social reform. But even in a salon he might observe some things which suggested the preferability of living in the twentieth rather than in the eighteenth century. The fact that all the women made liberal use of cosmetics would please by its familiarity, but he would be shocked to note that at least a quarter were heavily scarred by small-pox. He would learn that one's chances of escaping this disease were slight (though increasing, now that inoculation had been introduced) ; had not the King himself caught it in his palace of Versailles and died of it ? Should our modern man be spending a winter evening at Versailles itself, he would note that even in the great gallery, lit by 3,000 candles and filled with a magnificently dressed throng, cold winds blew boisterously, so that the faces of duchesses were blue with cold. Something of the splendour of the scene might fade because it was impossible to prevent the candles being blown out. And beneath the refinement and sophistication he would find lurking a curious barbarity. The Queen must bear children in public, with a motley crowd craning its neck to miss nothing of the spectacle, as though she reigned, not at Versailles, but in a cannibal island. Should anyone do hurt to the person of God's annointed, he was punished with a terrible and superstitious violence. In 1757 a weak-minded fanatic named Damiens stabbed the King with a knife, causing a painful, but not a dangerous, wound. The King soon recovered, but his assailant suffered a lingering and atrocious death. After being tortured to reveal the name of his accomplices, he was placed on a table in the Place de Grève and further tortured with burning tongs and molten lead. Ropes were attached to his limbs and horses were used in an attempt to tear him asunder, but, as this was not successful, he was slowly hacked to pieces. The whole proceedings, which occupied an hour and a quarter, were watched by an enormous crowd which filled the Place de Grève. For windows with a good view the price was as high as 20 livres.

The Parisians of the latter half of the eighteenth century prided themselves on the magnificence and orderliness of their capital. In truth, there was some excuse for their civic pride. The city was overflowing its ancient boundaries, as pleasant residential suburbs sprang up in its outskirts. Ancient and dilapidated streets and houses were being torn down to give place to buildings of greater comfort and con-venience. Rents were rising rapidly. A century before, Paris could boast of only a few eating houses ; in 1774 there were 600 cafés in which citizens could read their journals and discuss the latest news. There were two newspapers, containing some account of current events, but little political comment—when a question of political importance was exciting the public, that need was supplied, as in England, by a stream of sheets and broadsides, sold at street corners. But there were no provincial newspapers, and in the provinces the traveller would be fortunate if he were able to unearth a month old copy of one of the Paris journals.

The city was learning to amuse itself. Horse racing had been introduced from England, with Vincennes as an imitation Newmarket. The theatre was booming, and the latest play provided as interesting a topic of conversation to prosperous citizens as in our own times. The ecclesiastical ban on actors and actresses, by which these were denied the benefits of the sacraments, was no longer taken very seriously ; still nominally outcast, the profession was raising its social status. There was great delight in the newly introduced Italian opera. In construction, theatres were approaching their modern form, and the stage was no longer obstructed by the presence of a crowd of courtiers.

But there were other less satisfactory aspects of Parisian life. Much of the city was still essentially medieval. The citizen, as he walked through dark and narrow streets, would be assailed by fearful smells ; there were no pavements on which the pedestrian might take refuge from a recklessly driven aristocratic cabriolet, and down the centre of each street ran a foul gutter, to help in carrying off the accumulations of filth ; London streets had pavements, and were far cleaner. Much of the traffic was composed of water-carts, for there was no general pipe supply, and 20,000 men found employment in carrying water to private houses. Those engaged in acting as substitutes for sewers were almost equally numerous. The slaughter of cattle within the city limits added to the variety of smells and the refuse of the capital. Herds of cattle frequently blocked the streets. In the poorer quarters, thousands festered in unbelievable degradation, ridden with diseases which they passed on to more fortunate neighbours. To be admitted as patient to a hospital was almost equivalent to sentence of death.

The peasants were more fortunate than the slum dwellers in that the air they breathed was purer, but in little else. Clothed in rags, barefooted, haggard, dirty and wretched, they strove, by primitive methods, to wring enough to eat from the soil, and pay their crushing taxes. They lived almost exclusively on a cereal diet, without milk, eggs, or meat—a diet incompatible with health and physical efficiency. Their houses were but huts, small, filthy, leaky, and windowless. There was no beauty and dignity to be found in the countryside, few pretty village festivals, and no comely women. All were bent and scarred with unceasing toil. The misery of the peasant was in large measure artificial, the result of bad government ; he paid more than half what he earned in taxes to the Government, the church, and the seigneur possessing feudal rights over his parcel of land. But primitive barbarism is primitive barbarism whatever its cause. Noblemen as a class visited their estates as little as possible, for the sight of such savage misery was depressing to well cultivated and civilised minds.

Eighteenth-century France was elegant and intelligent, and at the same time dirty and inefficient. Lavoisier, as his knowledge grew and his mind developed, became a stalwart opponent of dirt and inefficiency. Other reformers might grow eloquent about the insolence of court officials and the iniquity of *lettres de cachet*, and doubtless Lavoisier liked such things no better than other members of his class. But he felt there were more urgent problems : the peasants must be taught how to farm their land ; Paris needed a new water supply ; the hospitals and prisons were in a dreadful state. It was a useful state of mind in a country whose dominant class was devoted to epigrammatic and endless conversation, to wholesale fornication, to the exquisite living of a meaningless existence. A few more Lavoisiers, and that society might not have met so gloomy an end.

The Lavoisiers lived in a circle which included the best brains in France, perhaps the best brains in the world of that time. Within that circle, in which the *bourgeoisie* predominated, though aristocrats were not unknown, hopefulness reigned. Its members congratulated themselves on living in a time of progress, reason, and high civilisation—in the greatest century of all. The advance of science was destined soon to destroy superstition and bigotry, and ensure prosperity and happiness for all mankind. Conversation flowed round stimulating new phrases and ideas—the social contract, the sovereignty of the people, the rights of man. It was that great moment of the social idealist when perfect social and political systems, which have never been put to the test of practice and never seem likely to be, can be hopefully and happily discussed, as the Fabians hopefully and happily discussed socialism in the 'nineties of last century. To give some slight substance to current optimism, behind the chatter of reform there was even some hint of real reform. Louis XV. had shrugged his shoulders and remarked, with commendable penetration, " *Après moi le déluge*," but with the advent of his successor it seemed, for a short time, as if the clouds had lifted. There was increase in general prosperity, particularly in the great cities, a certain activity in public works ; a network of fine main roads was being constructed by forced peasant labour, roads which greatly excited the admiration of Arthur Young in 1788, until he observed that there was hardly any traffic on them, and wondered whether shoeless peasants really required such magnificent causeways. In truth, the effort towards reform did not amount to very much ; the clouds had not retreated very far. But whatever storms were brewing, we may picture Antoine and Marie beginning their life together in a reasonably happy, gay, energetic, and self-respecting circle, in which enthusiasm and hard work were as much the fashion as good manners.

CHAPTER IV

JOSEPH PRIESTLEY

LAVOISIER's family was staunchly Catholic, and he had been well grounded in the Faith. His biographer, Grimaux, insists that his early religious beliefs and practices remained unchanged throughout his life, but offers no evidence in support of this except a conventional letter of thanks for a theological book sent him by Edward King, in which Lavoisier congratulates the author on his efficient defence of the Scriptures. Otherwise there are no facts on record suggesting that Lavoisier differed from the general run of French intellectuals of his day in his attitude towards the Christian faith. His real religion, in fact, was that of Voltaire and Thomas Henry Huxley—scientific humanism —the goal of which is a sane and ordered world, the regulation of human affairs according to the dictates of reason and scientific knowledge and not those of superstition and despotic expediency. But in turning to his great contemporary and rival, Joseph Priestley, we enter a very different religious atmosphere. The influence of Voltaire did not extend far into the West Riding of Yorkshire.

To the historian of science the name of Lavoisier is closely linked with those of two English contemporaries, Cavendish and Priestley, particularly the latter's. It is impossible to think of Lavoisier's scientific achievements without thinking at the same time of Priestley's, and indeed Lavoisier perhaps owed more to Priestley than to any scientist of his own nationality. Yet personally there was very little association between the two. Lavoisier met Priestley only once (Cavendish he never met) and the letters they exchanged dealt almost exclusively with scientific questions. They had few other interests in common. As human beings they were poles apart, differing not only in nationality and religious background, but also in character and philosophy of life. The only reason for including accounts of Priestley and Lavoisier between the covers of a single book is thát both contributed largely and simultaneously to chemical science, the work of one being in many respects complementary to the work of the other.

Joseph Priestley was born in 1733 in Fieldhead, a tiny Yorkshire village situated in the district which has been for centuries, and still remains, the heart of the English woollen industry. His father was a cloth finisher and his mother a farmer's daughter, both simple and pious Presbyterian folk to whom this world was a brief and unimportant prelude to eternity. His grandfather had been " famed for his heavenly conduct " and had passed away with the words : " See how a man of God dies " upon his lips. Like Lavoisier, Joseph lost his mother at an early age ; having given birth to six children in as many years, she died in the hard winter of 1739, when the Thames was completely frozen over above London Bridge. After her death he was sent to live with his grandmother. Three years later he was adopted by his aunt, Mrs. Keighley, " a truly pious and excellent woman," with no children of her own. Like Lavoisier's Aunt Constance, she looked after her nephew with more than maternal care.

The Keighleys lived at Heckmondwike, a village probably more picturesque in the eighteenth century than it is to-day. The industrial revolution had not yet ravaged the West Riding. In his youth Mr. Keighley had persecuted dissenters, but having one day secreted himself in a chapel during service to secure evidence of treason and heresy on the part of the worshippers, he saw a sudden light and was converted. After his death in 1745 his widow made her house, the Old Hall, a resort for all the dissenting ministers in the district. Religion, centring in the Independent Chapel, was the main interest of the family, not only on Sundays, but throughout the week. It permeated and filled each detail of everyday life. Priestley remarked later that " there was hardly a day in the week in which there was not some meeting of one part of the congregation," and twice a day his aunt led her household in prayer. He himself, at an early age, acquired a facility in the art of extempore prayer, and an interest in its technique. " At my aunt's," he says, " there was a monthly meeting of women, who acquitted themselves in prayer as well as any men belonging to the congregation. Being at first a child in the family, I was permitted to attend their meetings, and, growing up insensibly, heard them after I was capable of judging." The boy was accustomed to kneel down and pray, not only at bedtime, but at other times of the day. The Sabbath was kept with peculiar thoroughness ; chapel, religious reading, meditation and prayer were supposed to fill the day. The strict Sabbatarianism of Victorian Noncon- formity, which as a general observance disappeared only yesterday and may still linger here and there in the English provinces, was surpassed at two points—walking for recreation was not allowed, and no cooking was done.

Mrs. Keighley, being well-to-do, was able to send Joseph to various schools in the neighbourhood. Here he began what Brougham rather unjustifiably calls his " rambling and scanty " education. Rambling it certainly was, but not scanty, for the boy was avid of learning. At school he learned some Latin and Greek, acquiring during holiday time a smattering of Hebrew from a friendly minister. From another minister he had some training in geometry, algebra, and various branches of theoretical and practical mathematics, but he never made much headway with his mathematical studies. In his early teens he read a number of advanced works on philosophy. His aunt, noting his studious habits, naturally wished him to go into the ministry, but his health was at first not considered good enough for that arduous and exacting career. It was resolved, therefore, to put the boy into business. To qualify himself for a post in Lisbon, which had been promised by an uncle, he taught himself Italian, German, and French, not very effectively, if one may judge from his difficulties in making himself understood during a visit to Paris in later years. Joseph was an earnest youth and during his boyhood spent most of his recreation time in study. He had little opportunity for light reading, " Robinson Crusoe " being the only romance with which he was acquainted. He once snatched away a " book of knight errantry " which he found his younger brother Timothy reading ; he regarded Timothy, in fact, as frivolous, though the two had prayed together when scarcely past infancy. At the age of twelve Joseph is said to have bottled up some spiders in a closed jar to see how long they could live, an experiment sometimes quoted as evidence of an early-developing scientific bent. It must be remarked, however, that most intelligent boys perform such experiments.

During adolescence Joseph suffered, as might be expected, from religious doubts and difficulties. He had read and been told that conversion, a new birth, was necessary to salvation, but he was unable to be certain that he himself had really experienced anything of the kind. This caused him much distress ; at times God seemed to have forsaken him and he felt like the man in the iron cage in the " Pilgrim's Progress." But apart from such physiological religious troubles, he had others of a less familiar kind. He had been taught that " all mankind, by the fall of our first parents, lost communion with God, are under His wrath and curse, and so made liable to all miseries in this life, to death itself, and to the pains of hell for ever." This genial Genevese doctrine he found repugnant, while at the same time he felt distress that he could not feel a proper repentance for the sin of Adam, without which that sin could not be forgiven him. But his naturally vigorous and sensible mind soon broke free from such dreary shackles, for he discarded the pitiless doctrines of Calvin in favour of the saner tenets of Arminianism. Arminius had left a loophole. Man was not inevitably damned by the sin of Adam, to be rescued from eternal torment only by divine caprice, which saved those predestined to be saved. Helped by the grace of God, he could work out his own salvation, which depended on belief and repentance. The sovereignty of God was so exercised as to be compatible with the freedom of man.

Joseph, when he applied for admission as a communicant to the Independent Chapel, was found to be so unsound in his views about the sin of Adam, and the resulting damnation of all mankind, that the elders unhesitatingly rejected him.

At the last moment, when all preparations for the journey to Lisbon had been made, Joseph's health appeared to improve, so that it was decided, in spite of his non-acceptance by the elders, to revert to the original plan of a devotional career. He was therefore sent to a well-known dissenting academy at Daventry, one of several institutions which at that time supplied higher education to Nonconformists, excluded from the universities. During their first years at the Academy all students followed the same course of study, and it was not until the last year that they specialised for the various professions. An unexpected atmosphere of liberalism and free inquiry seems to have pervaded the Daventry Academy. It would appear that at a period when the ancient and orthodox universities were sunk in ignoble lethargy, a livelier spirit was to be found in the poverty stricken educational institutions of the dissenters. Priestley himself wrote, at a later date, in a letter to the Prime Minister, that " while your universities resemble pools of stagnant water secured by dams and mounds, ours are like rivers which, taking their natural course, fertilise a whole country." At Daventry students were taught to realise that most questions have two sides ; there was a continual discussion between pupils and teachers about theological and philosophical problems. " We were permitted," he says, " to ask any questions, and to make whatever remarks we pleased ; and we did it with the greatest, but without an offensive, freedom." In theological debates " Dr. Ashworth took the orthodox side of every question, and Mr. Clark, the sub-tutor, that of heresy, though always with the greatest modesty." In this brisk atmosphere two religious notions crystallised out in Joseph's mind. He became an upholder of Arianism, which exalts the First Person of the Trinity at the expense of the other two, and regards Jesus as a being created by the Father, and not co-equal with Him. Further, he adopted the comfortable faith that all things are guided and necessitated by the will of God, Who works behind the earthly scene for some obscure but glorious end.

His first appointment was as assistant to an old Presbyterian minister at Needham Market, in Suffolk, where he received as stipend only £30 per annum, though he had been promised £40. He was not a success in his new post; a stammer impeded his eloquence in the pulpit, and his Arianism was very soon discovered and resented. A journey to London to consult a quack who offered to cure all defects in speech resulted in the expenditure of £20, a very large sum for one in Priestley's circumstances, and no appreciable improvement in his stutter. At Needham, however, he made a number of stimulating acquaintances, receiving particular kindness from a certain Mr. Alexander, a Quaker, who owned a good library. He continued his theological studies and came to the conclusion that " the doctrine of atonement had no countenance either from Scripture or reason." Here he began his " observations on the character and reasoning of St. Paul," falling foul of the latter at a good many points. This work was not published till many years later. On the whole, Priestley was very unhappy during the three years of his first pastorate. He considered his calling the most honourable of any on earth and was anxious to distinguish himself in it ; but here he felt himself in a " low, despised situation," surrounded by indifference and hostility. Other ministers would not exchange pulpits with him, because the more genteel members of their congregations objected to his stammering delivery. But throughout this perplexing and disappointing period of his life he was sustained by his unshakeable faith that God was arranging everything for the best.

His poverty became so acute that he was forced to supplement his income by teaching, although, as he said, " he had conceived, like most other young men of liberal education, a great aversion to the business of a schoolmaster." He circulated the citizens of Needham with a proposal to teach their sons classics and mathematics, but without effect ; his views on the Trinity were too heretical. He made a little by lecturing to adults on " The Use of the Globes," but not enough to relieve his precarious situation. When a possibility of procuring a pastorate in Sheffield arose, and he was asked to preach a trial sermon, the prospective congregation found him " too gay and airy." At length he was recommended by a friend to a congregation in Nantwich in Cheshire, and thither he joyfully made his way in 1758. From the outset he found the atmosphere of Nantwich more agreeable.

Here Priestley met with a certain Mr. Eddowes, a grocer, and a sociable and sensible man, who persuaded him to learn the flute. He never became a proficient performer, but his flute provided him with a hobby which filled many hours of his life. The knowledge and practice of music, he says, is to be recommended to all studious persons, and if they have no ear for music, so much the better, for their sensibilities will be less easily offended. The detective story had not yet been invented as a pastime for the intelligentsia. In Nantwich, where the congregation was less interested in theological conflicts, he became a comparatively popular minister. He was not overworked and found time to set up a school, which generally consisted of about thirty boys, and included a separate room of about half a dozen young ladies. Here, for the first time, we learn of certain scientific interests. He bought a few scientific instruments—" a small air pump, an electrical machine, etc."—and amused himself and his pupils with some elementary experiments. He had always, he later said, had a taste for such things. But it was not till many years after that his real scientific career began.

At Nantwich, and afterwards at the newly founded Warrington Academy, where he accepted a full-time position as teacher of languages in 1761, Priestley became genuinely interested in education. The universities, he felt, supplied almost no knowledge of the kind which helped men to be of service to their country. " Formerly," he says, in an excellent passage, " none but the clergy were thought to have any occasion for learning. It was natural, therefore, that the whole plan of education, from the Grammar School to the finishing at the University, should be calculated for their use. If a few other persons, who were not designed for Holy Orders, offered themselves for education, it could not be expected that a course of studies should be provided for them only and, indeed, as all these persons who super-intended the business of education were of the clerical order, and had themselves been taught nothing but the rhetoric, logic, and school divinity, or civil law, which comprised the whole compass of human learning for several centuries, it could not be expected that they should entertain larger, or more liberal, views of education ; and still less that they should strike out a course of study for the use of men who were universally thought to have no need of study, and of whom few were so sensible of their own wants as to desire any such advantages." The orthodox universities did not include history in the curriculum ; a bright student might pick up a little Greek or Roman history from the study of the classics, but the history of England and Europe was not considered worth a gentleman's attention. Priestley was insistent that students should be taught the history of their own times, and he added, as a subject of equal importance, what he called " Civil Policy," which included the theory of laws, government, manufactures, commerce, naval force, etc., " with whatever may be demonstrated from history to have contributed to the flourishing state of nations, to rendering a people happy and populous at home, and formidable abroad." Students must be encouraged to ask questions, and the authorities on both sides of controversial subjects should always be quoted. He does not consider knowledge of the classics absolutely necessary to a student before entrance to the Academy, *i.e.*, to a student of university age (this in 1760 !), but he considers it desirable that " he should have such an insight into Latin as may enable a person to read the easier classics, and supersede the use of a dictionary, with respect to those more difficult words which are derived from the Latin " and the student " should

understand French very well " and have some knowledge of
the " more useful branches of mathematics." Such ideas,
with others equally characteristic, concerning the study of the
workings of Divine Providence in the direction of human
affairs, he included in " An Essay on a Course of
Liberal Education for Civil and Active Life," published
in 1766. It may have been partly due to Priestley's
influence that a considerable number of the pupils who
studied at Warrington Academy from 1760-80 afterwards
achieved distinction. The economist Malthus was a pupil
there, though some years after Priestley's departure. These
eighteenth-century Nonconformist universities, short-lived
and impecunious as they were, did invaluable pioneer work
in the educational field.

At Warrington Priestley published several books, the first
of an enormous series, for he developed into a fertile writer
whose works, edited by Rutt, fill twenty-five volumes.
Among the books written at Warrington were works on
" Oratory and Criticism " and the " Constitution of and
Laws of England." Of these Brougham remarks : " How
well he was qualified to write on oratory and English law,
we may easily conjecture, from the circumstance that he
could never have heard any speaking save in the pulpits of
meeting houses, and in all probability had never seen a
cause tried ; but even if he had been present at debates and
trials, it is difficult to imagine anything more adventurous,
than the teacher of an academy, who devoted his time to
teaching and to theology, promulgating rules of eloquence
and of jurisprudence to the orators and lawyers of his
country." It is a comment which, while doubtless justified,
does not come well from a lawyer of whom it was said that
if he had known a little law he would have known a little of
everything. A few years after the appearance of these
books, Priestley published his " History of Electricity "
which, in spite of certain evidences of haste and superficiality,
was on the whole an excellent piece of work and secured him
election to the Royal Society.

In 1762 he married Mary Wilkinson, an ironmaster's

daughter, whom he later described as " a woman of an excellent understanding, much improved by reading, and of a temper in the highest degree affectionate and generous." Mrs. Priestley seems to have fulfilled her somewhat difficult position with tact and skill, and the marriage proved an eminently successful one. During the betrothal she was generally described to those interested as orthodox, but Timothy, Joseph's brother, and in his way as remarkable a character, decided, after a brief conversation, that she was " no-dox "—an admirable religious standpoint, for the wife of Joseph Priestley. Their wedding was enlivened by the behaviour of Thomas Threlkeld, subsequently a distinguished Presbyterian divine, who, present to give the bride away, became so immersed in a Welsh Bible which he found in a pew, that he quite forgot to attend to his important duties.

CHAPTER V

WITCHES' CAULDRON

DURING the years 1770 and 1771 Lavoisier made two interesting experiments : he disproved the old chemical superstition that water can be transformed into earth and he showed that diamonds are combustible, an observation which required the co-operation of a generous and scientifically-minded jeweller. But it was not until 1772, the year after his marriage, that he began his life work in earnest. The conception which was to guide almost all his subsequent work in chemistry was already taking shape in his mind. He was then twenty-eight years of age, at the beginning of the best creative period of a man's life, when he has acquired sufficient knowledge and skill from others to be able to strike out on his own, and has not yet learned respect for established things ; when, moreover, he feels he has an unlimited time before him. It is in early manhood that great ideas are born. What a man accomplishes after thirty-five is usually a development or refinement of earlier work, often an improvement on earlier work, but it is the flower of a shrub whose roots have already been planted.

To understand the importance of Lavoisier's contribution to science it is necessary to make a brief incursion into the history of chemistry. Chemistry is as old as civilisation, in the sense that civilised man has always made use of certain processes essentially chemical in nature, such as dyeing and smelting. But while chemistry as an art was practised thousands of years before the Christian era, as a science it scarcely existed when Lavoisier was at school. Man's early attempts to explain the chemical processes which he observed and used were peculiarly unsuccessful. He did not possess enough facts out of which to build a satisfactory system. All history, including the history of science, teaches one to distrust reason when it leaves facts behind and begins to operate in the void ; working with infinite subtlety on insufficient material, the human mind produces monstrosities like astrology and the Hindu religion. But, for all that, explanations are psychologically necessary ; a suspense of judgment, in the presence of inadequate data, is distasteful to the human mind, and that doubtless for biological reasons. Man is a systematising animal. It would not be true to say that any explanation of puzzling phenomena, providing it does not involve the persecution by those who believe it of those who do not, is invariably better than no explanation at all, but at least a faulty generalisation may provide scaffolding for the construction of truth. A useful purpose can thus be ascribed to theology and academic philosophy, and the doctrine of Thales that water is the primal element from which all others are derived.

The idea of a primal element is found in many writers of antiquity, but the element chosen was not always the same. Earth, water, air and fire were all given the place of honour by different philosophers. At length the idea, first expressed by a follower of Empedocles, that all four are primal elements and form all varieties of matter, became the general belief. It was generally held that all four were mutually convertible. They were not, of course, elements in the later sense of concrete substances with definite unchangeable properties ; they were rather qualities—material substances were composed of so much airyness, so much wateryness, and so on. The atomism of Democritus was quite a different development of the Greek intellect.

The doctrine of the four elements, accepted and dignified by Plato and Aristotle, was destined to lengthy existence, for it influenced science right down to the end of the eighteenth century, and lingered as a popular belief until our own day. The writer, born in 1899, has a distinct recollection of a child's picture book which displayed the four elements, earth, air, fire, and water, on the frontispiece in diagrammatic form. It is still easy to find educated people who unthinkingly repeat this ancient and curious scientific doctrine, and the idea lingers in popular speech, as when we speak of a liner and an airship as operating " in different elements." As long ago as 1789 Lavoisier wrote, in the preface of his " Traité Elementaire de Chimie " :

" I may here observe, that the fondness for reducing all the bodies in nature to three or four elements, proceeds from a prejudice which has descended to us from the Greek philosophers. The notion of 4 elements, which, by the variety of their proportions, compose all the known substances in nature, is a mere hypothesis, assumed long before the first principles of experimental philosophy or of chemistry had any existence. In those days, without possessing facts, they framed systems ; while we, who have collected facts, seem determined to reject even these, when they do not agree with our prejudices. The authority of the fathers of human philosophy still carries great weight, and there is reason to fear that it will even bear hard on generations yet to come."

The dignified English of a contemporary translation of Lavoisier's book is quoted here.

The elements themselves, Aristotle taught, were formed by combinations of four fundamental attributes, heat, cold, wetness and dryness. Fire was hot and dry, air cold and wet, water cold and wet, earth cold and dry. All matter consisted of combinations of elements and attributes with the fundamental stuff of the universe, the quintessence. The doctrine of elements and attributes could readily be represented in the form of diagrams, and so easily taught to students of philosophy, as could the related doctrine of the four humours to students of medicine. Man had found his explanation of certain perplexing phenomena and remained satisfied with it for two thousand years.

" To fix quicksilver—of several things take 2, 3 and 3 ; 1 to 3 is 4 ; 3, 2 and 1. Before 4 and 3 there is 1 ; 3 from 4 is 1 ; then 1 and 1, 3 and 4 ; 1 from 3 is 2. Between 2 and 3 there is 1, between 3 and 2 there is 1. 1, 1, 1, 1, 2, 2 and 1, 1 and 1 to 2. Then 1 is 1. I have told you all." A hardy pupil, confronted with an alchemical formula of this nature, exclaimed " But, Master, I do not understand." The historian of alchemy is in the same position ; no rational account is possible of that strange aberration of the human mind. To the alchemist, the specific character of a metal depended on the proportion of sulphur and mercury which entered into its composition, these being qualities rather than substances. On the presence of the former depended the property of combustibility. The metals were related to certain heavenly bodies and shared with these the spiritual qualities with which the astrologers endowed them. Silver was the earthly representative of the moon, quicksilver of the planet Mercury, iron of Mars, tin of Jupiter, lead of Saturn. Gold, the noblest of all substances, was the earthly image of the sun.

By suitable alteration in the proportions of sulphur and mercury which they contained, the baser metals could be changed into gold. Metals themselves strove in this direction, for an impulse to obtain a higher state was inherent in nature, so that the essence of alchemy was to assist a natural process. But to effect the transformation or evolution in the direction of gold the philosopher's stone was necessary. In their dim laboratories the alchemists dimly sought the philosopher's stone, the quintessence, which existed in all things but always contaminated by impurities. Could these but be removed, there would be revealed at length the stone itself, capable, not only of turning metals into gold, but of healing all diseases and of ennobling all who touched it. It could renew youth and prolong life ; some claimed that it conferred immortality. Many of those who had seen it said it resembled a red pow-der, but Berigard of Pisa said it was of the colour of a wild poppy, while Paracelsus likened it to a ruby, transparent and brittle as glass.

We need not linger over the iatro-chemists, followers of the remarkable Paracelsus, who adopted from the alchemists the elements of mercury or liquidity and sulphur or com-bustibility, to which they added salt, and declared that all matter was composed of these three in various combinations. Clearly, this three-element theory is closely related to the Greek doctrine, which the respect of the schoolmen for

Aristotle kept alive. The iatro-chemists require mention here because their principle of combustibility, sulphur, developed into the *phlogiston* of Stahl. The famous theory of Stahl, which dominated chemistry for a century, was in fact a reversion to alchemy. When Stahl was in his infancy, Robert Boyle expressed in the " Sceptical Chemist " (1661) his unbounded contempt for the " vulgar stagyrists," as the iatro-chemists were called, and discarded their elements, sulphur, mercury, and salt, as well as those of the ancients. He defined an element simply as a substance incapable of decomposition, and left it for the future to decide what substances might be included under this description.

George Ernest Stahl was born at Anspach in 1660, and crowned a successful career in medicine and science by becoming physician to the King of Prussia in 1716. He contributed nothing to chemistry except a false generalisation, but, nevertheless, he retains a prominent position in the history of science. Since very early times human beings must have speculated on the nature of flame and what happens when a substance is burnt ; it is a problem which most boys find intriguing. Much of alchemy centred round this fundamental phenomenon. The alchemists said that a substance burned because it contained the sulphurous principle of combustibility. Stahl gave the principle a new name and an academic status.

According to Stahl and his followers all substances capable of being burnt possessed this one component in common, which escaped in the act of burning. All combustible bodies were therefore compounds, one of their constituents being phlogiston ; the differences between them depended on the proportions of phlogiston and other components which they contained. Sulphur, which burns leaving very little residue, was held to be pure, or almost pure, phlogiston ; phosphorus on burning becomes a white ash which gives an acid reaction ; it was therefore considered to be a compound of phlogiston and phosphoric acid. When a metal is heated strongly in the presence of air, changes take place in its nature and appearance which were ascribed to loss of phlogiston ; calcined metals or calces no longer contained the combustible principle. Therefore, metals were described as phlogiston plus calx. The fact that when calces are heated in the presence of charcoal the original metal reappears was thought to be due to the transference of phlogiston from the charcoal, a substance containing it in abundance. Atmospheric air was held to absorb the phlogiston given off by the burned or calcined substance, this being the only part assigned to it in the operation. The fact that air is necessary for combustion must have been part of general knowledge from very early times.

Some phlogistonists perceived a parallel between combustion and respiration. When a candle burns in a limited supply of air, it soon goes out ; when an animal is placed in a closed vessel, it soon dies. Respiration, like combustion, was considered to be a transference of phlogiston to the air, and both ceased in a confined space because the air became saturated with phlogiston.

The doctrine of phlogiston, held by almost all chemists of the first three-quarters of the eighteenth century, seemed to explain and co-ordinate many observed facts, and it acted as a useful working hypothesis. It is in conformity with common sense, for when a substance is burnt, something seems to escape. The discrepancies and shortcomings of the theory largely eluded notice. No one had ever seen phlogiston ; the only property which could be assigned to it was that it departed on combustion, but before blaming the chemists of the eighteenth century for their belief in so elusive a substance, it is well to remember that until very recently physicists believed in an ether which gave little proof of real existence. The most serious flaw in the phlogiston theory was the fact, which was observed in the seventeenth century by Boyle, Mayow, and Rey, that a metal on calcination actually increases in weight, but most phlogistonists ignored this difficulty. When they did not, it was explained by an ingenious subterfuge. Flame on leaving a substance passes upwards ; it therefore possesses the quality of levity or negative weight, and its departure from the burnt substance leaves the latter heavier in weight. Thus, the more phlogiston a substance contained, the lighter it should be. Mayow, a Cornishman, had, in 1688, published a book in which he developed the conception of a " *spiritus igneo-aureus*," the " more active and subtle " part of the air, which increases the weight of metals on calcination by combining with them. The fact that a candle in a closed flask was extinguished " although there was still contained in the flask ample abundance of air " led him to deduce the existence of this special part of the atmosphere. Further, he identified burning and breathing, both of which exhaust air of its " *spiritus igneo-aureus*." But Mayow's important observations were ignored by Stahl and his followers.

The phlogiston theory was the most important, indeed, the only important, generalisation in chemical science when Lavoisier was studying under Rouelle. Apart from this, there were plenty of accurate chemical observations on record, but they remained uncorrelated. The alchemists had made a number of useful discoveries in their search for the quintessence, particularly in connection with metals. Hales, to whose work Lavoisier invariably refers with great respect, had prepared a number of different gases, including hydrogen and marsh gas, and had developed a technique for handling them, but he made no serious attempt to study their properties ; he regarded them as being essentially atmospheric air modified in some degree by impregnation with foreign matter. Black had investigated the relation between chalk and quicklime and had discovered carbon dioxide. At this point the reader may be referred to any history of chemistry. But in spite of the labours of many ingenious and capable chemists, chemistry was not yet a science. The four elements of the Peripatetics—earth, air, fire and water, had not yet been finally dethroned ; the problem of combustion, closely associated with the problem of elements and the construction of matter, had not been satisfactorily solved. The shadow of alchemy lingered. One might perhaps compare the state of chemistry in 1772 with that of " psychic science " in our own day. In this bewildering field a vast amount of data, some of it scientifically controlled data, has been accumulated, but at the present moment it makes no sense. Clairvoyance, automatic writing, table turning, ectoplasm—all these need explaining in a rational manner. The one generalisation which covers them all—that they are the work of disembodied spirits—seems unsatisfactory to the scientifically minded. We await a more plausible hypothesis which will reduce each curious fact to its proper place.

In a private laboratory note, written in 1772, dealing with the whole question of the relation of combustion and calcination to atmospheric air, Lavoisier makes the following statement :

" However numerous may be the experiments of Messrs. Hales, Black, Magbridge, Jacquin, Cranz, Prisley and de Smeth[1] in this direction, they come far short of the number necessary to establish a complete body of doctrine."

It was that complete body which he himself sought, realising clearly that chemistry could make no advance until the fundamental problem of combustion was solved. " I feel bound," he adds, " to look upon all that has been done before me merely as suggestive : I propose to repeat it all with new safeguards, in order to link our knowledge of the air that goes into combination with, or is liberated from, other substances, with other acquired knowledge, and to form a theory. The results of the other authors whom I have named, considered from this point of view, appeared to me like separate pieces of a great chain ; these authors have joined only some links of the chain. An immense series of experiments remains to be made in order to lead to a continuous whole."

So Lavoisier, at the age of twenty-eight, envisaged his life work. He immediately set out to re-investigate the whole

---

[1] " It is truly painful," remarks Brougham in a characteristic footnote in his " Lives of Philosophers and Men of Letters in the Eighteenth Century," a work dedicated to the Prince Consort, " to find the determination of French writers never to take the trouble of giving the names of foreigners with any accuracy. Lavoisier always calls Stahl either Stalh or Sthal, and never once gives his right name."

problem *de novo*. One great principle guided him in all his research work, which, stated in his own words, is the following : " It is by the collection of a multitude of facts, and not by *a priori* reasoning, that new scientific theories must be established."

CHAPTER VI

OXYGEN

LAVOISIER'S first step was to repeat the experiment which Mayow had made a century before. (He was not at that date familiar with Mayow's work. Several years later, when his attention had been drawn to it, he tried to obtain a copy of Mayow's book, but unsuccessfully, for it had long been out of print.) Sulphur and phosphorus, Lavoisier found, increase in weight when burned, and he conjectured that the increase in weight was due to air, which during combustion combines with the burning substance. He was convinced that the increase in weight of metals during calcination was due to the same cause, and further experiment confirmed this hypothesis. He reduced litharge in a closed vessel by means of charcoal and noted that during the change from calx to lead a considerable quantity of air was liberated.

These experiments Lavoisier described as the most interesting made since the days of Stahl. He recorded them in a note which was sealed and deposited with the Academy on November 1st, 1772. From the start Lavoisier knew himself to be a great investigator, on the track of far-reaching discoveries, and he had no intention of letting the credit go to anyone else. Having assured himself of priority in the idea underlying his experiments, he proceeded to develop them in several directions.

His experiments on the calcination of lead and tin, though not very satisfactory in some respects, produced valuable evidence in support of his theory of combustion and calcination. When these metals were calcined in a closed vessel the metal gained in weight but the vessel did not ; therefore its increase in weight must come from the air enclosed in the vessel. When the vessel was opened the weight of the air that rushed in was found to be equal to the increase of weight in the metal. He observed that about one-fifth of the air was absorbed during calcination, and that the remaining air would not support combustion. But he did not realise that the air absorbed in calcination possessed the properties of oxygen, or understand the reaction which took place when calces were reduced in the presence of charcoal. For further advance he needed the assistance of another investigator.

We left Priestley attempting to provide a liberal education to nonconformist youth in Warrington Academy, and beginning his florid literary career with works on law and eloquence. He was accustomed at that time to spend a month every year in London, and here his growing reputation as a publicist enabled him to meet many of the active and original spirits of the day. He became friendly with Banjamin Franklin, still a British subject and resident in England, and with Canton, a schoolmaster with a distinguished scientific reputation. Under the influence of these two men Priestley's old hankering after " experimental philosophy " revived, and he offered to write a " History of Electricity," provided he could be supplied with the necessary books. His friends did this for him—actually most of the available material was to be found in the " Philosophical Transactions " of the Royal Society. Within a year the history was ready. Certain points were in dispute, and Priestley tried to settle some of them by experimenting on his own, having at that time " a pretty good electrical machine." The " History of Electricity " was a sound, if not remarkable, piece of work, and Priestley's own experiments on electricity of considerable originality and value, though not to be compared with his later chemical work.

Warrington Academy supplied Priestley with pleasant intellectual company, but it was a needy institution and paid him little money. As a bachelor he had lived on £30 a year, but now he found a salary of £100 a year, even when supplemented by the £15 paid by a few pupils who boarded in his house, insufficient for the support of a family. He therefore accepted an invitation to take charge of a congregation at Leeds, and moved there in 1767—thus relinquishing schoolmastering in favour of his earlier profession of minister. He had in some measure mastered the defect in his speech. Here at last he took up scientific research in comparative earnest, and it is a curious fact that the direction of his subsequent scientific career was largely determined by the fact that he took a house in Meadow Lane, next the brewery of Jakes and Nell. " Fixed air " or carbon dioxide is produced in large quantities during the brewing process. Priestley, finding a supply of an interesting chemical substance easily available, began to amuse himself—the expression is his own—experimenting with it, with results so fascinating that he abandoned " electricity " for the time being in favour of chemistry. He knew very little of chemistry ; his only knowledge, indeed, was that gleaned from a lecture course given by a tutor at Warrington. But ignorance never deterred Joseph Priestley from tackling any subject. Later he characteristically declared that in this case his lack of experience proved a distinct advantage to him. " I was led," he said, " to devise an apparatus and processes of my own, adapted to my peculiar views. Whereas, if I had been previously accustomed to the usual chemical processes, I should not have so easily thought of any other." To-day it is no longer possible for intelligent amateurs to make serious contributions to science, but it nevertheless not infrequently happens that sudden advances are achieved by workers coming freshly to a problem which has encrusted itself with an enormous mass of indecisive information. Those who have studied it for years cannot see the ship for the barnacles. One remembers Banting and diabetes. The irritation of the more learned and experienced when a beginner cheerfully and casually provides the solution for which they have laboriously sought in vain is easily understood and forgiven.

Priestley's first contribution to chemistry was the invention of soda-water. He first impregnated water with carbon dioxide by exposing it to the gas rising from fermenting wort. Later he adopted Lane's method of making the gas from chalk and sulphuric acid, leading it into the water by means of a flexible tube. As a result of this somewhat elementary work on " fixed air " he began to develop a technique of his own in handling gases, inventing his famous pneumatic trough for collecting them. The only person in Leeds who took an interest in his experiments was a surgeon, Mr. Hey. " Mr. Hey," he says, " was a zealous Methodist, and wrote answers to some of my theological tracts ; but we always conversed with the greatest freedom on philosophical subjects, without mentioning anything relating to theology." The mind lingers pleasantly over the picture of doctor and divine bending eagerly over the trough —"such a one as is commonly used for washing linen "—in which gas and water bubbled, and carefully avoiding the most casual reference to Salvation by Faith or the Trinity. One incident which occurred during Priestley's stay in Leeds shows him combining his two major *rôles*. A poor woman of his flock who imagined herself possessed by a devil, went to the minister for help. He had the reputation of being able to work miracles. Priestley attempted to reason with her, but the patient remained fixed in her delusion. The next day she returned, and the minister assured her that he had found a way of relieving her of her incubus. " His electrical apparatus being in readiness, with great gravity he desired the woman to stand upon the stool with glass legs, at the same time putting into her hand a brass chain connected with the conductor, and having charged her plentifully with electricity, he told her, very seriously, to take particular notice of what he did. He then took up a discharger, and applied it to her arm, when the escape of electricity gave her a pretty strong shock. ' There,' says she, ' the devil's gone. I saw him go in that blue flame, and he gave me such a jerk as he went off. I have at last got rid of him and I am now quite comfortable.' "[1]

---

[1] From Rutt's " Memoirs and Correspondence of Joseph Priestley," Vol. 2, p. 112.

Priestley's invention of soda-water—that "exceedingly pleasant sparkling water"—had an interesting sequel. MacBride had a few years previously put forward the idea that " fixed air " might prevent scurvy, and Priestley, having invented a method whereby " fixed air " could readily be swallowed, obtained an introduction to the First Lord of the Admiralty with a view to having his " sparkling water " tried out in practice. Scurvy was one of the major medical problems of the day. The Admiralty, inundated with reports from ships whose crews were sometimes halved by the ravages of the disease, and on which many of the survivors dragged themselves weakly about with putrid gums and bleeding tissues, was at its wits' end. The expansion of commerce, of the British Empire itself, was held up by scurvy ; advances in the art of navigation and the technique of shipbuilding were largely nullified. Clutching at a straw, the Admiralty asked the College of Physicians to report on Priestley's " sparkling water," and that body replied favourably, on grounds which typically illustrate medical mentality in the eighteenth century. It accepted without reserve MacBride's theories of the origin of scurvy. MacBride, in order to explain the fact, widely realised, even at that date, that a sufficient supply of fresh vegetables prevents scurvy, while a diet mainly composed of animal foods tends to produce it, assumed that more " fixed air " is produced during the digestion of the former than during that of the latter. Scurvy is therefore due to lack of " fixed air." Not only the College of Physicians, but the Royal Society itself, lent its support to the idea that a valuable antiscorbutic agent had been discovered. When the Copley Medal was bestowed on Priestley for his discoveries on " different kinds of air," Sir John Pringle, in making the award, specially alluded to the probability that his sparkling water could prevent and cure scurvy. Subsequently, two warships were fitted up with apparatus for producing it.

Priestley's contact with the Admiralty over the question of windy water (to use Mr. G. K. Chesterton's expression) led to a proposal being made that he should accompany Captain Cook on his second voyage to the South Seas, in the capacity of astronomer. The terms were so good that he accepted, but subsequently certain clerical members of the Board of Longitude objected to his religious principles (during his stay in Leeds Priestley became a Socinian, or, as we should say, a Unitarian) and another was chosen in his place—an episode in the history of England which has called forth so many witticisms that it would be superfluous to attempt another. Actually it was on this voyage that Captain Cook succeeded in keeping his crew entirely free from scurvy by rations of sweetwort and cabbage preserved in vinegar—thereby making a most important contribution to medical science—and he in his turn received the Copley Medal for the discovery of an antiscorbutic remedy. Had Priestley been a member of the expedition, he might have urged a trial of his " sparkling water," unfortunately devoid of vitamin C, with disastrous results had Captain Cook so far lowered his high scientific standards as to consent to it.

To have made the first published reference to india-rubber need not be numbered among Priestley's major claims to distinction. Should the reader be one of those unfortunate investors holding shares in rubber plantations he will learn with awe that in 1770 a cubical piece of india-rubber, half an inch long, cost three shillings.

" I am going on with my experiments on air with uncommon success," Priestley wrote about 1771, " for which I am not unthankful to the Giver of all Knowledge." He was indeed at the beginning of an extraordinarily fruitful period of scientific research. He made the fundamental observation that air in which a candle had burnt out could have its power to support combustion and respiration restored by green plants—a sprig of mint or even a piece of groundsel could effect this transformation. After the isolation of oxygen this process was further investigated by Ingenhousz, an Austrian scientist, and by Priestley himself, and its true nature made clearer. Equally remarkable was his discovery of nitric and nitrous oxide gases. The isolation of the former enabled him to evolve a simple method of estimating the proportion of a given sample of air fit for respiration, or, in other words, its oxygen content. Priestley was delighted with this invention of a method of " eudiometry," because it enabled him to be more economical of mice, which he had hitherto used for testing the purity of air. The modern scientific worker in need of mice tells his laboratory attendant to get him fifty or so from the breeding stock, but the animals used in Priestley's experiments came from the wainscots of his own house. " It is most convenient," he says, " to catch the mice in small wire traps, out of which it is easy to take them, and holding them by the back of the neck, to pass them through into the vessel which contains the air. If I expect that the mouse will live a considerable time, I take care to put into the vessel something on which it may conveniently sit, out of reach of the water. If the air be good, the mouse will soon be perfectly at its ease, having suffered nothing by its passing through the water. If the air be supposed to be noxious, it will be proper (if the operator be desirous of preserving the mice for further use) to keep hold of their tails, that they may be withdrawn as soon as they begin to show signs of uneasiness ; but if the air be thoroughly noxious, and the mouse happens to get a full inspiration, it will be impossible to do this before it will be absolutely irrecoverable. Two or three of them will live very peaceably together in the same vessel, though I had one instance of a mouse tearing another almost in pieces, when there was plenty of provisions for both of them."

We need not enlarge on his discoveries of nitrogen, sulphur dioxide, hydrochloric acid gas, silicon tetrafluoride, and ammonia. In all he discovered nine gases, of which only three had been previously known. Much of his success was due to the use of mercury instead of water in the pneumatic trough, for certain of the gases which he isolated had eluded earlier investigators because of their solubility in water. It is necessary, however, to linger for a moment over the familiar story of his crowning achievement, the discovery of oxygen.

At that time Priestley was heating all the chemical substances he could obtain in a closed vessel over mercury, the source of heat being a large burning glass. One of the substances investigated happened to be *mercurius calcinatus per se*.[1] The result, he noted, was a rapid expulsion of air, which was insoluble in water. " But what surprised me more than I can express, was that a candle burned in this air with a remarkably vigorous flame . . . and a piece of red hot wood sparkled in it . . . and consumed very fast." Mice, he found, lived longer in a jar filled with this air than in a jar full of common air, and on taking a few whiffs of it himself he fancied he felt a certain sense of exhilaration. His new air, he suggested, might be " peculiarly salutary " to the lungs in certain morbid cases (it is regularly used to-day in the treatment of pneumonia), " but it might not be so proper for us in the usual healthy state of the body ; for . . . we might, as may be said, *live out too fast*, and the animal powers be too soon exhausted in this pure kind of air. A moralist, at least, may say that the air which Nature has provided for us is as good as we deserve."

Priestley called the newly-discovered gas, which he found to be equally obtainable from lead calx, " dephlogisticated air." It was air avid for phlogiston, and it seized on the fiery principle when brought into contact with it—hence the brilliant and rapid combustion of a candle placed in it.

Actually, all these observations were not made simultaneously. In an experiment on August 1st, 1774, when the new air made its first appearance, Priestley put a lighted candle into it because he " happened to have one to hand at the moment." When he met Lavoisier in October of the same year, he knew only one property of his new air—that a candle burnt in it with a brilliant flame.

---

[1] Mercuric oxide made by heating quicksilver in air. Priestley sometimes calls it *precipitate per se*.

CHAPTER VII

PRIESTLEY AND LAVOISIER MEET

PRIESTLEY was happy enough during the six years of his Ministry at Leeds. He knew the people—it was within six miles of his home—and while his religious views were unpopular with many, he was better liked than he had been at Needham. Though he threw himself whole-heartedly into his duties, stimulating both the young and old of his congregation to new devotional exertions, he found he had sufficient time on his hands to write controversial works on theology and to experiment with " fixed air." But his family was growing in true ministerial fashion, and he began to find his salary of one hundred guineas a year, with a house thrown in, not enough. It was above the average salary paid to Nonconformist ministers, but seemed too small to provide any prospect of suitable education for the children.

He was therefore ready to listen to an offer of a post as " librarian and literary companion " to William FitzMaurice Petty, second Earl of Shelburne. He had been recommended to his lordship by Dr. Price, a liberal theologian who had won considerable distinction as a mathematician. Lord Shelburne, who had himself received a rather scanty education, and in middle life developed an overweening respect for literature and science and the arts, felt that the companionship of a man like Priestley would help him to make good his intellectual deficiencies. The duties of the post were slight, almost nominal ; Priestley was to be comparatively free to devote himself to theological and scientific pursuits. He hesitated. The post seemed to involve separation from his family, to which he declared he would never consent. He was too happy at home. But his lordship was reasonable. The offer was raised from £200 to

£250 a year, with a pleasant house at Calne in Wiltshire, where his family would live. Most of the year was to be spent in Calne, and only a few months of it in London. There was no objection to Priestley preaching whenever he had the opportunity. When he sought advice from his friends Priestley observed that " those who were acquainted with Lord Shelburne encouraged him to accept his proposal, but most of those who knew the world in general, but not Lord Shelburne in particular, dissuaded him from it "—a faulty judgment, as it happened, on the part of the former, for Lord Shelburne was not an easy man to get on with.

Priestley at length accepted, and the years spent at Calne proved to be the most fruitful, from a scientific point of view, of his life. It was here that he made his most important chemical investigations, subsequently published in six volumes under the title of " Experiments on Different Kinds of Air." Lord Shelburne, he says, " encouraged me in the prosecution of my philosophical enquiries, and allowed me forty pounds per annum for expenses of that kind, and was pleased to see me make experiments to entertain his guests, and especially foreigners."

In August, 1774, a few weeks after the experiment with mercuric oxide and the burning glass, in which air capable of making a candle burn very brightly was evolved, he set off with his patron on a continental tour. The journey, which took them into Flanders, Holland, Germany and France, was described by Priestley in a lively series of letters to Lord Shelburne's sons. On the whole the Yorkshireman was not impressed by foreign parts. The prosperity of Flanders attracted him—such beans were not to be found in England—but the women were badly dressed and ugly, and their habit of walking the streets in slippers slatternly and indelicate. He was surprised to see sheaves of poppies in the Flanders fields, until he learned that lamp oil was extracted from their seeds. The sight of a regiment in Lille performing drill evolutions introduced by the King of Prussia, caused him, he says, " a good deal of pain," not, as he somewhat surprisingly adds, " from any consideration of the mischief that this new discipline might enable the French to do us in any future war, but from a cold that I got at the time, which affected my teeth very much."

About Holland Priestley has little agreeable to relate. The wealth of the country impressed him, especially as evidenced by the magnificence of the houses of the great merchants. The number of ships in the harbour at Amsterdam he found astounding. But though, he says, " it must be allowed that Holland is a great curiosity, and well worth the transient visit of a statesman, or a philosopher, it is certainly the last in which a man of a liberal turn of mind would choose to live . . . I can hardly express how very low, beastly, and sordid, the manners of the common people in this country are . . ."

Germany was more attractive, in spite of rainy autumn weather which made the roads difficult. The Rhine Valley in parts was " exceedingly romantic," and in others so well cultivated that it resembled a rich garden. It must, of course, be remembered that Priestley was travelling in the company of a great nobleman, to whom all doors were open. The travellers were received with profound courtesy wherever they went. The politically great were anxious to entertain Lord Shelburne, and, in the various minor duchies, electorates and kingdoms which they passed, a call had to be made on the reigning family. Priestley himself, who had in a few years acquired an international reputation as a scientific investigator, was also something of a celebrity.

His remarks about Paris, which the travellers reached on September 30th, display no striking originality ; he saw the centre of European culture through the eyes of an English provincial Nonconformist. He was impressed by the spaciousness and magnificence of the public buildings, and greatly offended with the narrowness, dirt, and stench of the streets. He met some polite and agreeable people, but none that " appeared to be more polite than many I know in England, especially in the middle ranks of life." In conversation the Parisians continually interrupted each other, being " too much taken up with themselves to admit of that minute and benevolent attention to others which is essential to politeness." He also found them deficient in cleanliness and indeed inferior to the English in almost every respect. " Notwithstanding the French know more of other countries than they used to do . . . they still have that conceit of themselves, and that contempt of other people, which are the truest marks of barbarism."

Priestley was lionised in Paris as a great scientific discoverer, but he never forgot that he was first and foremost a minister of the Gospel. The reader of his memoirs soon realises that his primary interest lay always in religion. As a theologian, he was in the position of many modernists : he had too little Christianity for fervent believers, and too much for complete infidels. Catholic superstition appalled him, while at the same time he regarded atheists as lacking in knowledge and intelligence. The result was probably complete bewilderment on the part of the Frenchmen with whom he conversed. He told atheists that he could " easily account for their infidelity by the very corrupted state of their religion, farther than which they plainly had not looked, and that they could not pretend to have studied the subject as himself and other believers in England had done "—a point of view which was possibly somewhat novel to them. One pious young man embraced him in the joy of having discovered a single philosopher who was also a believer. But Priestley found the net result of all his discussions unsatisfactory. " I left them all as I had found them, and whether they think better or worse of me on that account I am very indifferent." He soon got bored with Paris, and took to spending his evenings at his lodging to avoid company (one suspects that he may have found his self-taught French an insufficient medium in which to expound his doubts of the divinity of Christ). Finally, growing homesick for his own fireside, and eager to be at work again, he left Paris some weeks before his patron.

During his stay in Paris he naturally came into contact with the Lavoisiers. Lavoisier at that date was completely familiar with Priestley's earlier work on gases, for he had

given a full account of it in his recently published " Opuscules Physiques et Chimiques." This book, Lavoisier's
first, was sent by its author to all chemists of note in Europe
and to the various academies of science. He had accumulated a great deal of material in 1772 and 1773, and was too
impatient to await its slow appearance in the Academy
Memoirs. The book contained, in addition to the results
of numerous original experiments carried out by the author,
an account of the work of earlier and contemporary chemists.
Priestley is given considerable space, the *résumé* of his
investigations being prefaced as follows :—

" To fulfil the object which I set myself in writing the earlier
part of this book, it is necessary to give an account of the numerous
experiments which were communicated last year to the Royal
Society of London by Mr. Priestley. This may be regarded as
the most painstaking and interesting work dealing with the
fixation and liberation of air, which has appeared since that of
Mr. Hales. No other piece of recent work has made me appre-
ciate more strongly how many new paths in physics and chemistry
still remain to be trodden.

" Since Mr. Priestley's thesis consists more or less of a web of
experiments, almost uninterrupted by any reasoning—an
assembly of facts, most new to us, either in themselves or because
of the novel circumstances which accompany them—it does not
easily lend itself to abstraction. I shall therefore be compelled,
in the account I am about to give of his work, to follow him step
by step, and my abstract will be almost as long as the original
treatise."

The passage illustrates Lavoisier's scientific mentality,
and incidentally his attitude towards Priestley. In Lavoisier's
memoirs one finds none of the lightheartedness, the simple
pleasure in pretty experiments, which Priestley displays in
his scientific writings. When Lavoisier wrote about chemistry
he was a serious man dealing with a serious subject—as
serious to him as religion to Priestley. Mr. J. W. Sullivan,
in his " Limitations of Science," remarks that Lavoisier,
compared with contemporary scientists working at the same
problems, seems like a professional among amateurs—an
excellent judgment, involving a touch of paradox, when one
remembers that Lavoisier spent more time in the offices of

the *ferme générale* than in his laboratory. In spite of a genuine admiration for Priestley's skill in unearthing new facts, Lavoisier cannot avoid a note of criticism and even disparagement. This is all very novel and ingenious, he seems to be saying throughout his account of Priestley's work, but what does it *mean* ? How does it fit in with the existing body of knowledge and help to further the progress of science ?

Lavoisier had observed that when calcination took place in a closed vessel, some of the air in the vessel, sometimes a fifth but usually less, disappeared, and he had explained this by saying that the vanished air had united with the metal. But he had been unable to recover this air. When he heated various calces or oxides in the presence of charcoal, the oxygen evolved from the calx united with carbon to form " fixed air " or carbon dioxide (a reaction which he later elucidated), and he knew that " fixed air " would not effect calcination or support combustion. The calces which he heated without the addition of charcoal were not those which can readily be deprived of their oxygen. He was, in fact, in an impasse of a kind only too familiar to all scientific workers.

The key was casually supplied by Joseph Priestley. While in Paris he was entertained by the Lavoisiers, and during a meal " at which most of the philosophical people of the city were present," he mentioned his recent and as yet unpublished discovery of an air in which a candle burnt better than in common air. " At this all the company, and Mr. and Mrs. Lavoisier as much as any, expressed great surprise." Marie Lavoisier was then only seventeen years of age, and it is interesting to find Priestley thus indirectly alluding to her position as her husband's co-worker. " I told them I had gotten it from *precipitate per se* (mercuric oxide), and also from red lead. Speaking French very imperfectly, and being little acquainted with the terms of chemistry, I said *plomb rouge*, which was not understood till Mr. Macquer said I must mean *minium*."

It must have been an entertaining scene : the stuttering

Yorkshireman painfully· explaining himself, the thin, keen, ambitious face of Lavoisier as he eagerly follows the halting monologue, the flushed excitement of the pretty young hostess, the interest of the company in this strange philosopher from beyond the seas. "*Plomb rouge? Mais qu'est-ce que c'est que plomb rouge? Ah, vous voulez dire minium? Ah, mais oui, minium.*"

Lavoisier repeated Priestley's experiment in November and again, more carefully, in March of the following year. The results were read to the Academy during the public session of Easter, 1775, and subsequently published in the Academy Memoirs, in a paper which, for a number of reasons, must be regarded as one of the most interesting in the history of science. Lavoisier first of all described earlier experiments in which he had heated calces in the presence of charcoal and obtained " fixed air." He goes on to speak of iron oxides. " The difficulties arising from the very nature of iron, due to the refractory nature of its calces, and the impossibility of reducing them without addition (of charcoal) I came to regard as unsurmountable. I therefore decided to study another kind of calx which would have the property of being reducible without addition. Mercury *precipitate per se*, which is none other than a calx of mercury . . . seemed to be eminently suitable for the purpose I had in mind."

The result of heating the mercuric oxide was an evolution of air which was insoluble in water and which was once more capable of effecting the calcination of metals. When animals were placed in it they did not die ; on the contrary, this air seemed eminently suitable for respiration. A candle was not extinguished, but burnt with a brighter flame than in common air, while all combustible bodies were consumed with great rapidity.[1]   This air, he concluded, must be

---

[1] " A taper burned in it with a dazzling splendour ; and charcoal, instead of consuming quietly, as it does in common air, burnt with a flame, attended with a decrepitating noise, like phosphorus, and threw out such a brilliant light that the eyes could hardly endure it." So Kerr translated Lavoisier's account of his investigation of oxygen in the " Traité Élémentaire de Chimie." Kerr's translation has often a grace not to be found in the pedestrian and unpretentious original.

regarded as the purest part of the atmosphere, as " highly respirable air."

These results, Lavoisier says, filled him with great surprise. From the beginning to the end of his paper there is no mention of Priestley. It must be remembered that the latter's discovery of a special kind of air given off from mercuric oxide under the action of the burning glass had not been published when Lavoisier obtained the results recorded in his memoir. Priestley, on returning to Calne after his continental tour, continued his experiments with mercuric oxide, but for some months he was in doubt as to the nature of the air in which a candle burned so brilliantly. At first he thought it might be nitrous oxide (which enlarges a candle flame) ; later he came to the tentative conclusion that it was " substantially the same as common air." But when he had investigated more fully the properties of the air in question, he realised that it was a new discovery, and he communicated his results to the Royal Society in a letter dated March 15th, 1775, which was read to the Society a week later. This was the first public announcement of the discovery of oxygen, to which Priestley gave the name " dephlogisticated air." While Priestley was elaborating the details of his discovery at Calne, Lavoisier, in Paris, was working on precisely the same lines.[1] The latter's investigation of the properties of oxygen, though actually less thorough than Priestley's, was therefore original ; what he borrowed from Priestley was the idea of using mercuric oxide as a source of it. If he had acknowledged this debt he would not have laid himself open to the charges of dishonesty

[1] Both may have been using the same specimen of *mercurius precipitate per se.* Priestley thought that the sample which he used in his experiment on August 1st, 1774, bought from a common apothecary, might be in fact red precipitate of mercury, *i.e.*, mercuric oxide prepared by the action of spirit of nitre on mercury. This would involve the possibility that the evolved gas was " nitrous air." *Mercurius precipitate per se*, on the other hand, which is prepared by heating mercury in the presence of atmospheric air, could not be suspected of being a source of " nitrous air." Priestley therefore obtained from Waltire a sample of *mercurius precipitate per se* " guaranteed pure." During the Paris visit, Cadet gave him a sample, which was used in the experiments performed during the next few months. Lavoisier got his *mercurius calcinatus* from Cadet, perhaps from the same bottle.

which have been made against him in connection with the discovery of oxygen. Lavoisier never claimed in so many words to be the first and sole discoverer of oxygen, though it might be held that the claim is implicit in his 1775 report. In a memoir which appeared in 1782 he refers to oxygen as " this air which Mr. Priestley discovered about the same time as myself, and even, I believe, before me," and subsequently in his " Traité Élémentaire de Chimie " he remarks that it was discovered by Priestley, Scheele and himself " almost simultaneously." One may suggest that his mind worked as follows : " this Englishman has made a lucky find whose significance he does not understand ; he calls it ' dephlogisti-cated air,' which means nothing ; I was on the verge of discovering it for years and had practically deduced its existence by reasoning from my own experiments ; I alone realise its importance to chemistry ; I isolated it experi-mentally before anything was published about it, and am therefore entitled to claim credit for its discovery."

It was Marat who first openly accused Lavoisier of stealing other men's results. With regard to oxygen, the brutal charges of dishonest plagiarism which have been made against him are exaggerated. Lavoisier did not press his claim with any persistence, and Priestley's priority has never been seriously in dispute. The truth of Lord Brougham's blunt remark " Lavoisier never discovered oxygen until Priestley discovered it to him " may be accepted, but one feels little sympathy for the tone of pompous rebuke in which that pushing publicist thought fit to discuss the character of the founder of modern chemistry. We have, of course, only Priestley's own word for it that he told the Lavoisiers in Paris about oxygen. Priestley's memory was extraordinarily fallible ; in later years he was capable of forgetting an earlier published experiment so completely as to repeat it, note the result with surprise, and attempt to re-publish it. But a bad memory will not lead a man to remember what has not happened. The episode of *plomb rouge* or *minium* could not be invented.

The Greek philosophers taught that atmospheric air is an

element, constant and indivisible. The discovery of oxygen, of a " highly respirable " portion of the atmosphere, showed the falsity of this conception (though there was no immediate general realisation that the old idea was untenable, for revolutionary new ideas in science are often slowly assimilated). A new problem therefore arose : if atmospheric air is not an element, what are its components ? It is interesting to compare Lavoisier's solution of this problem, after he had received a vital clue in the discovery of oxygen, and carried out further relevant experiments, with that eventually arrived at by the discoverer of oxygen himself.

In an experiment which was reported to the Academy of Science in 1777, Lavoisier, so to speak, took atmospheric air to pieces and put it together again. First, he deprived a given quantity of air of its oxygen :—

" I enclosed 50 cubic inches of common air in a suitable apparatus, which it would be difficult to describe without illustrations ; I introduced into this apparatus 4 ounces of very pure mercury and proceeded to calcine it, keeping it for twelve days at a heat almost sufficient to make it boil.

" Nothing noteworthy happened during the first day ; the mercury, though not boiling, was in a state of continual evaporation. On the second day, red specks began to appear on the surface of the mercury, and they increased in size and volume daily ; finally, at the end of twelve days, having let the fire out and allowed the vessel to cool, I observed that the air it had contained was diminished by 8 to 9 cubic inches, that is to say, by about a sixth of its volume ; at the same time there had been formed a considerable quantity, approximately 45 grains, of mercury *precipitate per se*, or calx of mercury."

The air that remained in the vessel, he found, would not support life or combustion. In this it resembled " fixed air " or carbon dioxide, but its non-identity with that gas was proved by the fact that it did not precipitate lime water. The residual air was, in fact, largely composed of the gas which to-day we call nitrogen.

Lavoisier's next step was to reduce the 45 grains of mercury *precipitate per se*, to repeat, in fact, Priestley's famous experiment, but from a quantitative angle :—

" The experiments of Mr. Priestley and myself have made clear that precipitated mercury is nothing else than a compound of mercury with about one twelfth of its own weight of a kind of air that is better, and more respirable, if I may use such a word, than common air ; it appears then to be proved that in the foregoing experiment the mercury absorbed the better and more respirable part of the air during calcination, leaving behind the noxious or non-respirable part ; the following experiment confirmed this truth yet further :

" I carefully collected the 45 grains of calx of mercury formed in the preceding calcination ; I put them in a very small glass retort, whose neck, doubly bent, was fixed under a bell-jar full of water, and I proceeded to reduce it without adding anything.

" By this operation I recovered almost the same amount of air as had been absorbed by the calcination, that is to say, 8 or 9 cubic inches, and on combining these 8 to 9 inches with the air vitiated by the calcination of mercury, I restored this air exactly enough to its state before calcination, *i.e.*, to the state of common air : the air thus restored no longer extinguished flame, no longer caused the death of animals breathing it, and finally was almost as much diminished by nitrous air as the air of the atmosphere."

As a result of this brilliantly conceived experiment, and others, Lavoisier was able to make the following extremely clear and satisfactory pronouncement :—

" I have established in the foregoing memoirs that the air of the atmosphere is not a simple substance, an element, as the Ancients believed and as has been supposed until our own time ; that the air we breathe is composed of respirable air to the extent of only one-quarter and that the remainder is a noxious gas (probably itself of a noxious nature) which cannot alone support the life of animals, or combustion or ignition. I feel obliged, consequently, to distinguish four kinds of air or air-like fluids :

First, atmospheric air ; that in which we live, which we breathe, etc.

Secondly, pure air, respirable air ; that which forms only a quarter of atmospheric air, and which Mr. Priestley has very wrongly called *dephlogisticated air*.

Thirdly, the noxious air which makes up three quarters of atmospheric air and whose nature is still entirely unknown to us.

Fourthly, fixed air, which I shall call henceforward, following M. Bucquet, by the name of acid of chalk."

What were Priestley's conclusions on the same question ? Having been led, he says, though very gradually, " to a complete discovery of the constitution of the air we breathe," he made his pronouncement :—

" Atmospheric air, or the thing that we breathe, consists of the nitrous acid and earth, with so much phlogiston as is necessary to its elasticity."

CHAPTER VIII

THE HONOURABLE HENRY CAVENDISH

Our third philosopher, Henry Cavendish, takes us with a bound far up the social scale. Lavoisier was good French bourgeois, a class which, then as now, had no small conceit of itself; the fine title which his father purchased, *Conseiller Secretaire du roi, maison, finances, et couronne de France,* could not really assimilate so solid a family with the parasitic aristocracy of birth. As a country squire who devoted his estates to experimental farming, Lavoisier resembled very little the landed gentry of France. Priestley was middle class and north country to the backbone; he conducted himself in society with ease but not elegance, and undoubtedly retained throughout his life touches of the self-made man. Henry Cavendish could trace his descent back through six centuries, by unbroken links to Sir John Cavendish, Lord Chief Justice of the King's Bench in the reign of Edward III. He was the grandson of a Duke by both parents, and the nephew and cousin of others, with connections on both sides of the family with the greatest of the English aristocracy. Many illustrious administrators throughout the centuries had borne his name. One may add that Henry Cavendish remained all his life quite uninterested in his ducal relations and singularly indifferent to the glories of his family history.

He was born in 1731 at Nice, where his mother, Lady Anne Cavendish, lived for the sake of her health. She gave birth to another boy and died when Henry was two years old. Our three philosophers thus all lost their mothers at early ages, but while Priestley and Lavoisier were both carefully and tenderly reared by aunts, no such maternal substitute from among his distinguished relations was found in the case of Henry Cavendish. Actually, details of the boy's upbringing are entirely lacking. We may, however, surmise from our knowledge of his adult character that his childhood was a strange and unhappy one. Parents in those days were not particular about those to whom they entrusted the care of their children, and some slattern with leanings towards sadism may have had the two little boys handed over to her.

At the age of eleven he went to a school at Hackney kept by Dr. Newcombe, a sound classical scholar and a strict disciplinarian. Probably it was a dismal and unhappy place. No record remains of Henry's schooldays, and details of his Cambridge career are almost equally meagre. He kept his terms regularly at Peterhouse for three and a half years, then left suddenly without taking a degree. His departure was due, in all probability, to a reluctance to submit to the strict religious tests then demanded of degree candidates.

Of the next ten years of his life nothing is known. He suddenly emerged upon the world in middle life as a remarkable scientist and an even more remarkable eccentric. One slight ridiculous episode remains from his younger days. He was travelling in France with his brother Frederick, and in a hotel in Calais they passed the open door of a room in which a corpse was laid out for burial. The brothers said nothing at the time, but during the next day's journey Frederick suddenly remarked " Did you see the corpse ? " to which Henry replied " I did." The rest of the journey was passed in silence. In later years the brothers held no intercourse at all.

In early manhood Cavendish was comparatively poor for the scion of so propertied a family. He received, it is said, an annuity from his father of £500 a year. Another account puts his allowance as low as £120. We have the story that when Cavendish, a man in early middle age, attended the weekly dinners of the Royal Society Club, he invariably brought with him exactly the amount necessary to pay for the dinner, namely, 5s. His father gave him this—not a penny more. Certainly he became accustomed in early manhood to very frugal fare, and when, over the age of forty, he was suddenly enriched by a large legacy, he made no attempt to change his habits of life. The legacy—£300,000, no less—came from a military uncle who, it is said, disapproved of the contemptuous attitude adopted towards Henry by his other relatives. To these he was an unworthy representative of a family whose members were expected to play a prominent part in public affairs.

As a wealthy and gifted eccentric, he spent the last half of his unhappy life. He owned three houses, in Soho, in Montague Place, and in Clapham, the first of which was devoted to a library, the other two being fitted out as laboratories and workshops rather than as dwelling places. It was in the house at Clapham that a titled lady (probably the only visitor of her sex who ever penetrated there) was startled to see a long row of chamber pots set out on a bench, being used, in fact, by Cavendish as highly convenient vessels for evaporating saline solutions. Should he have occasion to drive from one house to another, or to a meeting of the Royal Society, he would sit as far back in the corner of the carriage as possible, in order to avoid notice. His daily walk was always taken in the dusk of the evening and followed an invariable route in the neighbourhood of Clapham and Wandsworth Commons ; to avoid contact with the passers-by as much as possible, he always walked in the middle of the road. Such proceedings were naturally intriguing to the inhabitants of Clapham, and it was rumoured that this strange solitary gentleman, who fled in terror if spoken to, whose house was given over to inexplicable activities, was in fact a wizard.

His wealth accumulated. When he died he possessed over £1,000,000 in bank stock—being, in fact, the largest holder of bank stock in England—with other property worth £40,000 a year, and £50,000 on account with his bankers. This, as Americans used to say, is real money. During his lifetime the relentless swelling of his bank balance had caused some trouble. The story of his reply to the banker who, finding that Cavendish's current account amounted to no less than £80,000, came to ask his client what he should do with it, is well known :—

" Sir, there is a person below who wants to speak to you."

" Who is he ? Who is he ? What does he want with me ? "

" He says he is your banker, and must speak to you."

Mr. Cavendish, in great agitation, desires he may be sent up, and, before he enters the room, cries in his thin shrill voice, " What do you come here for ? What do you want with me ? "

" Sir, I thought it proper to wait upon you, as we have a very large balance in hand of yours, and wish for your orders respecting it."

" If it is any trouble to you, I will take it out of your hands. Do not come here to plague me."

" Not the least trouble to us, sir, not the least." [1]

Cavendish was an ungenerous man, in the sense that he was as a rule too much out of touch with humanity to realise that others might be in need. He was, nevertheless, quite capable of giving very large sums away in a spasm of irritation, to be rid, as it were, of the supplicator for ever. When asked to subscribe to a charitable object he would request the subscription list, note the largest donation, and write a cheque for exactly that amount—a practice of which unscrupulous secretaries of charitable organisations learned to take advantage in an obvious manner. On one occasion an acquaintance remarked to Cavendish, referring to an ex-librarian of his who had fallen on bad times, " We had hoped you could have done something for him, sir." Cavendish was genuinely surprised. What could he possibly do ? The other mildly suggested a little annuity, whereupon Cavendish pulled out his cheque-book and wrote a cheque for £10,000. When he died his enormous fortune was left entirely to an heir bearing his name who had little need of it. Not a penny was left to be devoted to the interests of science.

[1] Wilson, " Life of the Hon. Henry Cavendish," p. 175.

In society he cut a pathetic and ridiculous figure.   Having no knowledge of any subject but science, he could take no part in general conversation, and his excursions were confined to the meetings of the Royal Society at Somerset House and to weekly conversaziones at the house of its President, Sir Joseph Banks.   To this rule he made one strange exception : he would attend christenings of his cousins at Devonshire House or at some other of the great houses of his relatives.   But even when the company was exclusively scientific, Cavendish was not at his ease.   He would stand for a long time outside the door of the place of meeting, trying to gather courage to open the door and face the company.   When someone else arrived and he was forced to take the plunge, he would slip in as unostentatiously as possible in the wake of the newcomer.   " He would often," says Brougham, " leave the place where he was addressed, and leave it quickly, with a kind of cry or ejaculation, as if scared and disturbed."   A sudden remark, or the fixed regard of an interlocutor, would throw him into a state of genuine agitation.   Those who wished to hold Cavendish in conversation were warned by the knowing to gaze into vacancy over his head.   A group of acquaintances talking among themselves would attract and repel him at the same time, so that he would sidle up with the nervous stealthiness of an animal attracted by a bun and yet afraid of the donor.   A sudden movement on someone's part, or the sight of an unfamiliar face, would send him scurrying away.   At one of Sir Joseph Banks' parties, Dr. Ingenhousz, a somewhat pompous man, committed the *gaffe* of suddenly introducing a strange Austrian gentleman to Cavendish, mentioning the titles and qualifications of his compatriot at great length. The stranger, rising to the occasion, told Cavendish that his principal purpose in coming to London was to converse with him—one of the greatest ornaments of the age, and one of the most illustrious philosophers that ever existed.   Two pompous Austrians at one time—it was too much.   Cavendish stood silent with his eyes cast down, " quite abashed and confounded."   Then, spying an opening in the crowd, he fled from the house, sank into the darkest corner of his carriage, and drove straight home to solitude and peace. Eccentricity has its privileges.

While Cavendish was ill at ease in the company of men, contact with women was quite intolerable to him. He shunned the female sex as circumspectly as a fourth century hermit. To avoid chance encounters with housemaids, he had a back staircase built in his Clapham home, and should an unfortunate maid show herself by mistake, she was immediately dismissed. He ordered his meals on a slip of paper left on the hall table, so that no speech with the housekeeper should be required. His daily walks at Clapham were ruined by the behaviour of two ladies who, having observed that Cavendish took the same route every day, brought their friends to watch so remarkable a figure passing by. One day, while getting over a stile, he saw to his extreme horror that he was being watched, and that by members of the female sex. Henceforward he took his exercise under cover of darkness. During one of the meetings of the Royal Society Club, a very pretty girl leaned out of a window on the opposite side of the street to watch the philosophers at dinner. Sensible men and fathers of families, they abandoned scientific conversation and went to the window to study beauty. Cavendish, on joining the group, shrank away in disgust when he saw the object of their attention. He had thought, poor fellow, that they were observing the moon.

Such figures as Henry Cavendish are to be found in any lunatic asylum, harmless miserable creatures who draw away if spoken to with a sort of terrified distaste. What was remarkable about Cavendish was not his psychoses, but the fact that they co-existed with intellectual ability of the highest order. Intellectual achievement and so marked a degree of maladjustment rarely go together. But this dirty, semi-insane old aristocrat, shuffling about in clothes fifty years out of fashion, was really one of the foremost chemists and physicists of his day. He was the first fully to describe hydrogen, he discovered the chemical composition of water,

H. Cavendish

THE HONOURABLE HENRY CAVENDISH.
From a drawing by Alexander.

[*To face p.* 76.

he discovered nitric acid, he made a remarkably accurate calculation of the density of the earth. Memoirs on heat and electricity, found after his death among his papers, anticipate discoveries made half a century later. His approach to chemical and physical problems was always strictly mathematical, for, Brougham says, " he was a most complete and accomplished mathematician . . . his papers relate to various branches of optics, of physical and practical astronomy—to the theory of mathematical and astronomical instruments—of mechanical and dynamical sciences, both theoretical and practical—to pure mathematics in all its branches, geometry, the integral and differential calculus, the doctrine of chance and annuities . . . that he had the most familiar and masterly knowledge of the calculus is plain throughout all his investigations." We might, indeed, make use of a familiar and, as generally used, meaningless word, and say of Cavendish that he had a mathematical complex. The practice of counting and measuring, even when conducted for its own sake alone, seemed to give him some deep psychological satisfaction. When he performed a chemical experiment he measured the quantities used of all the reagents, whether such facts had any bearing on the ultimate result or not. He had a *way-wiser* attached to the wheels of his carriage, which enabled him to reckon the miles covered. When attending the Royal Society Club he always hung his hat on the same peg ; to have moved it one peg to the right or the left would have given a different mathematical bearing to the action and stirred up deep resistances. His servants in Clapham had learnt, doubtless as the result of painful scenes, that his boots must always be placed at one particular spot outside the dining-room door, with his stick in one particular boot. He ordered new suits (always the same suit, grey in colour, for, like a certain Great Lady of our own times, he took no heed of passing fashions) not when his old ones were worn out, but in accordance with a regular time system. His tailor was instructed to appear at certain regular intervals, and Cavendish would consult the calendar to know when the next visit might be expected. The universe, in fact, was to him only a number of objects which could be weighed, counted and measured, and he made scarcely any contact at all with its less ponderable and measurable aspects.

A great brain, and a very small man ! A psychiatrist might find it interesting to guess at the early experiences which made full human development impossible, allowing one small part of his being to hypertrophy, and the rest to waste away.

CHAPTER IX

WATER

Somewhere about the year 1780, Priestley, at that time resident in Birmingham, became interested in hydrogen, then known as "inflammable air." "Inflammable air" had first been thoroughly studied by Cavendish. In one of his experiments, Priestley placed some minium in a tall cylinder containing hydrogen, and heated the minium by means of a burning glass. The result was a transformation of the calx into metal, while the volume of "inflammable air" in the cylinder rapidly diminished. In the course of some similar experiments with oxide of mercury, he noted that moisture appeared within the cylinder. Lavoisier at this date would have realised that the oxide, during its reduction to metal, was giving off "highly respirable air" or oxygen, though he would not have understood that oxygen was uniting with hydrogen to form water. Priestley, though familiar with Lavoisier's ideas about calcination, explained the phenomena observed along quite different lines. "I could not doubt," he says, "that the calx was imbibing something from the air ; and, from its effects in making calx into metal, this could be no other than that which chemists have unanimously given the name of phlogiston." Following Cavendish, he identified "inflammable air" and phlogiston. The fatal flaw in his explanation, well understood by Lavoisier, that the reduction of calx to metal resulted in a loss, and not a gain, in weight, escaped him. When he discovered a loss of weight, he explained it by sublimation of the calx.

In some further experiments Priestley exploded common and "inflammable" air together in a vessel by means of an electric spark. After the explosion the walls of the vessel were found to be covered with moisture, but Priestley paid little attention to this phenomenon. The experiment was a " random one," made " to please a few philosophical friends " and not to test some particular hypothesis. One of the philosophical friends, a certain Mr. Warltire, lecturer on Natural Philosophy in Birmingham, conceived the idea that such an experiment might solve the question of whether heat has weight. He therefore repeated it several times, weighing the flask before and after the explosion. The flask seemed to weigh less after the generation and loss of heat due to the explosion, so that Warltire came to the conclusion that heat is a ponderable body—thus providing, as he thought, further support for the phlogiston theory. Cavendish, hearing of this experiment and the important conclusion based on it, thought that, " if there were no mistake about it, it would be very extraordinary and curious." He therefore repeated it with the infinite care of which he was capable, but could find no appreciable difference between the first and second weighings. He was immediately interested, however, in the phenomenon which both Warltire and Priestley had disregarded—the deposit of moisture within the vessel. " I could never," he said, " perceive a loss of weight of more than one-fifth of a grain and commonly none at all." But " in all the experiments the inside of the glass became dewy," and the dew he found to be pure water.

Here was something which gave promise of a most satisfying series of weighings and calculations. Cavendish immediately embarked on experiments in which he burned common air and " inflammable air " together in differing amounts, reaching the conclusion that " when inflammable air and common air are exploded in proper proportions, almost all the inflammable air, and near one-fifth of the common air, lose their elasticity and are condensed into dew." Later he substituted Priestley's " dephlogisticated air," which Lavoisier was beginning to call " *oxygène*," for common air. The gases were mingled in the proportions of about 19,500 grain measures of " dephlogisticated air," and 37,000 of " inflammable air," or about two volumes of hydrogen to one of oxygen, and after the explosion it was usually found that the gases disappeared entirely in the formation of water. In certain experiments nitric acid was formed, a phenomenon which puzzled Cavendish for some time, and held up the publication of his results, until he realised that the acid was derived from a small quantity of atmospheric air which remained in the globe after exhaustion by the air pump. From all this Cavendish drew rather meagre and disappointing conclusions. " I think," he said, " we must allow that dephlogisticated air is in reality nothing but dephlogisticated water, or water deprived of its phlogiston ; or, in other words, that water consists of dephlogisticated air united to phlogiston." This round-about and involved explanation of the composition of water in terms of the phlogiston theory seems to have satisfied him. Superior to Lavoisier in technical ability as an experimenter, he lacked the Frenchman's capacity for interpretation.

Cavendish was never in a hurry to give the world the results of his work. After his death valuable scientific observations, which he had not troubled to publish, were found recorded in his manuscripts. He experimented, one feels, mainly for his own edification and would have continued to experiment if the Royal Society and its " Philosophical Transactions " had never existed. In the present instance, apart from his temperamental indifference to publication, the fortuitous appearance of nitric acid during the course of the investigation had interested and delayed him. Actually his experiments on the composition of water, performed in 1781, did not appear in print until 1784. In the meantime much had happened.

Between 1781 and 1783, Priestley, hearing from Cavendish of the direction in which the experiments originated by Warltire and himself had been developed, proceeded to try something similar himself. His work in this instance was inaccurate, because he used, not only hydrogen, but gas derived from heated charcoal, a mixture of carbon monoxide, carbon dioxide, and methane. Some moisture was obtained, the weight of which was measured by a very primitive method involving the use of blotting paper. This experiment was published in 1783, Priestley giving full credit to Cavendish for the idea on which it was based. In the same paper he describes some equally faulty experiments which purported to show that water could be converted into air. All these results were communicated privately to James Watt, who, having studied them, made the following statement in a letter which he intended to be read to the Royal Society : " Are we not then to conclude that water is composed of dephlogisticated air and phlogiston deprived of part of their content or elementary heat ; that dephlogisticated or pure air is composed of water deprived of its phlogiston and united to elementary heat and light, etc. ? "

It was on this slender basis—this somewhat hazy statement founded on faulty experiments performed by a worker who fully acknowledged his debt to Cavendish—that Watt later claimed to be the discoverer of the composition of water. Actually his letter to the Royal Society was never read, because Priestley soon detected the fallacies in his experiments and induced Watt to withdraw it—not, however, before it had been read by certain members. But the letter was destined to play an important part in the great Water Controversy, a term which suggests a conflict between an urban district council and a borough surveyor, but was, in fact, the title given to one of the most prolonged and boring battles about priority in scientific discovery which has ever taken place.

Lavoisier was more closely connected than Watt with the discovery of the chemical composition of water. In 1781 he had actually burned oxygen and hydrogen together, but he had not noticed the formation of water. Though the question of the non-elementary nature of water was in the forefront of his mind at this time, he did not succeed in devising a crucial experiment which would clarify the problem. Rumours of Cavendish's experiments crossed the Channel, for the small scientific world was close-knit at this period, but it was not until after the visit of Blagden to Paris that Lavoisier fully realised their importance and repeated them. Blagden at that time was Cavendish's assistant. In one of his peculiar fits of generosity, Cavendish had presented him with a perpetual annuity of £500, in return for secretarial and scientific duties. Blagden, elected Secretary of the Royal Society in 1784, was a good scientific worker but, it seems, a trifle over-precise and prosy in his conversation, a characteristic which annoyed his friends but won the respect of Samuel Johnson. His connection with Cavendish was severed a few years later, for indeed the position of secretary to such a man was an impossible one.

In June, 1783, the worthy Blagden was in Paris, where he gave Lavoisier and his colleagues a full account of his employer's experiments on water, of which previously the French workers had heard only rumours. As before in the case of oxygen, Lavoisier immediately realised the importance of the discovery, and hastened to carry out the synthesis of water himself. It is at this point that he committed the most unworthy action of his career. Having repeated Cavendish's experiment in a rough and ready way on June 24th, in the presence of Blagden and certain members of the Academy of Science, he gave the Academy the very next day a brief account of his experiment, which is recorded in the minutes as follows :—

" MM. Lavoisier and de Laplace announced that they had lately repeated the combustion of combustible air with dephlogisticated air ; they worked with about sixty pints of the air and the combustion was made in a closed vessel : the result was very pure water."

In a fuller account of this and similar experiments given a little later (actually Lavoisier was the first to describe the synthesis of water in print) he mentioned that Blagden was present on June 24th, but he omitted to say that the experiment was performed at the latter's instigation. He makes it appear as though Blagden, having watched the synthesis of water taking place in the Arsenal laboratory, casually remarked that Cavendish had been able to do much the same thing in London. In point of fact Blagden had stressed the

exact quantitative nature of Cavendish's experiments—a
vital part of the discovery which Lavoisier slurred over, for
he makes Blagden say vaguely that Cavendish obtained
" a considerable quantity of water." He himself did not
obtain quantitative results until later, and then his figures
were less accurate than those of Cavendish. In a paper
written in collaboration with Seguin and published in 1789,
he enumerates a number of newly-discovered facts which
had revolutionised chemistry, including that of the non-
elementary nature of water. " Water," the authors remark,
" is not an element, not a simple substance, as the ancients
believed. It is composed of 14,338 parts of oxygen and
85,668 parts of hydrogen." And they proceed to say:
" M. Lavoisier, one of the authors, established all these
facts in a series of memoirs presented to the Academy."
Altogether it was a strange lapse on the part of a man of
integrity into meanness and folly—folly because he had no
real chance of obtaining credit for Cavendish's discovery.

Lavoisier did, however, make one extremely useful and
original contribution to the subject. He made a partially
successful analysis of water. Steam from water boiling in
a weighed retort was passed through a heated gun barrel ;
hydrogen gas emerged at the other end, while the iron
inside the barrel was oxidised. The weight of the hydrogen
gas produced, added to the weight acquired by the gun
barrel in the process of oxidation, was found to be nearly
equal to the weight lost by the retort. This was clearly a
very pretty and very satisfactory experiment. Bergman
had previously shown that when iron is placed in distilled
water, it is transformed into " ethiops martial " (iron oxide)
and hydrogen is set free, and Cavendish's synthesis had
already demonstrated the components of water, but, for all
that, Lavoisier's analysis, involving the careful use of the
balance, was a masterly piece of work. We must remember,
of course, that while Cavendish described the synthesis of
water in terms of the phlogiston theory, Lavoisier was able
to describe it accurately in accordance with his own system,
and his priority in this respect is unquestionable.

Cavendish was the undoubted winner of the Water Handicap. Not so very far behind, striving very hard and running an excellent race, but inclined to foul a little at the corners, came Lavoisier. Far out of sight, faint but pursuing, Watt made a very poor third. But he needs no sympathy, having plenty of victories to his credit. Watt, it seems, had suffered so much from piracy in connection with his commercially valuable invention of the steam engine, that he had become over prone to suspect others of stealing his ideas. We can best so explain the following unworthy letter, written by him to Mr. Fry, of Bristol, in May, 1784 :—

" The papers which I mentioned to you that I had written, on the composition of water, have been read at the Royal Society, I am told with great applause. But I have had the honour, like other great men, to have my ideas pirated. Soon after I wrote my first paper on the subject, Dr. Blagden explained my theory to M. Lavoisier at Paris ; and soon after that M. Lavoisier invented it himself and read a paper on the subject to the Royal Academy of Science. Since that, Mr. Cavendish has read a paper to the Royal Society on the same idea, without making the least mention of me. The one is a French financier, and the other a member of the illustrious house of Cavendish, worth about £1,000,000, and does not spend £1,000 a year. Rich men may do mean actions. May you and I always persevere in our integrity and despise such things."

When Watt wrote this, he was well on the way to affluence and scarcely entitled to see himself as representing honest poverty in a struggle against the machinations of wicked rich men. But, indeed, the letter does him less than justice.

The discovery of the composition of water marks the birth of modern chemical science. Water, like air a few years previously, was shown to be non-elemental, and the long lived doctrines of the Peripatetics were thus finally disproved. What was of more immediate importance, the phlogiston theory received its death blow. Why should phlogiston and dephlogisticated air unite to form water ? There was no longer any sense in it. In fact, the whole idea of phlogiston suddenly became unnecessary, since phenomena previously explained by its help could be much more simply and

naturally explained without it.   Lavoisier's new generalisation did not win immediate recognition, but from 1784
onwards there was a steady trickle of converts over to his
side, until ten years later only a few diehards remained in
the opposite camp.

This fundamental change in chemical ideas, involving the
dethronement of the prophet Stahl, was not received with
any enthusiasm in Germany.   In Berlin, students burnt
Lavoisier in effigy, but such gestures were no more effective
than the arguments which Galileo's opponents brought
forward to prove that the new planets and moons, actually
visible through his telescope, had no real existence.   A
ceremony arranged by the Lavoisiers symbolised more
accurately the true state of affairs.   With Madame Lavoisier
in the appropriate *rôle* of high priestess, Stahl's " Chemicæ
Dogmaticæ et Experimentalis Fundamenta " was solemnly
burnt on an altar.   The book had perhaps fulfilled a certain
purpose, but now the bonfire was the only place for it.

Though Lavoisier eliminated phlogiston from chemistry,
he himself retained the belief that heat is a material though
imponderable entity which enters into combination with all
substances possessing it.   Certain of his contemporaries
inclined towards the modern conception of heat as a
product of molecular activity.   Lavoisier was aware of their
views, and treated them with respect, but nevertheless held
fast to his own, elaborating these with great ingenuity in his
" Traité Élémentaire de Chimie."   The results of this error
were not serious, for an imponderable body could be disregarded in experiments essentially dependent on the use
of the balance.

Having disproved the ancient superstition that water and
air are elements, Lavoisier made no attempt to dogmatise on
the problem of elements, to construct a new system to replace
the old.   He took up, in fact, a position precisely similar to
that of Boyle :—

" All that can be said upon the number and nature of
elements is, in my opinion, confined to discussions of a meta-
physical nature.   The subject only furnishes us with indefinite

problems, which may be solved in a thousand different ways, not one of which, in all probability, is consistent with nature. I shall, therefore, only add upon this subject, that if, by the term *elements*, we mean to express simple and indivisible atoms of which matter is composed, it is extremely probable we know nothing at all about them ; but, if we apply the term *elements* or *principles of bodies*, to express our idea of the last point which analysis is capable of reaching, we must admit, as elements, all the substances into which we are able to reduce bodies by decomposition. Not that we are entitled to affirm, that these substances which we consider as simple, may not themselves be compounded of two, or even of a greater number of more simple principles ; but since these principles cannot be separated, or rather since we have not hitherto discovered the means of separating them, they act with regard to us as simple substances, and we ought never to suppose them compounded until experiment and observation have proved them to be so." (Preface to the " Traité Élémentaire de Chimie," Kerr's translation.)

It would certainly be difficult to discover, in the whole range of modern scientific writing, a passage which more aptly illustrates the correct attitude of the scientific worker towards an unsolved problem. Lavoisier did not always live up to his own high principles, for on occasion he allowed pre-formed ideas to lead him astray—he held, for example, to his theory that oxygen is the acidifying principle quite against the evidence. But in spite of certain human inconsistencies, he must be given a high place, not only amongst those who have contributed to science by observation and experiment, but amongst those who have helped to create the scientific spirit and philosophy which, for good or ill, exert an ever-increasing influence over the destiny of mankind.

CHAPTER X

LAVOISIER AS REFORMER

By the year 1784 Lavoisier had won a commanding position in the scientific world of the day. His reputation extended beyond the boundaries of France. The laboratory at the Arsenal was a meeting place for French scientists and an object of pilgrimage to distinguished foreigners visiting Paris, who, even if ignorant of chemistry, could observe with interest its glittering apparatus, and learn with awe how much it had cost. As the reader can assure himself by a visit to the *Conservatoire des Arts et Métiers* in Paris, Lavoisier spared no expense on the construction of laboratory apparatus. The best workmen in France were at his disposal, and everything was of the very solid best.

Arthur Young, who visited Paris just before the Revolution, has left us an interesting account of a meeting with Lavoisier in the Arsenal laboratory.

" To the arsenal, to wait on Monsieur Lavoisier, the celebrated chemist, whose theory of the non-existence of phlogiston has made as much noise in the chemical world as that of Stahl, which established its existence. Dr. Priestley had given me a letter of introduction. I mentioned in the course of conversation his laboratory, and he appointed Tuesday." . . . " To Monsieur Lavoisier, by appointment. Madame Lavoisier, a lively, sensible, scientific lady, had prepared a *dejeuné Anglais* of tea and coffee, but her conversation on Mr. Kirwan's ' Essay on Phlogiston ' which she is translating from the English, and on other subjects, which a woman of understanding that works with her husband in his laboratory knows how to adorn, was the best repast. That apartment, the operations of which have been rendered so interesting to the philosophical world, I had pleasure in viewing. . . . I was glad to find the gentleman splendidly lodged, and with every appearance of a man of considerable fortune."

But the time which the owner of the laboratory could find to spend in it was limited. He had so much else to do. We will now leave Lavoisier's major scientific work on one side for the moment, to consider some of his other activities. As the years passed he became a public figure, immersed in manifold duties, propping up with restless energy and enormous executive ability the undermined, staggering social organisation of his country. Competently and critically he surveyed many important social institutions, found them wanting, said so in a sub-acid but not too unkindly manner, and showed how reform might be effected. He wished to see all human affairs conducted with the calm precision of one of his own laboratory experiments. On reaching a position of influence in the Revenue Farm— *i.e.*, when elected to its Committee of Administration, which negotiated directly with the government—he made attempts to clean out even that most dirty of stables. He drew up a code instructing the employees of the Farm in their duties, in which those who brought unpopularity on the company by frequent legal actions against recalcitrant taxpayers were severely lectured. Early in his career he attacked the ridiculous system whereby certain articles were taxable in one province and not in another, which made smuggling a profitable trade. To combat smuggling, he pointed out, the Farm had to maintain numerous agents at large expense. It is characteristic of Lavoisier that the reforms he proposed usually involved a curtailing of un-necessary expenditure. His common-sense efforts here proved in the main fruitless, but he succeeded in obtaining the abolition of a curious and brutal tax upon the Jews. Any Jew wishing to travel through the district of Clermontois had to pay an imposition, known as the tax of the cloven hoof, which amounted to thirty pieces of silver. Swine were also liable to the *droit du pied fourchu*. Not unnaturally, Jews stayed away from Clermontois, and business suffered. As a result of Lavoisier's efforts this piece of eighteenth-century Hitlerism was finally done away with in 1786.

In one instance his desire to reduce the affairs of the Farm to order led him into unpopularity. The Farm had the right to collect dues on certain goods entering Paris, but it was not difficult for smuggled articles to find their way into a straggling city. In 1780 it was reckoned that about one-fifth of the goods exposed for sale in the shops was contraband. To check this drain on the Farm's revenues, Lavoisier suggested that a wall should be built round the city, and after some delay his proposal was adopted. The task was entrusted to a grandiose architect, who expressed his personality in enormous turrets at the various barriers. The Parisians were annoyed at what they considered a despotic curtailment of their supply of good country air, and Lavoisier was hotly attacked for his share in the matter.

No efforts could make the Revenue Farm a satisfactory institution from any point of view. Lavoisier, however, fully succeeded in regularising the affairs of another quite similar organisation. Until 1775 gunpowder had been supplied to the government by the *Ferme des Poudres*, a private monopoly run for the profit of its members, with the result that France had several times been obliged to sue for peace for want of munitions of war. In 1775, Turgot created the *Régie des Poudres*, and appointed four commissioners, of whom Lavoisier was one, to take charge of it. It was at this time that Lavoisier took up residence in the Arsenal. From its very inception, the *Régie des Poudres* was a miracle of efficiency. Only qualified assistants were employed, methods of manufacture were improved, and the output of gunpowder rapidly rose. As the result of a study of foreign methods and of experiments conducted by himself (one of which led to a severe explosion in which he and his wife only escaped by a lucky accident, two employees being killed) Lavoisier was able to produce a powder giving cannon balls an extra carry of about 50 per cent. It was later reckoned that during the fourteen years of its existence the *Régie des Poudres* saved the Treasury some 28 million livres. The appointment supplemented Lavoisier's income by 17,000 livres a year.

Among Lavoisier's circle of friends were two men specially

interested in his experiments on gunpowder—Pierre and Irénée du Pont, father and son. The du Ponts had business interests in America, and eventually Irénée took up residence in Wilmonton, in Delaware. Here he founded a tiny gunpowder factory which was destined to grow into the largest concern for the manufacture of gunpowder in the United States. There is thus a direct link between Lavoisier and the great modern firm of Dupont de Nemours, still owned by the descendants of the men who watched the experiments at the Arsenal.

Lavoisier was a humanist who realised, perhaps more fully than many of the frothy intellectuals who chatted of reform in Parisian salons, the true needs of his stricken country. His travels on scientific and financial business had taught him that the population of France was mainly composed of peasants, and that those peasants were in a very bad way. Their misery, he observed, was partly due to short leases, lack of credit facilities and unjust taxation, but also to the inefficiency of their agricultural methods. The fiscal policy of the country was designed to benefit the merchant and manufacturer at the expense of the peasant. (It is interesting to reflect that precisely the opposite holds in France to-day.) " If commerce," Lavoisier said, " has been given more attention and protection than agriculture, it is because the profession of merchant is followed by citizens of a better class, who can speak and write, who live in towns, who bind themselves into organisations, and thus can make their voices heard. The unfortunate cultivator grumbles in his cottage ; he has neither representative nor defendant, and no department of state exists to look after his interests."

A Committee of Agriculture existed in Paris, whose purpose was to advise the government on agricultural affairs. Lavoisier became a member in 1785, was immediately elected secretary, and forthwith became the committee. This invariably happened whenever Lavoisier was appointed secretary of a committee. In his secretarial capacity he drew up reports on the cultivation of flax, potatoes, wheat and maize, he investigated suitable methods for penning sheep, and studied the value of peat ash as manure. He also prepared schemes for the establishment of experimental farms, for the collection and distribution of agricultural implements, and for the better adjustment of tithes and rights of pasturage. He attacked monopolist organisations, " possessing the art of 'disguising their own interest under an appearance of acting in the public interest," which refused to pay the peasant a fair price for his live-stock. The cities might temporarily benefit, but ultimately artificially lowered prices would lead to scarceness and dearness, since the livestock in question would be no longer worth the trouble of producing.

On the subject of experimental farms, Lavoisier could speak from personal experience, because he originated an extremely successful one on his own estate at Frechines, in the district of Blesois. When he bought the estate in 1778 he found that agriculture in Blesois was in a deplorable condition ; manure was scarcely used at all, annual crops were only about five times greater than the amount of seed sown, and the peasants were unable to grow sufficient fodder to feed their cattle during the winter. Lavoisier, with the resources of scientific method and wealth at his disposal, proceeded to show what could be done. He set aside three areas of eighty hectares, from the worst land in his domain, which were farmed by M. Lefèvre, of Blois, according to his instructions. Everything done was recorded with strict laboratory precision. Trial areas were measured out exactly, and full records kept of seed sown, crops harvested, expenses involved, and so on. After some preliminary difficulties all went well. He introduced the potato into the locality, disproved the superstition that sheep grazing damages the soil, and procured sheep from Spain and cows from Chanteloup to improve the local breeds. By 1793, the income produced by the experimental farm was about 25,000 livres, crop yields had been doubled, and the land was capable of supporting five times as much livestock as formerly. In presenting an account of his agricultural experiments to the Committee of Agriculture in 1788, Lavoisier strongly urged that the wealthy should invest money in land. The rate of interest might not equal that promised by speculation in stocks and public funds, but the investment was reasonably safe, and brought with it the blessings of the poor. Apart from his efforts at agricultural improvement, Lavoisier built a school for the children of his tenants. Not infrequently he gave small personal loans to those in need. When, in 1789, the neighbouring town of Blois got into financial difficulties following a bad harvest, he made a generous loan without interest, which was in fact never repaid. Grimaux, writing a century later, says that Blesois peasants still retained the memory of Lavoisier as their benefactor.

In 1787 he became a member of the Assembly of Orleans. In this capacity we find him still carrying on his unwearying, hopeless struggle for progress and prosperity. Making use of his wide knowledge of finance he introduced schemes for the founding of discount banks and insurance societies ; he urged the creation of nursing establishments, the digging of canals, the exploitation of mineral wealth. All his plans came to nothing, for it was the eve of the Revolution. Lavoisier, though only a member of the Third Estate in a parliament including nobility and high dignitaries of the church, was the guiding spirit of the Assembly. His name appears on almost every page of its records, and most of the reports subsequently published in its name were actually drawn up by him. In the field of pure science Lavoisier was always eager to secure full credit for work he had accomplished, and even, on occasion, for work he had not accomplished, but in his administrative and reforming capacity he was content with anonymity.

We need make only brief reference to his successful attempts to reform the constitution of the Academy of Science, of which he became Director in 1785. The constitution of the Academy had not been altered since its inception a hundred years previously, so that reforms were overdue. Here again, it was a case of progressive common sense on one side and prejudice and traditionalism on the other.

In modern times a scientific discoverer is apt to be rewarded by a professorship which compels him to devote most of his time to teaching second year medical students. Lavoisier escaped that fate, but he could not escape the secretaryships and seats on commissions which were thrust on him from all sides. After the commencement of the Revolution he was forced to desert science almost entirely, and devote his energies to public service. Efficiency is a dangerous gift for a man of genius to possess. Probably he found pleasure in writing precise and accurate minutes, and in being the only sensible and clear-minded man on any given committee ; he knew, moreover, that the state of France called desperately for the help of such men as himself, and may have felt that science must give place to urgent social necessity. But scientific research was his true *métier*, the glamour of which never dimmed as he passed into middle age. In later years he must often have yearned for his retorts and bell-jars with real sickness of soul.

Of his numerous reports to the Academy we will mention here only two. One is his most enlightened and humane report on prison reform, a subject which the efforts of Howard had brought to the notice of the civilised world. As a member of a commission of five, Lavoisier inspected a number of prisons in Paris, not without strenuous opposition from authorities who considered such visits an impertinent intrusion. The commission was horrified at the conditions it observed, and in admirably restrained language pointed out their inhumanity. The prisons were stinking dens in which human beings, covered with vermin, were crowded together in the utmost filth. A further report on the construction of new prisons, mainly drawn up by Lavoisier himself, embodies highly original recommendations with regard to sanitation, fumigation and cleanliness. Unfortunately the minister who had originated the enquiry, Necker, lost his position soon afterwards and the question of prison reform was shelved.

Enough has been said to illustrate Lavoisier in his capacity of progressive social reformer. The only other Academy report which we will mention here is of a rather different nature, but presents in itself a number of entertaining features. It is that which the Academy was asked to draw up on the activities of Mesmer, who, having been expelled from Vienna as a result of the efforts of the Austrian College of Physicians, took up residence in Paris in 1778, and after a few years became a roaring success. Orthodox medicine, however, was soon on his track, and roused the authorities to action. In April, 1784, Lavoisier received the following dignified commission : " *Le Roi a fait choix de vous, Monsieur, pour procéder, avec plusieurs autres personnes distinguées par leurs lumières et leur experience, à l'examen de la méthode où pratique tirée des prétendues connaissances du sieur Mesmer.*" One may surmise that it was a job after Lavoisier's own heart, for what could be more satisfying to a man with a passion for scientific method than the opportunity to expose one who was regarded by the informed as a dishonest and dangerous quack ? Mesmer's own explanation of his philosophy and technique left something to be desired. There existed in the universe, he said, a magnetic fluid capable of producing remarkable phenomena, including the cure of the sick. This fluid, he cautiously added, was easier to feel than to describe. Newton called it the Ether, Descartes, the Universal Mover, the alchemists, the Universal Principle or Quintessence. Through it light, sound and smells were propagated, and in all probability its operations could be explained by the laws of matter and motion. It was true that it was hard to believe in a fluid whose existence was not always immediately apparent to the five senses, but what about love ? Lovers experienced all kinds of mysterious attractions and repulsions due to a force which was difficult to analyse, the existence of which was nevertheless recognised by all human beings.

Mesmer's *exposé* was not of a nature calculated to appeal to the scientific mind. But it was his practice rather than his precept which aroused the wrath of the medical profession.

All individuals, he declared, were charged with magnetic fluid in varying degrees, and when suitable contact was made between two individuals, fluid inevitably passed from the more highly charged to the less highly charged, usually with enormous benefit to the latter. For treating actual disease, the highly charged operator and the patient sat opposite each other on two chairs, with the former's knees outside the patient's knees and in contact with them; their opposing poles were then in contact, and an exchange of magnetic fluid resulted. As a rule, however, Mesmer preferred mass methods, less time-consuming and more lucrative. He was accustomed to group his patients round a covered tub, containing bottles which he himself had charged with magnetism by rubbing them with his hands. From the tub there issued a number of flexible iron rods which the patients applied to the affected part. Each sufferer carried a little iron bar to increase his receptivity. There was a piano in the room, on which soft music was played, and sometimes songs were sung. Mesmer had found, he said, that the music of an instrument which had been charged with magnetism could re-transmit the fluid, and possibly the song of a highly magnetised individual produced the same result. Clothed in the dress of a magician, Mesmer moved quietly among the assembled patients, touching one with his wand, fixing another with his gaze, making solemn passes with his hands before the eyes of a third. The patients were wont to laugh, cry, cough, and hiccup, and some of them would faint or go into convulsive seizures.

The president of the investigating commission was the celebrated Franklin, at that time resident in Paris; it was in his house at Passy that the greater part of the enquiry was carried out. The astronomer Bailly, destined to play a tragic *rôle* in the history of the Revolution, was an active member. The commission included medical men (one of whom was the ingenious Dr. Guillotin), but from the start the scientific members decided that to investigate alleged cures would be waste of time. In its final report, written in the style of Lavoisier—the original is actually in his handwriting—there is some rather plain speaking about medicine and science. Nature, it is pointed out, cures most patients, and it is quite impossible, by observing a few cases, to decide whether a particular form of treatment is effective or not. Such a decision, the report says in effect, can only be made by strictly statistical methods. Unfortunately, very few people (and no doctors, it seems to imply) are capable of understanding and using statistical methods. The quarrel between the scientist and the physician is a familiar one, which still reverberates from time to time in the columns of the medical press. The scientist demands that the strict methods of the statistician and the laboratory worker should be imported into the practice of medicine, while the physician, as a retort, acidly begs his critics to come and try. Faced with recalcitrant and all too human experimental material, working continually in an atmosphere of worry and emergency, how can he be other than an empiricist snatching at therapeutic straws ? Graphs and figures are all very well, but what can be more accurate than the clinical impressions of a lifetime ? The scientist thereupon calls the physician a mediæval relic, but gives the latter the last word by rushing terror-stricken to his consulting room next time he is ill to sit humbly and thankfully at the feet of medical omniscience.

At the time when the commission of enquiry began its work, Mesmer had an assistant and collaborator named Deslon, and it was decided that Deslon rather than Mesmer should provide material for the investigation. Deslon, a prominent physician, professor at the University, had completely succumbed to the fascination of the remarkable Austrian and his therapeutic methods, with the result that he had been expelled from the College of Physicians and the Faculty of Medicine. Apparently the Academy Commission considered it more seemly to deal with a man who had at least once belonged to the orthodox fold of French medicine, than with a foreign charlatan. Deslon, it seems, was as convinced as Mesmer himself of the existence of animal magnetism, and was delighted to co-operate in the investigation. After some discussion, the range of the enquiry was limited to two points : first, the commission wished to discover whether it was possible to produce the reported effects of animal magnetism without using animal magnetism, and secondly, whether such effects could be produced on a patient who was unaware that she (for the patients were mostly female) was being magnetised at all.

It was speedily discovered that the symptoms which the patients exhibited at Mesmer's seances could easily be produced without the use of iron rods or magnetised bottles and the rest of the paraphernalia, for certain patients, when sitting in the circle around the copper tub, went off into convulsions before the rods even touched them. As a conclusive test, one of Deslon's patients, a girl highly susceptible to the mysterious influence, was put in a chair with her eyes bandaged. She was then told that Dr. Deslon was about to be fetched, and a moment later one of the commission entered the room imitating the doctor's walk. Another investigator politely asked the non-existent Dr. Deslon to begin his demonstration. In a few minutes, the blindfolded girl was in the midst of a convulsive seizure, though nothing had been done to her. Similar experiments with other patients produced similar results.

Another type of experiment provided equally conclusive evidence against the existence of animal magnetism. A susceptible patient, a washerwoman, was asked to sit in a certain chair and a member of the commission, a stranger to her, engaged her in conversation about trivial matters. The chair had been placed in a doorway from which the door had been removed, the opening being covered with a large sheet of carboard. Behind the cardboard Dr. Deslon strove might and main to magnetise the washerwoman, but she proceeded with her chat for half an hour quite unaware of the invisible figure a few feet away, and in full possession of her five senses. Animal magnetsim, Mesmer had said, could easily pass through wood and stone, so why not cardboard ?

The commission was triumphant, but one thinks sympathetically of poor Deslon, straining and sweating behind the cardboard partition. It reported that Mesmer's magnetic fluid was non-existent; imagination, without magnetism, could produce convulsions and the rest of the phenomena; magnetism, without imagination, could produce nothing. It further added that the violent crises which occurred in patients under treatment by Mesmer's methods were probably harmful, both to the victim and to spectators, who might be affected in the same way because of " the imitative faculty which is a law of nature." As a result of the report, Mesmer and Deslon lost a great part of their wealthy clientèle. Mesmer himself lived on in comparative obscurity in Paris for some years; eventually, after various wanderings in Germany and Austria, he retired with an ample competence to Switzerland, where he lived in peaceful retirement until his death in 1810. He had made a discovery of great importance, which is indeed one of the very foundations of modern psychological science, but he came to grief in trying to explain it in terms of physics. He understood as little as his patients or the Commission of Enquiry itself the strange hinterland of the human mind in which he was groping.

It is of interest to compare the exposure of Mesmer at the hands of Lavoisier and his colleagues with that of the physician Elliotson in 1838. The enquiry in this case was instigated by the gifted and truculent Thomas Wakley, founder and first editor of the *Lancet*. Elliotson, a thoroughly sound physician, one of the founders of University College Hospital, had a craving for originality; the limited and stereotyped therapeutics of the day bored him. Coming into contact with a Frenchman named Dupotet, who had experimented with " Mesmerism " in Paris, Elliotson threw himself heart and soul into the study of the subject. But hypnotic phenomena are amazing and bewildering on first contact, and Elliotson quite failed to keep his head. Not content with investigating the therapeutic possibilities of " mesmerism," he embarked on a series of outlandish

BIBLIOTHECA
Ottaviensis

H 2

experiments with subjects of whose good faith the outside
world had no proof. Two girls, Elizabeth and Jane O'Key,
were put through the most remarkable performances. They
were thrown into convulsions by means of " passes " made
at a distance, or by the touch of " magnetised " metals ;
when in the hypnotic trance, they were asked to prescribe
treatment for themselves and other patients. At this
unexpected violation of its proper sphere, the medical
profession was immediately up in arms. Elliotson, convinced like Mesmer of the reality of the phenomena observed,
was ready to submit his experiments to the fullest enquiry.
Wakley, of the *Lancet*, took up the challenge. It was
arranged that five persons chosen by Wakley and five chosen
by Elliotson should investigate the genuineness of the
reactions displayed by the O'Key sisters. One of them,
Elliotson said, would fall into convulsions when touched by
a piece of metal, but remained placid on contact with lead.
At the enquiry he began by handing pieces of lead and nickel
to Wakley. Wakley covertly passed the piece of metal to a
friend, who put it in his pocket. The lead was applied to
the girl's hand, while a bystander by arrangement audibly
whispered, " Take care you do not apply the metal too
strongly." The result, of course, was that the girl fell into
strong convulsions. Elliotson was delighted, and could
hardly believe Wakley's statement that the piece of nickel
had remained in someone's pocket throughout. Subsequently the nickel itself was applied, but the girls remained
passive, which they did when water " magnetised " by
Elliotson was given them to drink, while water straight from
the pump sent them into convulsions.

Wakley's not very penetrating conclusion was that the
two girls were imposters, the implication being that Elliotson
was less a knave than a fool. A short time later the Council
of University College passed a resolution forbidding the
practice of " mesmerism " in its hospital, and Elliotson,
deeply involved, had no choice but to resign his position on
the hospital staff. Though he continued to carry on a large
practice in London for some years afterwards, from the

point of view of professional distinction he was a ruined man. His fine career came to an abrupt close.

If Mesmer and Elliotson were a little too credulous, the investigatory committees which exposed them were a little too cocksure of their ground. Looking back, we perceive that in the long run the laugh is not altogether on the side of Wakley and Lavoisier. Both succeeded in disproving the existence of animal magnetism, and thereby rendered a service to science, but at the same time they seem to have been curiously unimpressed by the phenomena of hypnotism. Later investigation of these phenomena, by Charcot, Janet, and others, gave the subject the stamp of respectabi'ity, and eventually led to great enlargement of psychological knowledge.

CHAPTER XI

THE SCIENCE OF NUTRITION

It is not proposed to give here an account of all Lavoisier's important contributions to science, such as his discovery of the composition of carbon dioxide, his pioneer work in connection with chemical equations and organic chemistry. We may mention briefly the new system of chemical nomenclature, drawn up in 1787 by Lavoisier in collaboration with de Morveau, Berthollet and Fourcroy, which is the basis of the system used by the modern chemist. He regarded this reform as being of the first importance to science. " The impossibility of separating the nomenclature of a science from the science itself," he wrote, " is owing to this, that every branch of physical science must consist of three things : the series of facts which are the objects of the science ; the ideas which represent these facts ; and the words by which these ideas are expressed. Like three impressions of the same seal, the word ought to produce the idea, and the idea to be a picture of the fact. And, as ideas are preserved and communicated by means of words, it necessarily follows, that we cannot improve the language of any science, without at the same time improving the science itself ; neither can we, on the other hand, improve a science, without improving the language or nomenclature which belongs to it. However certain the facts of any science may be, and however just the ideas we may have formed of these facts, we can only communicate false or imperfect impressions of these ideas to others, while we want words by which they may be properly expressed." [1]

Some of the new terms, he added, might seem at first sight uncouth and barbarous. " But we considered," he says,

---

[1] Kerr's translation, " Traité Élémentaire de chimie."

" that the ear is soon habituated to new words, especially when they are connected with a general and rational system. The names besides, which were formerly employed, such as *powder of algaroth, salt of alembroth, pompholix, phagadenic water, turbith mineral, colcothar*, and many others, were neither less barbarous nor less uncommon. It required a great deal of practice, and no small degree of memory, to recollect the substances to which they were applied ; much more to recollect the genus of combination to which they belonged. The names of oil of tartar per diliquum, oil of vitriol, butter of arsenic, and of antimony, flowers of zinc, etc., were still more improper, because they suggested false ideas ; for in the whole mineral kingdom, and particularly in the metallic class, there exists no such thing as butter, oils, or flowers ; in short, the substances to which these fallacious names were given, are rank poisons." [1]

A poet might have regretted the assassination of such gorgeous words as pompholix and colcothar, but there was nothing of the poet about Lavoisier.

One branch of Lavoisier's work is of exceptional interest to us to-day, and seems to deserve special mention. During the later years of his scientific career he investigated the relation between respiration, animal heat, and the combustion of foodstuffs and thus laid the foundation of the science of nutrition.

The idea of the body as a machine which derives its heat and energy from the combustion of fuel is a highly obvious and familiar idea to us. But it was not so obvious in 1780. It was naturally realised, as a matter of common sense, that food sustains and replenishes the body, but how ? Similarly, it was obvious that breathing is necessary for life, but why ? Aristotle and others had surmised that the purpose of breathing was to refresh and cool the blood in the lungs. Robert Hook, in 1667, investigated respiration by a brutal experiment in which he kept a dog alive, after removal of its ribs and diaphragm, by blowing air into the windpipe with bellows. He showed that the movements of the lungs, their

---

[1] Kerr's translation, " Traité Élémentaire de chimie."

expansion and collapse, are not necessary for life, since when holes were picked in the surface of the lungs, and a continuous current of air blown through the windpipe, the animal remained alive. When it eventually died, Hook concluded that it was not the movelessness of the lungs which caused death, but the want of a sufficient supply of fresh air.

In a confined space a candle soon goes out; a living creature dies. The first phenomenon had been explained on the ground that when air becomes saturated by the fiery principle given off by a burning substance, the increase of pressure prevents further emission of phlogiston; the second as being due to a loss of elasticity in the air, which, when fouled by exhalations, becomes incapable of dilating the alveoli of the lungs. But although attempts had been made to explain the two phenomena on different lines, the existence of some analogy between a living creature and a burning substance had been vaguely realised. Even the poets, as Lavoisier pointed out, had often likened life to a flame.

The disciples of Stahl had maintained that the effect on air of respiration, combustion, and calcination of metals, is essentially the same; air becomes impregnated with phlogiston. Nitrogen, which will not support any of the three processes, was known as " phlogisticated " air. It had no further capacity, so to speak, for receiving phlogiston. Venous blood, Priestley maintained, gave up its phlogiston in the lungs, where it was transformed into bright red dephlogisticated blood.

The substance of the preceding paragraphs is given by Lavoisier in one of his papers on respiration. He wrote in the past tense, for such ideas were obsolete, and he (and he alone, as he points out rather frequently) had made them so. He had given unshakable proof that in combustion and respiration " vital air " or oxygen is absorbed, and " fixed air " or carbon dioxide given off. In one experiment he eliminated, by means of potash, the " fixed air " produced by the respiration of a bird in a closed vessel, and, by adding oxygen to the residual air, reconstructed atmospheric air.

METABOLISM EXPERIMENT AT THE ARSENAL LABORATORY. MADAME LAVOISIER TAKING NOTES.

Drawn by Madame Lavoisier.

[*To face p.* 104.

" Fixed air " had actually been discovered by the Scotch chemist Black, who had shown, by simple and ingenious experiments, that it is produced during the burning of charcoal and is present in expired air. Priestley, too, had made the capital discovery that air " vitiated by breathing " could have its salubrity restored by the action of green plants. But it was Lavoisier who demonstrated that " fixed air " is a compound of carbon and oxygen, and through that observation was ultimately able to extend his great generalisation in chemistry into the infant science of physiology.

The fact that absorption of oxygen and evolution of carbon dioxide take place in respiration as in combustion led Lavoisier to the original conception that animal heat is derived from oxidation ; that the same oxidative process goes on in the body as in a hearth fire, only more slowly. This hypothesis was put to the test of experiment. As a rule, Lavoisier's co-workers seem rather shadowy creatures, whose names appear on the title pages of reports written in his own style and containing accounts of experiments obviously designed by himself. But in his work on animal heat he enjoyed the collaboration of a scientist whose genius and reputation equalled or even excelled his own. Laplace was indeed primarily a mathematician, not a laboratory worker, but in the present instance he contributed his full quota to the experiments ; many of the laboratory notes are in his hand, and not in Lavoisier's—a rare occurrence in the history of the latter's collaborations. Their joint papers, as finally published, contain formidable equations which one unhesitatingly ascribes to Laplace, for Lavoisier was a poor mathematician. Laplace, the " Newton of France," five years Lavoisier's junior, was already famous ; as not infrequently happens in the case of distinguished mathematicians, who are born and not made, his powers had developed very early. When scarcely twenty he had written a letter to the geometer d'Alembert on the principles of mechanics which had so impressed the latter that he immediately found an appointment for the young genius as Professor of Mathematics at the École Militaire. Here he remained many years, and had, in 1785, the task of examining the cadet Bonaparte in mathematics. Laplace took great pleasure in being famous, but scientific achievement did not completely satisfy his ambitions ; he desired to distinguish himself in the field of administration. When Napoleon was First Consul he rashly appointed his old professor Minister of the Interior, but so incompetent did he prove that he had to be sacked at the end of six weeks. The result of giving Lavoisier a similar appointment would have been more satisfactory. Laplace's servility, first to revolutionary leaders, later to Napoleon, and finally to Louis XVIII. after his accession in 1814, did not endear him personally to his contemporaries, but his position as the foremost living mathematician remained unchallenged throughout his life. His greatest achievement was, perhaps, the reduction of the Solar System to mathematical order ; all apparent anomalies were eliminated by his genius, and it is said that his activities in this branch of science languished because there was nothing left to explain. No further mathematical analysis could be made until new facts were observed.

This was the man who became Lavoisier's co-worker in experiments with heat. The first essential was a device for measuring heat, a calorimeter. Various unsatisfactory calorimeters had been invented by earlier workers ; the device used by Lavoisier and Laplace (probably invented by the former) was a definite advance on former models. The criterion adopted for measurement of heat was capacity to melt ice. Their apparatus consisted of a vessel like a large pail divided into three circular compartments, one inside the other, the middle compartment containing a weighed amount of ice. The heat-producing process under investigation took place in the innermost chamber, while the outer was filled with snow to prevent melting of the ice by the heat of the room. The experiments, therefore, necessarily took place in winter when ice and snow were obtainable.

The amounts of ice melted by the combustion of certain substances, and by the presence of a guinea-pig for various periods, were noted. This was in itself valuable and original information. But Lavoisier and Laplace developed their experiments further by measuring at the same time the amount of oxygen used up, and the amount of carbon dioxide given off, during the process under investigation. The whole quite complicated apparatus, which must have cost Lavoisier a small fortune, is excellently illustrated in the report of the experiment. Several calorimeters, made on this plan, are included in the collection of Lavoisier's instruments on view at the *Conservatoire des Arts et Métiers* in Paris.

One of the final results was as follows : In the combustion of coal, 10 ounces of ice were melted in the production of 224 grains of carbon dioxide ; a live guinea-pig, in the production of 236 grains, melted 11 ounces. The authors apologised for the roughness of these results ; it was impossible, they said, considering the technical difficulties, to hope for closer correspondence. But in reality the degree of parallelism observed was a happy fluke, for the problem of the production of animal heat is much more complicated than Lavoisier realised. Later he recognised that the heat production of an animal cannot fully be gauged by its output of CO_2, because another process involving the evolution of heat also takes place : namely, the combination of oxygen and hydrogen to form water. For the time being, however, the experimental data, inaccurate and incomplete in many respects as they were, served to establish his main point. " When," wrote Laplace and Lavoisier, " an animal is in a state of rest, so that during the course of several hours its vital activities remain unvaried, the conservation of animal heat is due, in great part at least, to the heat produced by the combination of oxygen inspired with the base ' fixed air,' supplied by the blood. . . . Respiration is a process of combustion, which, though it takes place very slowly, is perfectly analogous to that of the combustion of coal. Combustion takes place in the lungs without any emission of light, because the fiery matter evolved there is immediately absorbed by the humidity of those organs. The heat developed in combustion is communicated to the blood flowing through the lungs which carries it to all parts of the body." These may seem somewhat primitive ideas, but they were nearer the truth than anything previously put forward.

It was clear that the combustible material—which Lavoisier erroneously regarded as elemental carbon—must ultimately be derived from food. " In respiration," Lavoisier remarked in a later paper, " it is the substance of the animal, the blood, which supplies the fuel. If the animal did not receive habitually from food what it loses by respiration, the lamps would soon run short of oil, and the animal perish, as a lamp goes out when its fuel is exhausted."

Lavoisier found guinea-pigs very suitable as experimental animals in his earlier work on respiration and animal heat. " They are tame, healthy creatures," he says, " easy to feed and big enough to inspire and expire air in quantities suitable for measurement." But later he conceived the bold idea of experimenting directly on human beings, and for this purpose he secured the collaboration of a young scientist, Seguin, who had already performed some useful work on respiration. " However laborious, disagreeable or even dangerous the experiments might prove to be, M. Seguin wished that they should all be performed on himself." Anti-vivisectionists, had any existed in 1789, would have applauded the statement. In reality, however, the experiments involved little more than the discomfort of wearing an air-proof brass mask and breathing oxygen supplied through a tube for short intervals. The main point which Lavoisier and Seguin wished to investigate was the intake of oxygen during varying conditions of activity.

The late Professor Graham Lusk, whose text-book, " The Science of Nutrition," is one of the standard works in English on the quantitative side of nutrition, continually expresses amazement at the penetration of Lavoisier's experiments. He tabulates the results obtained by Lavoisier and Seguin as though they were the latest product of a modern scientific institute equipped with Atwater-Rosa-Benedict calorimeters and such expensive devices for studying

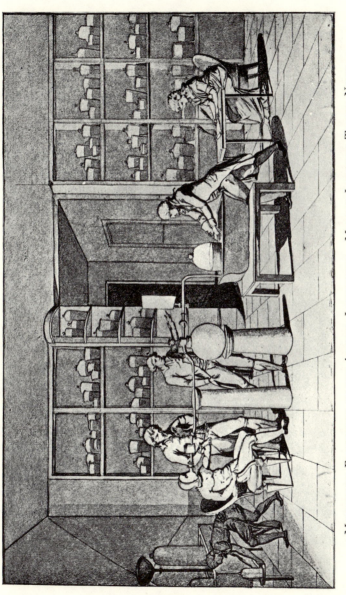

Metabolism Experiment at the Arsenal Laboratory. Madame Lavoisier Taking Notes.
Drawn by Madame Lavoisier.

[*To face p.* 108.]

human energetics. The following is taken directly from the latest edition (1928) of Lusk's work :—

RESPIRATION EXPERIMENTS ON MAN
(Lavoisier and Seguin)

Condition.	Environmental Temperature.	Oxygen absorbed per hour.	
	Degrees Centigrade.	Cubic inches. (Pouces.)	Expressed as litres (Lusk.)
1. Without food . . .	26	1,210	24
2. Without food . . .	12	1,344	27
3. With food . . .	12	1,800–1,900	38
4. Work (9,195 foot pounds) without food. . .	12	3,200	65
5. Work (9,750 foot pounds) with food . . .	12	4,600	91

" These remarkable results," Lusk goes on to say, " are in strict accord with the knowledge of our own day. We know more details, but the fundamental fact that the quantity of oxygen absorbed and of carbon dioxide excreted depends primarily on (1) food, (2) work, and (3) temperature, was established by Lavoisier within a few years after his discovery that oxygen supported combustion."

Lavoisier and Seguin gave a general account of their experiments in an Academy Memoir of 1789, but the details of the experimental methods employed have never yet been published. (These may still exist among the unpublished Lavoisier documents in the possession of his wife's family.) We have, however, some record of their technique in the form of two spirited drawings by Madame Lavoisier. Both of these show Seguin breathing into a mask to which is attached a rigid tube, presumably connected at the farther end with a supply of oxygen. In one drawing the subject is at rest ; in the other he is performing a measured amount of labour by depressing a foot pedal, while an observer counts his pulse. Among the relics preserved in the family collection at La Champfortière, Sarthe, is a brass mask which is in all probability that actually used in these experiments.

Lavoisier was clearly delighted with his work on oxygen consumption—on metabolism, as we should say nowadays—work which would indeed be sufficient in itself to make the name of a lesser man. It seems significant that of all his experiments this was the one which Madame Lavoisier chose as a subject to draw. In the Academy memoir a note of exultation enlivens his usually pedestrian style. Here and there he philosophises on his results in a way that reminds one of Priestley, always an incorrigible moraliser. His experiments had established a relation between oxygen consumption and work performed. Might it not, therefore, be possible to evaluate and compare the effort expended on different forms of work—that of an orator, or a musician, for example ? One might even investigate the mechanical effort put out by a philosopher wrapped in thought, an author as he writes, or a musician as he composes. The first suggestion has been amply justified—it has proved possible to investigate the energy expenditure involved by many different activities, including the playing of musical instruments. The second remains a problem for the future, since we have not yet developed satisfactory methods of studying the physical changes which must occur as a result of mental activity.

These reflections on oxygen consumption in relation to occupation suggested a new line of thought to Lavoisier. A man while working inspires more oxygen ; his flame, so to speak, is burning more brightly, and it follows that his substance is being more rapidly consumed. The harder he works, the more need there is of fuel to replenish the flame. But fuel comes from food, and food costs money.

" As long as we considered respiration simply as a matter of consumption of air," Lavoisier continued, " the position of the rich and the poor seemed the same ; air is available to all and costs nothing ; the labourer has indeed better opportunities than most of obtaining this gift of nature. But now we know that respiration is in fact a process of combustion, which consumes each instant some of the substance of an individual ; that this consumption increases as the rate of the pulse and of breathing accelerates, that, in fact, it increases in accordance with the labour and activity of an individual's life ; a whole host of moral questions seems to spring into being from observations which are themselves purely material in nature.

" By what mischance does it happen that a poor man, who lives by manual work, who is obliged, in order to live, to put forward the greatest effort of which his body is capable, is actually forced to consume more substance than the rich man, who has less need of repair ? Why, in shocking contrast, does the rich man enjoy an abundance which is not physically necessary, and which seems more appropriate to the man of toil ? "

An unfortunate mischance indeed ! We may still reflect with advantage on the fact that as a rule it is those whose energy requirements are greatest who have the greatest difficulty in securing a sufficiently varied and adequate diet, while those who spend most of the working day in well-padded chairs have every inducement to stuff themselves with rich and unnecessary food. At this point Lavoisier makes a quaint and unexpected excursion into politics.

" Let us refrain," he says, " from putting the blame on nature, and from upbraiding her for ' mistakes ' which are indeed part of her very essence. Let us rather rely on the progress of philosophy and humanity, which unite to promise us wise institutions, which will tend to equalise all incomes, to raise the price of labour, and to ensure its just reward ; which will obtain for all social classes, and particularly for the indigent, pleasure and happiness in greater abundance. Let us rather seek to ensure that the facile enthusiasms and exaggerations to which men met together in large assemblies are prone, the passions which so often lead human beings to act in defiance of their own interests—windy passions from which sages and philosophers are no more immune than other men—do not wreck an enterprise with so fair a beginning, and bring to naught the hopes of our country."

The revolution had dawned. Lavoisier, who understood better than most of his fellow-countrymen the shortcomings of the old *régime*, had welcomed it. But somehow he did not like the look of things. The talkers, the windbags, the little empty men who traffic in the emotions of the crowd, seemed to be thrusting themselves into prominence. How, in such an atmosphere, could the healing reforms, for want of which the country was wasting away, be soberly put into operation ? How, in such an atmosphere, could the calm and beneficent advance of science continue ?

At a moment when chattering patriots occupied most of the limelight, Lavoisier thought it advisable to point out, in the concluding paragraph of the memoir, that there are other useful forms of human activity.

" Il n'est pas indispensable, pour bien mériter de l'humanité et pour payer son tribut à la patrie, d'être appelé à ces fonctions publiques et éclatantes qui concourent à l'organisation et à la régénération des empires. Le physicien peut aussi, dans le silence de son laboratoire et de son cabinet, exercer des fonctions patriotiques ; il peut espérer, par ses travaux, de diminuer la masse des maux qui affligent l'espèce humaine ; d'augmenter ses jouissances et son bonheur, et n'eût-il contribué, par les routes nouvelles qu'il s'est ouvertes, qu'à prolonger de quelques années, de quelques jours même, la vie moyenne des hommes, il pourrait aspirer aussi au titre glorieux de bienfaiteur de l'humanité."

This was Lavoisier's last great contribution to science. A few more years of strenuous activity remained to him, but the opportunity of undistracted work " in the silence of the laboratory " never returned, and it was left to others to explore the entirely new territory which, in the final effort of his genius, he had discovered. He opened a door, and saw in a brief glance a vista of new and enthralling researches. He himself never passed through. It is fitting that this last fine memoir should conclude with a passage which may be regarded as his confession of faith.

A further quotation from Lusk's " Science of Nutrition " may be added here :—

" The modern era of the science of nutrition was opened by Lavoisier in 1780. He was the first to apply the balance and the thermometer to the phenomenon of life, and he declared ' *La vie est une fonction chimique*.' The work of to-day is but a continuation of that done a century and more ago. Lavoisier and Laplace made experiments on animal heat and respiration. The great German chemist Liebig received his early training in Paris, residing there in 1822. Liebig's conception of the process of nutrition fired the genius of Voit to the painstaking researches which laid the foundation of his Munich school. These have been repeated and extended by his pupils, of whom Rubner is chief, and by others the world over. Thus the knowledge often transmitted personally from the master to the pupil, to be in turn elaborated, had its seed in the intellect of Lavoisier."

CHAPTER XII

INTERRUPTIONS

NATIONS, like individuals, are horribly bound by sins of past commission. The great day of repentance dawns; evil is solemnly expelled; it remains only to live happily ever after. But things do not happen like that. Ordered sanity of behaviour can be expected only of a society in which the idea of ordered sanity of behaviour has been deeply implanted. The law of the conservation of matter, understood and expounded by Lavoisier, has its counterparts in the field of political morality. Moral output can never exceed moral intake, and the latter is a slow process. Real revolutions, real progress, must take place slowly in the minds of common men and women; it is not enough that a few inspired prophets should point the way. We foolishly expect the idea of internationalism to flower suddenly in a world overgrown with the weeds of national prejudice, or a nation of individualists, whose minds through long habit move automatically along individualist lines, to adopt immediately a system of state socialism at the instigation of a single man. In our reading of history we take wiser views. When we consider the state of France of 1789, we realise at once the pathetic folly of those who hoped that a new era of happiness and prosperity must dawn because the King had granted a constitution, and a worthless aristocracy had been expropriated. In spite of the drama of the tennis court, in spite of the eloquence of Mirabeau, in spite of the symbolic fall of the Bastille, France remained a country of wretched and ignorant peasants, surrounded by hostile neighbours, with her cities at the mercy of a brutal and despairing mob, with no adequate civil service, with no class trained to govern, with only a tiny sprinkling of educated and progressive men prepared to work soberly and quietly in the interests of their country. Such were the elements in the retort from which it was hoped there would crystallise out, in defiance of natural law, the philosopher's stone of universal happiness.

Lavoisier was deeply involved in the revolution from its beginning. His father had purchased noble rank, but politically he belonged to the powerful group which directed the finances of the kingdom, and temperamentally to the intelligentsia of the capital. The real aristocracy of birth centred at Versailles, and not in Paris, a separation which tended to accentuate the gulf between the solid merchants of the city and the class which regarded the court as the centre of all things. In the Orleans Parliament, held in 1787, Lavoisier had served as a member of the Third Estate, and had not relished the subjection of that estate to the nobility and clergy. The Third Estate—the Commons —outnumbered the other two Orders put together, but if, according to custom, voting was by Assemblies, each Assembly having one vote, it was liable to defeat on every issue. Only if all the members sat and voted together could the Third Estate make its numbers felt. In 1789, when the States General was about to be summoned after an interval of 109 years, we find Lavoisier actively interested in this burning question of votes and assemblies, which was hotly and bitterly discussed during the months preceding the election. Presumably as a result of his political experience, he was chosen to represent the nobility of Blois in the States General, but only in the capacity of substitute deputy ; it is said that his family's elevation to the nobility was too recent to warrant his election as full deputy. One of the senior deputies of the department of Blois was the Vicomte de Beauharnais, whose wife, Josephine, was destined to be Empress of France. It does not appear that Lavoisier, as substitute deputy, took any part in the historical events of that summer at Versailles ; later in the year he personally entered an active political field when he was elected as representative of the district of Culture Saint Catherine in the Assembly of the Commune of Paris. We may infer, however, that in spite of his position as representative of the Second Estate, his sympathies were entirely with the Third Estate in its struggle for power and position. He must have followed with burning interest the story of the humiliation of its members from the day they were commanded to appear before the King in black coats and waistcoats, knee breeches and stockings, to be snubbed by the nobility and badgered by insolent court officials, until the day when they found the doors of their customary meeting place locked, and proceeded in exasperation to a tennis court to take an oath not to separate until a constitution was granted. His friend and fellow academician, the astronomer Bailly, who had assisted in the exposure of Mesmer, acted as chairman on that august occasion.

The National Assembly which was formed as the result of the rebellion of the Third Estate commanded the support of the middle classes. It soon became obvious, however, that there was a menacing factor in the situation—the Paris mob. The labouring class in Paris was illiterate, underpaid, and miserable ; the city was choked with unemployed who existed no one knew how. In consequence the slums were like a mine packed with dynamite which the smallest spark would explode. Early in the summer, the mob had broken loose and wrecked the property of a wealthy manufacturer, Reveillon, who had unwisely remarked that there was no starvation among the people, and that a man could live on three sous a day. A more malignant scoffer had forfeited his life. Foulon had declared that, for all he cared, the people might eat grass ; he had been captured by a hungry mob and dragged before the conscientious and high-minded Bailly, newly-elected President of the Assembly. Bailly, quite incapable of dealing with such a situation, stammered that he should be tried by the proper authorities. Old Foulon clung to the President's knees, but he was soon torn away and hanged on a lamp-post before the Hotel de Ville. Later the mob decapitated the body, stuck grass in the mouth, and carried the head in triumph through the streets.

At the taking of the Bastille—that symbolic gesture so charged with world-shaking consequences—the mob had given further evidence of its ferocity. For three days in July it had held the city in its virtual control. In August of the same eventful year, Lavoisier—who had just published his great text-book, the " Traité Élémentaire de Chimie," and was engaged in his fundamental investigations with Seguin—barely escaped being the victim of its primitive fury. A large supply of gunpowder, which had been manufactured in the Arsenal for Rouen and Nantes, was being loaded on to a barge in full view of passers-by. The authority for the removal had been signed, in the absence of Lafayette, by a subordinate official named La Salle. Suddenly a rumour circulated that the powder was destined to be sent to " the enemies of the nation." Messengers came running to Lafayette and Bailly to inform them that the people was being betrayed, and these, without further enquiry, and in ignorance of the fact that the removal had been duly authorised, issued an order to stop loading the vessel and to return the powder to the Arsenal. The sight of this proceeding confirmed the suspicions of the mob that the Arsenal authorities had been guilty of treachery. Next day Lavoisier easily explained the whole matter to a commission of enquiry, which issued a report that no irregularity had taken place. But the mob was aroused and cared nothing for official reports. An angry crowd surged round the Arsenal demanding the blood of Lavoisier and his fellow officials. The authorities, under pressure, arrested him and another Arsenal official, and brought them to the Hotel de Ville—a perilous journey through streets lined with a shouting and threatening crowd. Acting with admirable sangfroid, Lavoisier again explained the nature of the whole transaction to the Assembly. Hearing that this body was satisfied, the mob suddenly decided that he was guiltless, but concluded that there must have been dirty work somewhere. It turned its attention to the man who had originally signed the order—La Salle. La Salle, fortunately warned that he was being hunted, managed to escape with his life.

Incidents of this nature were incompatible with civilised existence. The mob, which had materially assisted in the overthrow of the old *régime*, was beginning to show a taste for pillage, and had somehow to be quelled. The propertied middle classes, horrified by the daily increasing exhibitions of mob violence, proceeded to take measures to safeguard their existence. Lafayette's National Guard was essentially a middle-class body designed to combat proletarian anarchy. Each member had to buy his own uniform, and the regulations enforced the wearing of a uniform so expensive that no very poor man could afford it. As an adjunct to the National Guard a battalion of volunteers was formed, in which each trooper had to provide his own horse and arms. This pre-eminently bourgeois organisation began immediately to drive the tiger back into its cage. Before the end of the year Paris was reduced to something like order, and in the provinces branches of the National Guard soon taught the excited, over-hopeful peasantry, by wholesale executions, that freedom has its limits. The peasants had burned the castles of their late masters, the aristocrats, often with the motive of destroying, not so much the buildings themselves, as the legal documents relating to leases, tenancies, and tithes, which they contained. It was as though a man should attempt to wipe out his debts by burning bills as he received them. Actually, the newly-formed National Assembly did remove some of the heavier impositions from which the peasants suffered, while the latter had in future the satisfaction, doubtless considerable, of knowing that the money wrung from them went into the national exchequer and not into the pockets of feudal lords.

For the time being, the bourgeois and their National Guard triumphed. They had beaten the King and his unenthusiastic mercenaries, they had mastered the peasantry and the proletariat. Lavoisier himself, though in his middle forties, was a member of the National Guard, in which capacity he was called to serve as sentry on several occasions. When the revolution dawned he was at the summit of his career, rich, honoured beyond the borders of his country, surrounded by admiring and devoted friends. His laboratory at the Arsenal was the centre of the scientific life of France. His chemical discoveries had won general acceptance from scientific workers, and had penetrated so far into the general consciousness that the new chemistry was beginning to be taught in the schools. But in spite of having possessed a position of such dignity under the old aristocratic system, Lavoisier had accepted the revolution as necessary. While deploring the antics of patriots in parliament assembled, the irresistible flood of fine oratory which the revolution had loosened, he was nevertheless prepared to work loyally for the new *régime*. Privately, however, though he had no aristocratic sympathies, he inclined towards the extreme right. He considered, for example, that the arming of the public had been rather overdone. In a letter to Franklin, written in 1790, he expresses the view that the aristocratic party was definitely broken, but at the same time he deplores the putting of too much power into the hands of those whose function it is to obey. The people who had kept their heads in the midst of the general confusion—and, he might have added, *fermiers généraux* with large fortunes to lose—considered that things were going rather too fast and too far. In other letters written at this time he expresses his general misgivings at the trend of events, laying particular stress on one point ; the upheaval was definitely checking the advance of science in France.

None the less, in the early creative phase of the revolution he played a full and active part. The circle in which the Lavoisiers moved contained nearly all the trained constructive minds of the country. He became a member of the famous '89 Club, a club unique in those troubled times in that its objects were not primarily political. It was concerned, indeed, to develop and defend the principles and freedom of the new constitution, but its main purpose was to further the progress of social reform. The club, which included such men as Mirabeau, Bailly, Monge, and André Chenier, was definitely an association of the

intellectually superior, while its high annual subscription
of five golden louis excluded all but the relatively prosperous.
It is scarcely to be wondered that it never achieved the
affection of the dispossessed. The mob had other cham-
pions. A few years later mere membership of the '89 Club
was to involve danger of the guillotine.

In 1791, Lavoisier drew up for the authorities a careful
report on "*La richesse territoriale de la France,*" which contained the most valuable statistical data relating to population, industry, and agriculture. This was the first satisfactory work of its kind in France. He calculated the
national income and demonstrated, somewhat to the dismay
of the revenue authorities, the limits of national taxation.
His population statistics were of topical and political interest
in that they showed how tiny, numerically speaking, had
been the proportion of nobles to the rest of the population.
They also caused some surprise. There had seemed to be
so many nobles. Was it possible that so small a group had
caused so much noise ?

" It is not possible," remarked a reviewer in the *Moniteur*,
" to give an abstract of this work. We will confine ourselves to quoting an extremely patriotic calculation (*un calcul
très patriotique*) whose arithemetical exactitude seems
unquestionable. The ci-devant nobles formed 3 per cent.
of the population of the kingdom, their number, including
men, women and children, being only 83,000, of whom
18,323 were capable of bearing arms. Those classes of
society, which were formerly referred to as the Third
Estate, contained 5,500,000 men capable of bearing arms."

At this period of his life Lavoisier developed into a sort
of official adviser to the Government on scientific and
financial matters. As a member of a Treasury Commission,
set up in 1791, he introduced into national finance an
element of unprecedented and probably highly unpopular
efficiency. The system of book-keeping which he established made it possible for Ministers of Finance to discover
at any given moment the exact state of the national
exchequer. Later he assisted the Treasury from a rather

different angle, by giving advice on the type of paper and printing to be employed in the manufacture of the money bills known as " *Assignats*."

In the introduction to a memorandum on the financial situation in France, published in January, 1792, he expressed himself as follows :—

" At a time when everything, good and evil alike, is liable to exaggeration, when everybody looks at things through distorting glasses which make them too great or too small, too near or too distant, and no one seems capable of seeing them in accordance with their proper size and position, I thought it would be of use if someone would undertake to discuss the situation calmly, and submit the finances of the state to rigorous mathematical analysis."

Lavoisier considered it prudent not to put his name to the memorandum, but we can scarcely imagine that its authorship remained a mystery, for who could mistake that slightly acid style, that insistence on clear and unbiassed thought, that fully developed contempt for political emotionalism ? We need scarcely wonder that his unpopularity with demagogues of all parties grew. To the end he never seems to have understood why he was on the whole a failure in politics, never seems to have realised that a man of his type tends to be regarded by popularity seekers and political windbags with fear and hatred.

Among Lavoisier's interests was one which has not yet been mentioned—education—a subject which tends sooner or later to attract the attention of men who find human dirt and muddle irritating. He had established a model school for his tenants at Frechines. In the preface to the " Traité Élémentaire de Chimie," a work designed as a text-book, he had included some reflections on the psychology of learning. Talleyrand recognised Lavoisier's authority as an educationalist by sending him the draft of his famous and influential report on public education for criticism and advice. Now this interest was to involve him in further laborious public work. The Bureau of Arts and Crafts, of which he was a member, was asked to draw up a scheme of national education, and this task, like many others imposed upon the Bureau, was confided to Lavoisier. Needless to say, the admirable if Utopian scheme which he formulated was never put into practice, but it remains of interest as an exposition of his own views on education. He was strongly biassed towards the practical. Like Priestley, he insists that children should be taught things which will be of genuine use to them in after life : how to read a map, how to keep account books, how to use indices and dictionaries. Country boys should be taught the principles of agriculture, and girls housekeeping, needlework, cooking, nursing, and the care of infants. When he comes to deal with high schools and *lycées*, his temperamental indifference to the arts is clearly manifest ; though he does not neglect these, the emphasis is all on science. Each high school, he recommends, should be equipped with a library, a case of scientific instruments, models of machines, astronomical instruments, and collections illustrating natural history, as well as a garden for the study of botany and agriculture. The natural history collections, he adds, should be as complete as possible. As an educationalist he seems nearer akin to Sanderson of Oundle than to Arnold of Rugby. There is no mention of religion in the report, but he proposes that children should be taught the elementary principles of morality, and should receive instruction about the rights and duties of man and the " social contract " generally. He makes one curious concession to contemporary idealism in suggesting that transgressors should be tried by juries chosen from among the children themselves, which will return a verdict of guilty or not guilty ; subsequent punishment, if necessary, being inflicted by the authorities.

All this was taking Lavoisier farther and farther from the realm of laboratory research. One of his most important official activities at this time, however, had closer connections with experimental science. On the motion of Talleyrand, at that time devoting some of his enormous ability to social reconstruction, the Assembly passed in May, 1790, a decree which conferred on the Academy of Science the task of setting up a rational system of weights and measures. It was intended that the system should be an international one, and the Assembly envisaged an international commission to establish it. But a request for the co-operation of the Royal Society of London, though presented in the form of a letter from King Louis to King George, met with an unenthusiastic response. The Royal Society felt that the proposal smacked somehow of red revolution. As a legacy of its caution we still retain our antiquated and irrational system of weights and measures, spend irritating hours with conversion tables, and are perpetually embarrassed in the presence of foreigners genuinely surprised at the barbarism of our practice in this matter.

Lavoisier himself was especially concerned with the establishment of a standard of weight, and with Haüy began the investigation of the weight *in vacuo* of a volume of distilled water at 0° C. Other members of the Commission undertook the study of the unit of length, for which ·000004 of the earth's meridian was proposed. To further the accurate determination of this unit, it was decided to measure exactly the distance between Dunkirk and Barcelona, a task which was entrusted to Delambre and Méchain. Lavoisier was treasurer and, indeed, general organiser of the Commission, whose fortunes were shortly to become closely bound up with those of the Academy of Science. Later we shall have to tell of the enormous difficulties it encountered.

During the early years of the revolution, while Lavoisier was becoming every day more closely entangled in a net of public activities, the social life of the capital proceeded much as before. The rich remained rich, and the poor, poor. There were occasional alarms and excitements ; the National Assembly provided animated scenes and gorgeous oratory about the Rights of Man ; the King, with a reduced court, lived in the Tuileries and not at Versailles. But in spite of his diminished prestige he remained a king, and a king as powerful as any in Europe. Nor had a clean sweep been made of monarchical institutions. The Revenue Farm itself, perhaps the most universally detested of these, survived until March, 1791, when its contract was cancelled by the Assembly. Its disappearance was not at that time a severe blow to Lavoisier ; he had made his pile,[1] and moreover retained his well-paid post at the Arsenal.

But if the sea was smooth for the time being, the glass was falling ; storms murmured in the distance. The mob, still hungry, still half-clothed, still savage from lack of all human decencies, had got nothing out of the revolution. The fall of the Bastille had not lowered the price of bread. If the great lords and their impudent lackeys had disappeared from the streets, there still remained Lafayette and his National Guards. Suddenly the mob found a spokesman to express its sense of frustration, its greed to share. That spokesman was Jean Paul Marat, who himself felt, with all the concentration of an unbalanced mind, the bitterness of the unsuccessful and dispossessed. Marat's whole life had been a struggle against poverty. For many years he had been employed in a subordinate position by an aristocrat, and so enabled to study at close quarters the advantages of wealth which he could not enjoy. He was clever but not quite clever enough. His " Philosophical Essay on Man " showed enormous erudition, but somehow failed to throw fresh light on the problems of philosophy. By profession a doctor, he had made a few minor contributions to medical science and received an honorary degree of M.D. from the University of St. Andrews. After enjoying for a short period a reputation as fashionable physician to court and aristocracy, he had achieved a permanent appointment as medical officer to the guards of that insolent and impossible Bourbon, the Comte d'Artois. He had striven hard to earn a reputation in science, but unfortunately backed the wrong horse. In his " Researches on Flame," published in 1780, he had maintained that a candle goes out in an enclosed space because the air, dilated by the flame and

---

[1] Grimaux estimates that he made about 1,200,000 livres during his twenty-three years' connection with the farm.

unable to escape, compresses the flame and smothers it. Naturally the Academy of Science, with Lavoisier as its guiding spirit, gave an upholder of such unfashionable ideas little encouragement. Marat had further spoiled his chances of receiving a sympathetic hearing from the mandarins of science by differing from Newton with regard to certain optical phenomena. Some have held that the frigid attitude of the Academy towards him was unjustified ; certainly, like all such organisations, it was suspicious of amateurs outside its own dignified portals. But it does not appear that Marat was a genuinely gifted scientific worker. For the rest, he was only 5 feet high, with huge arms and an ugly yellow face, and entirely lacked decent manners. He had curious tics, such as a habit of walking on tiptoe. For all the disadvantages inflicted upon him by nature and society he was destined to take a terrible revenge.

The revolution was Marat's opportunity. Abandoning science and medicine he threw himself into politics in the character of an unappeasable *enragé*, a party of one. He became the opponent of Lafayette and Bailly and the prosperous and educated man who had assumed control of the Assembly. "*Nous sommes trahis*" was his perpetual cry, a cry to which the mob was very ready to listen. His paper, the *Ami du Peuple*, contained weekly denunciations of this individual or that in the manner of *John Bull* during the Great War. If anyone suspected a politician of dishonesty or treachery, he had only to write to the *Ami du Peuple* about it and Marat did the rest. It made excellent reading for the mob, but not for those who were attacked. As these were for the most part men of power and position, the editor of the *Ami du Peuple* led an uncomfortable existence in cellars and sewers, and his paper was printed under circumstances of extreme difficulty.

One of the most virulent denunciations in the *Ami du Peuple* was directed against Lavoisier. Marat hated Lavoisier, partly because, in his capacity of leading chemist in the Academy, he had contemptuously dismissed Marat's scientific work as worthless, but chiefly because he had everything that Marat had not : wealth, scientific renown, good looks, a pretty wife.

" I denounce this Coryphæus of the charlatans, Sieur Lavoisier, son of a land grabber, chemical apprentice, pupil of a Genevese stock-jobber, fermier général, régisseur of powder and saltpetre, administrator of the Discount Bank, Secretary to the King, member of the Academy of Science !

" Would you believe that this little gentleman, who has an income of 40,000 livres a year, whose only title to public gratitude is his achievement of having put Paris into prison, of having intercepted its supply of air by a wall which cost the poor 33 million livres, of having conveyed powder from the Arsenal to the Bastille on the night of July 12th, is now actually clamouring like a demon to be elected departmental administrator of Paris ? Would to heaven he had been hung on a lamp-post on the 6th of August ! The electors of la Culture would not then have to blush for having elected him."

In another number Marat denounced Lavoisier as a scientific charlatan and plagiarist.

" Lavoisier, the putative father of all discoveries which are noised abroad ! Having no ideas of his own, he steals those of others, but since he hardly ever knows how to evaluate them, he abandons them as lightly as he takes them up, and changes his systems like his shoes."

It is interesting that Marat should have made the charge of plagiarism against Lavoisier, since it shows that considerable discussion must already have taken place as to the exact part which Lavoisier had played in the discovery of oxygen and the composition of water, and in the chemical revolution.

For the time being Lavoisier could afford to disregard Marat and his like. The day of the Jacobins had not yet dawned ; pressure of war was required to drive the country into the hands of the extremists and bring the Terror into existence. The times were uncertain and anxious, but he shouldered manfully his burden of public business, and hoped for quieter days to come.

CHAPTER XIII

BIRMINGHAM AND THE BASTILLE

PRIESTLEY's position as Lord Shelburne's librarian was an easy and profitable one ; it was during his residence at Calne that his best scientific work was done. But after some years a certain coolness arose between Priestley and his patron. The coolness was on his lordship's side, and Priestley wrote later that he never understood the cause of it. Here he was showing a curious *naïveté* which sometimes appears in his writings, for the cause of his lordship's displeasure was plain to everyone else. Shelburne, politically ambitious, was beginning to find a librarian so outspoken on controversial political and religious issues something of an embarrassment.

His lordship generously continued to pay Priestley an annuity of £150 after their connection was severed. This was something, but not nearly enough, he found, to support adequately a family which now contained six members. There was talk of granting him a Government pension, but he abruptly declined all offers of this kind, saying that he wished to preserve himself independent of everything connected with the court. He was quite ready, however, to accept charity from his friends—a contradiction which grievously shocked Lord Brougham. Even at Calne, where his financial position was tolerably comfortable, he received £40 a year from friends who thought that Lord Shelburne's allowance did not fully provide for the expenses of his experiments. When, after leaving Calne, he went to London, he most thankfully received larger charitable subscriptions which came both from those who wished to see his scientific work continued, and from those who appreciated his powers as a theological disputant. All his life he was ready and willing to be the recipient of donations from friends and admirers.

His next move was to Birmingham, where lived his brother-in-law, John Wilkinson, the iron-founder. John Wilkinson was a well-known man, a pioneer of the industrial revolution, who had been closely associated with James Watt and his partner Boulton in their production of a commercially satisfactory steam engine. Possibly Priestley hoped that the wealthy manufacturer would eventually find positions for his sons in his business. Apart from the presence of so satisfactory a relative, Birmingham had the appeal for Priestley that it contained a group of scientists and inventors of distinction. Its Lunar Society, a scientific society founded by Boulton, so-called because it dined monthly at the time of the full moon, included Erasmus Darwin, Josiah Wedgwood, and Samuel Galton—ancestors of great English scientific families. Priestley rapidly became an influential member of the Lunar Society, so influential, indeed, that as a body it continued to support the theory of phlogiston long after it had been generally discredited. Apart from its scientific advantages, Birmingham was attractive to him in that it was a stronghold of dissent.

Though Priestley was now enjoying a great reputation as a natural philosopher, he turned again to the profession which he considered the noblest. The congregation of New Meeting, said to be the most liberal in England, asked him to become its minister. With alacrity he accepted. Doubtless these worthy Dissenters were gratified at hearing every Sunday the voice of a scientist of European renown raised in prayer or expounding the scriptures, while the minister himself was never so happy as in the pulpit. One may imagine that his sermons abounded with illustrations from the field of natural philosophy, for to Priestley scientific research was a righteous pursuit which made clear the works of God. He could understand, he said, why the Church of Rome feared science. It feared it as it feared all enlightenment. As the result of long experience, he had developed a quiet and persuasive pulpit manner; he avoided all

JOSEPH PRIESTLEY.

[*To face p.* 128.

declamation, gestures, and oratorical flourishes, talking to his congregation as one friend conversing with another. He gave much time and care to the religious instruction of the children of his flock.

In the part of his memoirs covering this period Priestley gives some account of his private life. He was now well advanced towards middle age and becoming settled in his habits of body and mind. He had lived with the aristocracy, by no means unhappily, but had definitely come to prefer a middle class *milieu*. " There is not only most virtue, and most happiness," he says, " but even most true politeness, in the middle class of life." The emphasis here seems to be on the word " true " ; it is as though he carried uncomfortable recollections of his insufficiency in the superficial politenesses of high society. He had been contented enough while living with Lord Shelburne, but preferred Birmingham and the hearty singing of his congregation.

He enjoyed excellent health, and a singularly placid temperament ; nervous irritation was unknown to him. " It has been a great advantage to me," he says, " that I have never been under the necessity of retiring from company in order to compose anything. Being fond of domestic life, I got a habit of writing on any subject by the parlour fire, with my wife and children about me, and occasionally talking to them, without experiencing any inconvenience from such interruption. Nothing but reading, or speaking without interruption, has been any obstruction to me. These are useful habits, which studious persons in general might acquire if they would ; and many persons greatly distress themselves, and others, by the idea that they can do nothing except in perfect solitude or silence." We may note here a touch of that placid unawareness of the feelings of other people which was an important element in Priestley's character and explains many chapters in his life history. " I have never found myself," he proceeds, " less disposed or less qualified for mental exertion of any kind at one time of the day more than another ; but all seasons have been equal to me, early or late, before dinner or after." His ease of mind and body further showed itself in a capacity for refreshing sleep. " It has been a singular happiness to me, and a proof, I believe, of a radically good constitution, that I have always slept well, and have awakened with my faculties perfectly vigorous, without any disposition to drowsiness. Also, whenever I have been fatigued with any kind of exertion, I could at any time sit down and sleep ; and what-, ever cause of anxiety I may have had, I have almost always lost sight of it when I have got to bed, and I have generally fallen asleep as soon as I have been warm." As the cause (or effect) of such tranquillity of disposition, he carried with him throughout life a profound belief in the guiding and sustaining hand of God.

In the congenial atmosphere of Birmingham, Priestley continued his scientific pursuits ; it was here that the experiments with Warltire which provided Cavendish with useful hints were performed. But he had already passed the zenith of his scientific achievement, and at this later period of his life the religious controversialist begins to take precedence over the natural philosopher. In 1872 he published a huge tome on " The History of the Corruptions of Christianity," which he considered the most valuable of all his writings. This was an opinion not generally shared, for not all contemporary theologians agreed with Priestley that the corruptions of Christianity were those doctrines opposed to the Unitarianism of the minister of New Meeting. His " History of Early Opinions concerning Jesus Christ," developed precisely the same ideas, as did his " General History of the Christian Church to the Fall of the Western Empire." These works were hotly attacked, not only by orthodox theologians of the Church of England, but by Lutherans and Calvinists. At Dort, in Holland, the " History of the Corruptions of Christianity " was burnt by the common hangman. Theologically his position was not uninteresting. He did not propose, as a medium of escape from later incrustations, a return to the New Testament, a difficult book which had been interpreted one way by Catholics, another by Arians, and a third by Anglicans.

Such differences of interpretation he held to be inevitable, because the New Testament was written, not for all time, but for a little group of persons who lived long ago in the first century. It was far easier for them, than for later readers, to understand its phraseology and metaphor, to decipher its difficult passages. It followed, therefore, that the ideas about the Trinity and other religious questions held by the earliest Fathers of the Church were probably nearer to the teaching of Christ and of the New Testament than subsequent interpretations, and it behoved all to study them. Investigation would show that the theology of the Fathers was very similar to that of Joseph Priestley.

In private life Priestley was the best tempered of men. He numbered among his personal friends some who were bitterly opposed to him on questions of politics and religion. He was rarely resentful, harboured few grudges. " The connection that all persons, and all things necessarily have, as parts of an immense, glorious, and happy system (and of which we ourselves are part, however small and inconsiderable), with the great author of the system, makes us regard every person, and every thing, in a friendly and pleasing light. The whole is but one family . . ." But his manners in controversy did not suggest this universal affection. When his attacks on orthodox theology and the Establishment had brought upon him the wrath of the bishops, he did not increase his popularity in episcopal circles by remarking that " Bishops are recorded in all histories as the most jealous, the most timorous, and, of course, the most vindictive of men." As a rule he made enemies of the powerful and distinguished : Gibbon and Burke, for example, were both made the objects of his attacks ; but he also succeeded in making himself an object of hatred and suspicion to the orthodox clergy of Birmingham by the establishment, in that city, of a library containing a distinctly unorthodox selection of books. This was denounced as " a fountain of erroneous opinions, spreading infidelity and schism through the whole neighbourhood." By the end of a decade of energetic religious controversy and political propaganda on behalf of Dissenters, Priestley had acquired an almost diabolic reputation among staunch upholders of church and state. The orthodox felt him to be really wicked, malignant, and destructive—regarded him, in fact, as many worthy people in 1900 regarded the kindly and harmless Mr. Bernard Shaw. He himself was probably quite unaware of the depth of feeling he had aroused against himself. In a memoir written at about the period he remarks : " I esteem it a singular happiness to have lived in an age and country, in which I have been at full liberty both to investigate, and by preaching and writing to propagate, religious truth." He was soon to find that the liberty was less complete then he supposed.

In one of the many pamphlets—thirty in all—which Priestley published during the years spent in Birmingham, he likened the dynamic force of truth, as represented by himself and his fellow Dissenters, to that of an explosion. " We are, as it were, laying gunpowder, grain by grain, under the old building of error and superstition, which a single spark may hereafter inflame, so as to produce an instantaneous explosion ; in consequence of which that edifice, the creation of which has been the work of ages, may be overturned in a moment, and so effectively as that the same foundation may never be built upon again." The simile was a good one, aptly describing the way in which steady criticism and ridicule may bring about the disintegration of apparently secure and long established institutions. It was exactly thus that Rousseau, Beaumarchais, and the Encyclopædists destroyed the crazy edifice of the French monarchy. But words are easily twisted for the benefit of fools, not only by knaves, but by honest political antagonists. Priestley's enemies found it easy to spread among the illiterate the rumour that a plot was on foot to blow up the churches. Opposition pamphleteers nicknamed him " Gunpowder Priestley."

One of the early acts of the revolutionists in France was the establishment of religious liberty. Under the old *régime* the lot of the Huguenots had been hard, and English Dissenters had regarded them as companions in misfortune.

DOCTOR PHLOGISTON,
The PRIESTLEY politician or the Political Priest.

[*To face p.* 132.

But now that France had taken the lead towards toleration, and, further, had expropriated her established church, those who suffered from religious disabilities in England naturally hailed the Revolution as a glorious victory for freedom of conscience, and held up the changes in France as an example to the world. Priestley himself was far too English an Englishman to understand or sympathise with the French spirit ; in Paris he had been like a fish out of water ; but the lofty principles of the Revolution captivated his imagination. From Lavoisier he had learnt of the attitude of the educated middle classes in France in the early days of the upheaval. Lavoisier had remarked, in the course of a professional letter relating to chemistry, that while there had been some excesses, these had been committed for the love of liberty, philosophy and toleration, and that there was no danger of such things being done in France for an inferior motive—a judgment which, written for the benefit of a foreigner, scarcely conveyed his own private views. Priestley's son William was actually in Paris during the summer of 1789, a fact which had caused some anxiety to his parents ; he returned safely to tell a stirring story of the birth of the new order. In October of the same year, Priestley wrote thus to Mr. Adam Walker :—

" My son and brother-in-law were in Paris during all the great scene, so that I had very minute accounts of all that passed. There is indeed a glorious prospect for mankind before us. Flanders seems quite ripe for a similar revolution ; and other countries, I hope, will follow in due time ; and when civil tyranny is all at an end, that of the church will soon be disposed of. You saw what was taking place in Flanders when you were there ; but I hope the revolution will be less bloody than you then forfended. Our court and the courtiers will not like these things, and the bishops least of all."

Priestley was quite right ; the court, courtiers and bishops did not like such things. Neither did that gifted Dublin snob, Mr. Edmund Burke, whose " Reflections on the French Revolution " Priestley was at some pains to refute. Mr. Burke was inclined, he said, to amuse himself with the shadow and wholly neglect the substance. " His conduct is best accounted for by his leaning towards the court." " I do not wonder," Priestley remarked in a letter to Dr. Price, " at the hatred and dread of this spirit of revolution in kings and courtiers. Their power is generally usurpation, and I hope the time is coming when an end will be put to all usurpation, in things civil and religious, first in Europe and then in other countries."

Feeling between the Church and State Party and the friends of the Revolution, mainly drawn from the ranks of the Dissenters, ran particularly high in Birmingham. A crisis was precipitated when the Francophiles proceeded to organise, on July 14th, 1791, a dinner in commemoration of " the auspicious day which witnessed the Emancipation of Twenty-six Millions of People from the Yoke of Despotism." At the same time a provocative pamphlet appeared which urged the people to " Remember that on the 14th of July the Bastille, that ' High Altar and Castle of Despotism,' fell." " Is it possible to forget," it went on to say, " that your own Parliament is venial ? Your ministers hypocritical ? Your clergy legal oppressors ? The reigning Family extravagant ? The crown of a certain great personage becoming every day too weighty for the head that wears it ? " And so on in the same strain. The Tories, highly incensed, meditated revenge on the Dissenters on the occasion of the forthcoming celebrations. It happened that the mob, understanding little of the issues involved, but instinctively on the side of King George and England against anything French and foreign, was Tory in its sympathies. The Church and State Party determined to use this dangerous weapon against its enemies. Whispers were circulated that the authorities would be highly gratified if the Dissenters were taught a lesson. The Birmingham poor were only too ready to listen. Apart from politics, the chance of a little destruction and murder with official sanction was naturally appealing.

As it happened, the commemorative dinner at Dadley's Hotel passed off uneventfully ; it began at three o'clock and broke up at six, when the diners dispersed, without interference, to their homes. Priestley himself was not present, but later that evening a mob collected round Dadley's Hotel, raised the cry of " Church and King," and tasted the first delights of destruction by smashing the windows. Someone in the crowd shouted " To New Meeting," and the crowd rushed off and set fire to that building. After another dissenting chapel—the " Old Meeting "—had been burnt out, the mob looked round for something else to destroy. This time the cry was " To Dr. Priestley's."

The police, in the modern sense of the term, did not exist. The magistrates, whose duty it was to maintain order, had remained at home during the early part of the evening, enjoying the preliminary success of their plans. It was now too late to interfere, even had they so desired, for the mob was thoroughly out of hand. It is said that one Church of England clergyman had earlier in the day secured the key of the building where the fire engine was kept, and handed it to his clerk, from whom it was retrieved with difficulty and delay.

Priestley had spent the day at home. In the evening, while he was playing his customary game of backgammon, a friend arrived breathless with the news that the mob was setting fire to his chapel, and that he himself and his own house was in danger. He flatly refused to believe it. Under persuasion, however, he walked to the house of a friend called Russell, a mile farther from town at Showell Green. On the way there he saw in the distance the flames rising from the burning chapels. His son William remained behind to put out the kitchen fire and to place certain valuables and manuscripts in a cache not far away.

At midnight the mob reached the house. Crying " God save the King," " Down with the Dissenters," " No false rights of man," and similar patriotic slogans, it gleefully set to work to smash everything in sight. The instruments in the laboratory were battered to pieces, as was all the furniture ; everything breakable was in fact broken. Books and manuscripts were scattered to the four winds. But the house was not set on fire because the rioters found themselves without a source of flame. For a time some of them tried to start a fire by means of sparks from the doctor's electrical apparatus, but without success.

Meanwhile Priestley and his wife had been hurried to another friend's house at Mosely Green, half a mile farther away. It was a warm, still, moonlit summer night, and from Mosely Green Priestley could hear clearly the shouts of the mob and the sounds of destruction at his house. It scarcely disturbed him. "Tranquil and serene," an admirer wrote long afterwards, "he walked up and down the road with a firm yet gentle pace that evinced his entire self-possession." The ways of God might at times seem puzzling, but in the long run He knew best.

At four o'clock in the morning the mob began advancing towards Showell Green, and the Priestleys were driven to Heath Forge, five miles away. Here they thought them-selves safe. They were preparing to go to bed when news came that the rioters were still pursuing. Priestley ignored this, but later in the morning more definite warnings were received and he himself, with a servant, rode to Bridgnorth in Shropshire. From here he proceeded, after two hours' sleep, to Kidderminster, and later to Heath, where he hoped for a full night's rest. But finding the Dissenters there in momentary expectation of a riot, he was forced to ride back again along the Kidderminster road. During the night he and his servant got lost in the dark. At dawn they found themselves on Bridgnorth race ground, " having ridden nineteen miles, until we could hardly sit our horses." After a few hours' rest in Bridgnorth, he set out again on horseback and, by hiring a chaise in Kidderminster, he was able to get to Worcester just in time to catch the London coach, on which there was one place vacant. He arrived in London on the morning of the 18th, and at last enjoyed an opportunity for sufficient rest and sleep. It had been a strenuous four days for a man nearing his sixtieth year.

Not only the property of the Priestleys, but also that of a number of their friends, suffered at the hands of the rioters before these were eventually, after a week's glorious orgy, dispersed by the military. No one, as it happened, was lynched. Later, fairly adequate compensation was paid by the municipality, and the authorities unenthusiastically sought to bring certain of the mob's ringleaders to justice. In the end two of these were hanged. The general feeling of the country towards the Dissenters, whose houses had been burnt, was " serve them right." The King himself, in a private letter, expressed himself as pleased that Priestley had been a sufferer, though disapproving of the means employed.

Within a few days of his arrival in London, Priestley wrote a " letter of expostulation " to the citizens of Birmingham, and began to compose a sermon on forgiveness. Before the extent of the disorders in Birmingham had become apparent, he had planned to return and deliver, in the ruins of his chapel, a sermon on the text " Father, forgive them, for they know not what they do." Fortunately the course of events prevented this procedure, which would surely have maddened his opponents beyond endurance. Mrs. Priestley was less high-minded. She did not consider that in such circumstances " God can require it of us as a duty, after they have smote one cheek, to turn the other." She, poor lady, was much more shaken than her husband at the destruction of their home and household effects, and even when safe in London, could not throw off the fear that at any moment a shouting, destroying mob might descend on them again. She began to urge her husband to emigrate to America.

It was with some difficulty that the Priestleys at length found a house in Hackney, for landlords, fearful of their property, were unwilling to accept them as tenants. But once settled in his new home, Priestley, quite undisturbed by his recent experiences, and the fact of being the most widely-hated man in England, resumed his usual placid and cheerful existence. Generous friends came forward with donations ; he built a new laboratory, the apparatus of which was furnished free by Thomas Wedgwood, and declared

himself happier than he had ever been in his life. He began
to preach in the Dissenting conventicles of the neighbourhood. But his enemies were unappeased; there were
persistent rumours that his house was to be attacked again.
Servants refused to stay for any length of time; patriotic
tradespeople hesitated to take his custom. He was attacked
by a virulent series of pamphlets and caricatures, and burnt
in effigy along with another well-known supporter of the
French Revolution, Tom Paine. As the news from France
grew more outrageous in the eyes of the outside world, his
position became more unpleasant and precarious. After
the Birmingham affair he had received letters of condolence
from a number of revolutionary leaders, including Con-
cordet, who hailed him in grandiloquent prose as a sufferer
in the name of liberty. He had the honour of French
citizenship conferred on him, and was actually asked to sit
in the National Assembly as member for the Department of
the Orne.[1] This offer he declined on the polite grounds of
insufficient acquaintance with the French language. His
son William was presented to the National Assembly as a
French citizen by M. Français of Nantes, on June 8th, 1792.
Priestley's first knowledge of this event came from the public
press, but naturally he was accused of having arranged it.

Members of the Royal Society began to shun his company.
" My philosophical friends here," he wrote, " are cold and
distant. Mr. Cavendish never expressed the least concern
on account of anything I had suffered, though I joined a
party with which he was, and talked with them some time."

---

[1] Tom Paine likewise accepted French citizenship at about the same
time, and on being elected as deputy for the Pas de Calais, actually took
his seat in the National Assembly. He opposed the execution of Louis,
thereby falling foul of Marat and the Jacobins. The following year he
threw in his lot with the Girondins and made a mortal enemy of
Robespierre. In December, 1793, he was arrested as a citizen of a
country at war with France and imprisoned in the Luxembourg. During
the height of the Terror he was marked down for execution by Robespierre and the Committee of Public Safety, but the disorganisation of
those months enabled him to escape the guillotine by a lucky chance. A
chalk mark scribbled on the door of his cell by an official of the Revolutionary Tribunal, as a sign that he was to be brought to trial, was over-
looked by the officers whose duty it was to convey prisoners from the
Luxembourg to the Conciergerie.

(In all probability Cavendish had never heard of the Birmingham riots.) Less wise than Lavoisier, Priestley had thought that scientists were above the political hatreds of common men. After the Royal Society had further angered him by rejecting an otherwise eligible candidate on account of his political principles, he cut himself off from it altogether and ceased to publish in its " Philosophical Transactions."

At length, in 1794, he decided to emigrate to America. War had broken out between France and England and Priestley felt that he, whose French sympathies were notorious, might at any time be made the victim of further persecution on the part of the Government or the populace. An unwary utterance in the pulpit might lead to imprisonment for sedition. The fact that his three sons, including William the French citizen, were already in America, driven thither by the difficulty of finding employment in Europe, fortified his decision to emigrate. Amid lamentations on the part of a handful of the faithful, the Priestleys embarked at Gravesend on the *Samson*, on April 7th, 1794, and safely reached New York on the 4th of June. Mrs. Priestley was seasick most of the voyage and scarcely able to interest herself even in the " mountains of ice, larger than the Captain had ever seen before," which they passed. But though the cooking was bad, and the captain swore much, and was given to liquor, her husband enjoyed every moment of it. He wrote two sermons on the causes of the prevalence of infidelity, though with difficulty ; he read the Greek testament and the Hebrew Bible ; he undertook some light reading which included Ovid's " Metamorphosis " and the " Dialogues of Erasmus." He conducted services for passengers and crew when the weather permitted it. He took thermometer readings of the heat of water at various depths. When at length the travellers found themselves safely on shore in America, he declared that he would willingly have sailed round the world.

CHAPTER XIV

THE FALL OF THE ACADEMY OF SCIENCE

Towards the middle of 1791, Lavoisier, like many other Frenchmen of his class, began to find his path encompassed with difficulties and dangers. In this defensive period of his life he showed fine fighting ability. He strove to save French science from the general shipwreck, to preserve what he could of his own wealth and position, and ultimately to save his life.

When the Revenue Farm was abolished in March, 1791, he was promised the position of Administrator of the Customs. This he was particularly anxious to obtain since such an appointment would be in itself a testimonial to his honesty as an administrator of the Farm. He failed to secure it, his enemies removing his name from the list submitted to the King. Shortly afterwards, however, he was nominated Commissioner of the National Treasury, and in this capacity performed, as previously mentioned, valuable services to his country. On receiving the appointment, he wrote to the press to say that he was accepting no salary for it, since the salary he already received as *Régisseur des Poudres* was sufficient for his needs. This move was partly a politic genuflection to the spirit of the times, but it was also intended to make his tenure of the post at the *Régie* more secure. This latter purpose it failed to fulfil. Five months later the number of *régisseurs* was reduced to three, and Lavoisier was not included in the new directorate. With some difficulty he secured from the King the privilege of retaining his laboratory at the Arsenal, the equipment of which had cost a large sum of money. In February, 1792, on resigning from the Treasury, he was unexpectedly reappointed to the *Régie des Poudres*, but almost immediately he resigned this position also, offering, however, to continue his researches on gunpowder at his own expense. In order to cut himself off altogether from a much criticised government department, he finally gave up his rooms in the Arsenal and took a house in the Boulevard de la Madeleine. His caution was amply justified. Three days after his departure the Arsenal was invaded by the police, and the remaining *régisseurs* arrested. One of these, overcome with terror, killed himself.

Lavoisier had made up his mind to avoid in future all salaried public appointments. When the King, in June, 1792, a few weeks before the storming of the Tuileries, offered him the post of Minister of Public Contributions, he hastened to decline that honour. In his carefully worded letter of refusal, he expressed the desire to serve the state in a more humble capacity. He was determined, in fact, to leave public life altogether and devote his time to purely scientific pursuits. Inclination, and a sense of imminent danger, combined to fortify him in this decision.

A letter written by Lavoisier to Robert Kerr, the translator of the " Traité Élémentaire de Chimie," illustrates his frame of mind at this period. The letter, dated January 6th, 1793, a reply to one of Kerr's, is as follows :—

" Sir.—It is true that the printer entrusted with the publication of my ' Elements of Chemistry ' has just issued a second edition of that work, but this was without my knowledge, and without my having made the smallest correction. It is a ' pirated,' rather than a second, edition.

" I note with gratitude your intention to undertake the English translation of a second edition, but I hope that you will reserve your good offices for a later occasion ; for since I made up my mind to retire completely from all public acitvities, and to give all my time to science, I have planned the production of the ' Elements of Chemistry ' on a much greater scale. I do not think that the new work will be ready for publication for two years, and I shall not fail to send you copy—leaf by leaf, if you like—as soon as the printing is begun ; but this will not be for a year or more. I shall then ask you to indicate what you consider the most expedient channel of despatch.

" I received recently the copy of your excellent translation which you so kindly sent me. I find nearly all of it clearer than my own text.

" The reason for my not writing to you was that I was engaged in occupations of a very different nature ; at that time one could hope to do useful service in administrative positions ; but to-day, with France given over to the strife of factions, it is becoming extremely difficult to get anything done in this field, and the man who aspires to a great position must either be very ambitious, or very crazy.

" I have the honour to be,
" Sir,
" Your most humble and obedient servant,
" Lavoisier."

Lavoisier and his wife spent the summer and autumn of 1792 on their estate at Frechines. Several reasons may be given to explain so unusually long a holiday. He needed rest, for the strain of the last years must have told on a man no longer young. He may have wished, by a prolonged stay in the country, to emphasise his desire to retire altogether from the political arena, and have planned an unobserved return to Paris as a private citizen. Or, perhaps, the wild disorders which took place in the capital that autumn made him hesitate to leave his rural retreat.

The earlier part of the year had seen a massing of enemies on the frontiers of France. The King and Queen, impenetrably stupid, incapable of learning or forgetting even under the spur of personal danger, awaited rescue in the Tuileries, the palace which they had come to regard as a prison. Should the rescuers not arrive in time, the King was placidly ready for martyrdom, but the Queen, less passive, was eager to escape, could she but find satisfactory accomplices. Flight to Rouen was suggested ; the Duc de la Rochefoucald-Liancourt was mayor of that city and prepared to give sanctuary to royal fugitives. But no, the Duc was a constitutionalist. Lafayette, in command of an army at Namur, wished to play the *rôle* of saviour to the King, but Lafayette, royalist though he might be, had been in sympathy with the revolutionary movement from the start, and Marie Antoinette could not bear the sight of him. Her dislike of him dated, indeed, from earlier days, for Lafayette, as a young officer at Versailles, had in his humourless, self-sufficient way indicated his contempt for the expensive imbecilities of the Queen and her entourage. So she passed her time in correspondence with ineffective rescuers of unimpeachable antecedents, while every day the pressure on the frontier grew greater, and the suspicion and hatred of the mass of the people became more intense. There was a demonstration against the palace on June 20th. A few weeks later Paris was enraged beyond bearing by the proclamation of the Duke of Brunswick, the leader of the army of Prussia, declaring that Paris was to be destroyed by fire and sword if the Royal Family was harmed, that if, indeed, submission to the Royal Family were not made at once, Prussia and Austria would take an unforgettable vengeance, and Paris be given up to military execution and subversion, and the guilty rebels put to the death they deserved. On July 27th the Federals from Marseilles, singing their great song, marched into the city. The monarchy was doomed. The next few weeks saw the fall of the Tuileries, the imprisonment of the royal family in the Tower of the Temple, and a great swing of political power in the direction of the militarists and Jacobins.

With the imprisonment of the King, a new and violently republican organisation came into power—the self-elected Paris Commune, of which Danton was the leader and Marat a prominent member. The latter's chance had come at last. One of the first uses to which he put his membership of the Commune was to acquire the royal printing press for his journal; he longed for fine paper and lordly type, for the *Ami du Peuple* had hitherto been printed anyhow on odd scraps of paper. Soon he was able to strike at some of his enemies. A general search for arms and suspects was ordered, and accordingly, on August 30th, the gates of the city were closed, every street was illuminated, and a house-to-house visitation carried out by the National Guard, now in the hands of the extremists. The search made a deep impression on peaceable and prosperous citizens, some of whom realised for the first time that the Revolution was capable of invading their private lives. It was controlled by Dr. Marat himself, and though most of the individuals seized were royalists and anti-revolutionaries, some were arrested for purely personal reasons. The gaols of Paris, and not only the gaols, but also a number of temporary houses of detention, were filled with prisoners to the number of over 3,000.

The problem of dealing with so large a mass of suspects was a grave one, to which a convenient solution was found in the massacres which took place a few days later. Small but well-organised groups of men broke into the various gaols and murdered a large proportion of the prisoners. Some escaped by chance, others by ready wit ; here and there the murderers showed a rough sense of justice. But on the whole they did their work thoroughly and without too fine a sense of discrimination, for 1,100 prisoners in all were despatched. At the Abbaye, the murderers, growing hungry and thirsty as the result of such strenuous exercise, were compelled to call a halt, during which they sent out for food and wine. Behind and directing the massacres, it is said, was a small committee, of which Marat was the leader.

That month France became a republic. Lafayette, the hero of the wealthy middle classes, slipped across the frontier into Belgium in time to save his neck. In the newly-elected Assembly, now called the Convention, the Jacobins, supported by the Commune, began their struggle with the Girondins. The youth of France rushed to join the colours. As the military situation grew more desperate, the single-minded extremists, the Montagnards, supported by the mob, advanced steadily towards supreme power in the state.

Possibly Marat would have attempted that August to pay off old scores on Lavoisier, had the latter not been out of sight and mind at Frechines. It was not until November that Citoyen and Citoyenne Lavoisier returned to Paris, for the opening meeting of the Academy of Science. By that time Paris had settled down again. France was at war, her

King was in prison, this time a genuine prison, the political atmosphere was explosive, but through it all the life of the capital still proceeded on something very like normal lines. For a time Lavoisier was able to realise his intention of a return to laboratory work, but not fully. Two exhausting and time-consuming tasks—his treasuryships of the Academy, and of the Commission of Weights and Measures —absorbed much of his energy. That winter, a few weeks before the execution of Louis Capet, he received the news that the Royal Society of London had conferred on him its highest honour—the Copley medal.

The Academy of Science had received a shock in April, 1792, when one of its members, Fourcroy, had quite unexpectedly put forward a motion that certain members, *connus pour leur incivisme*, should be removed from its register. There was general horror at this introduction of politics into a scientific meeting, and also some alarm. Members nervously recalled the uncomplimentary remarks which they had passed on occasion about the new *régime*. Fourcroy himself, a scientific worker of some distinction, the first chemist in France to teach the reformed chemistry in school, was ever eager to stand well with the ruling powers. We shall hear more of him. In putting forward his motion, he realised clearly which way the political wind was blowing. Several members objected very strongly to Fourcroy's motion, on the obvious ground that the Academy had no concern with the politics of its members, but it was not considered advisable to reject the motion altogether. As a way out of an embarrassing situation, it was proposed that the list of Academicians should be sent to the Minister of the Interior, who could revise it as he thought fit. A number of noble *emigrés* were still on the Academy roll.

When the Minister of the Interior returned a revised list early in 1793 (it does not appear that any members except *emigrés* were struck off), the Academy of Science felt that it had received a sort of official recognition from the new republican authorities. But it was a monarchical institution, and as such knew itself suspect. In an effort to consolidate its position, the Academy of Science staged a ceremony in which a general account of its work, and, in particular, an account of the progress of the Commission of Weights and Measures, was presented to the National Convention. The scientists, proceeding *en masse* to the Convention, were favourably received and publicly thanked for their labours. All now seemed well. But the Academy had formidable enemies in the Convention, and three days later a decree was passed forbidding it to elect any new members until further notice.

During the early months of 1793 it continued to meet, but rather nervously. A certain constraint hung over the proceedings. Yet, though frowned at by certain extremists, the Academicians had never before been so occupied by public work. The inexperienced and sorely tried ministers of the Republic sought scientific advice on a great variety of subjects. But though some of the authorities still found it useful to have a body of tame scientists at their disposal, to whom technical problems might be referred, the educated wealthy society which had supported science by its spontaneous interest and approval was disintegrating. Further, the fact that there was a war on gave all unpractical and non-military activities an unpatriotic flavour.

Certain members of the Commission of Weights and Measures had particular reason to deplore the chaotic state of the country. The standard of length, later called the metre, had been defined as the four-millionth of the earth's meridian, and in order that the latter might be determined with unimpeachable accuracy, Delambre and Méchain were entrusted with the task of re-measuring the meridian between Dunkirk and Barcelona. It was decided that the former's survey should extend from Dunkirk to Rodez, the latter's from Rodez to Barcelona. In the entire history of science there can scarcely be another such story of maddening difficulties and superhuman endeavour. The survey began in May, 1792, more than a year after the Assembly had approved of the undertaking. Méchain, on his way to the south, was arrested a few miles from Paris, but succeeded in establishing his *bona fides ;* at the Franco-Spanish frontier he was again in difficulties, but once in Spain all was comparatively plain sailing as far as geodesy was concerned. Unfortunately war shortly broke out between France and Spain, so that he was unable for more than a year to return to France with his records. His colleague, Delambre, had more remarkable adventures, of which he gave a sprightly and amusing account some years later. He tells how, on August 10th, 1792, he arranged with M. Lefrancais Lalande that the latter should light a beacon at Montmartre as an observation point, but when night fell there was no sign of the beacon, for that happened to be the day of the attack on the Tuileries, and Lalande, on his way out of the city to Montmartre, was held up at the barrier by the guard. Ignorant peasants suspected Delambre and his assistant of witchcraft and chased them and their theodolites out of their villages ; local authorities, less logical and no less ignorant, suspected them of mysterious counter-revolutionary activities. Everywhere Delambre had to explain at length to local communes, guards, and all kinds of minor bureaucrats, who had never heard of the official Commission of Weights and Measures, exactly what he was doing and why. Geodesy is not a simple subject to explain to a bucolic audience. They were arrested again and again. At Saint-Denis Delambre was in genuine danger from a revolutionary crowd. The town was full of volunteers waiting for arms before proceeding to the frontier, and these were in a menacing mood. Delambre succeeded in obtaining the support of an educated *procureur-syndic* from a neighbouring town, and he and this gentleman began to argue their case with the authorities of Saint-Denis.

" While we were there our carriages were searched, and letters were found addressed to all the departments which the meridian crosses. The crowd wished to break the seals, which was opposed, however, by the National Guard, who affirmed that they bore the official stamp of the Assembly. Shouts were heard ; the *procureur-syndic* and myself were wanted. As we went out, the *procureur* showed me a place to hide, and advised me to remain there a few moments, and, should he not return, to make good my escape. He returned to say that there was no danger. I was wanted to break the seals of the letters. Actually each envelope contained a circular letter signed by the Committee of Public Instruction of the National Assembly, introducing us to departmental administrations. Six already had been read ; they wished to hear all. But the reader was weary and demanded breathing space. I proposed that a letter should be chosen at random from those that remained ; I would vouch for it with my head that they were all the same. The proposition was accepted. But after the examination of the letters was over, the crowd turned its attention to the instruments. These were strewn all over the place. I found myself forced to begin again the course of lectures on geodesy of which I had given the first lessons at Epinai : My audience was not responsive. The day was failing ; it was growing almost impossible to see. My audience was very large, and while the front ranks heard and saw without under-standing, those farther back heard and saw nothing at all. Impatient murmurs became more pronounced ; several voices proposed putting into practice one of those measures which were the custom of the times, and which solved all doubts and difficulties. The *procureur*, however, hit on the happy idea of postponing the enquiry till the next day, putting on a great appearance of severity to impress the crowd."

The next day confirmation of Delambre's statement was obtained from Paris, and the incident was closed.

When Delambre and his assistant began the survey, they carried royal passports, but with the establishment of the republic these became worse than useless, for they rendered their bearers objects of suspicion. Delambre was afraid to return to Paris to apply for republican passports, because he thought it probable that the authorities would veto the continuance of the survey in such disturbed times. Eventually, however, he was forced to return, and actually succeeded, after plagueing various members of the Convention for weeks, in obtaining the necessary passports and permission to proceed. At one period his name was temporarily removed from the Commission of Weights and Measures, and he was ordered to hand over all the records and instruments. His house was searched by republican guards, who, however, found no definite evidence of counter-revolutionary activity. They lingered for a long time over a diploma of the Royal Society, written in Latin, which bore the name of George III. and the royal crest, and gave rise to the suspicion that he was in treasonable correspondence with a foreign monarch. At length the gallant surveyors, buffeted by wind and weather, subject to perpetual question and arrest, with scarcely sufficient money to buy enough to eat, grew so ragged, sick, and woebegone that villagers took them for returned prisoners of war.

It was the task of Lavoisier, as Treasurer of the Commission of Weights and Measures, to transmit salaries and expenses to Delambre and Méchain and other members of the Commission. As Treasurer of the Academy of Science, he was generally responsible for the payment of the salaries of the Academicians. To secure the necessary funds he began what was to be a lengthy struggle with the authorities. On several occasions, when urgently required money was not immediately forthcoming, Lavoisier advanced it from his own pocket. When Méchain was interned in Spain a cheque for 30,000 francs, endorsed by Lavoisier personally, was sent to him through a Swiss banker. He was in continual correspondence with the embarrassed and persevering Delambre. As the turmoil of the times increased, so did his determination that French science should survive. This became at last the main object of his life. His scientific colleagues were for the most part impecunious, unpractical, and retiring men, while he was thoroughly at home in the worlds of business and officialdom. Leadership was thrust on the one man capable of leading.

May arrived and the Academy grant for 1793 was not yet paid. Lavoisier appealed to the patriotism of certain members of the Convention, reminding them how eagerly foreign nations would take advantage of the non-payment of distinguished scientists to entice them into lucrative positions abroad. He insisted on the fact that the Academy of Science did a great deal of work for very little. He found in the Convention a very useful ally in Lakanal, an energetic young man whose main interest was education. Lakanal had an enormous admiration for Lavoisier and was flattered at being asked to render him service.

" Citoyen," Lavoisier wrote to Lakanal on May 12th, " the matter is urgent. A great many of our Academicians are suffering ; several have already left Paris, because their means do not permit them to remain. Science, if not soon rescued, will fall into a state of decadence from which it will be difficult to raise her."

Lakanal did his best. With great effort he persuaded the finance committee of the Convention, strenuously engaged in trying to save France from bankruptcy, to include the Academy grant for 1793 in its budget. His task was not made easier by the fact that the members of the Academy of Science were widely regarded as reactionaries. There was some truth in this view, for the scientists had on occasion audibly and publicly regretted the quiet security they had enjoyed under the monarchy. The promise to pay was not fulfilled. When the end of June came and no money was forthcoming from the government, Lavoisier paid the salaries of his colleagues out of his own pocket.

The rumour spread that the Convention intended to suppress the Academy of Science altogether. This was in July. Lavoisier, in fine fighting trim, rapidly drew up a memorandum calculated to convince the dullest and most provincial politician of the necessity for its continued existence. This memorandum, which was clearly written under emotional strain, he sent to Lakanal for distribution to the members of the Convention. In a private covering letter he declared that not only were the interests of the public and of science involved in this question, but the good name of the Convention itself. If that good name was to be maintained in the eyes of the world, it was essential that the temple of science should remain standing in the midst of the surrounding ruin.

It was unnecessary, the memorandum began, to insult the intelligence of the representatives of France by a lengthy exposition of the value of science to a great country. All mass-industry, such as had given England her great wealth, was ultimately founded on the labours of scientists. French science had done much for French industry—the development in Paris of the manufacture of mathematical and astronomical instruments, previously an English monopoly, could be cited as an example. In the realm of pure science, France had out-distanced her rivals. In the mathematical sciences, for example, England, in spite of the great lead given by Newton, had definitely fallen behind, while French chemistry had recently " given laws to all nations." Such successes could never have been won without the existence of the Academy of Science.

" Under an arbitrary government," Lavoisier tactfully added, " France enjoyed great advantages from science, because, even under the old *régime*, science was, as it were, organised on republican lines, and the respect in which it was held protected it against despotic interference."

Why was it essential to have a society of scientific workers at all ? Because co-operative effort was essential to scientific advance. The man of letters could work on his own ; his material existed in the great world around him. The historian could seek his data in libraries without assistance from anyone. But the physicist, the chemist, and the engineer all required each other's co-operation, while often the services of the mathematician were necessary to appraise the results of their experiments. Isolated scientific workers could do very little.

Government support of scientific endeavours was essential. Scientific instruments were expensive—how few private astronomers, for example, could afford to build observatories ? A reasonable livelihood, and means to purchase the instruments necessary for their work, must be assured to those who devote their lives to research.

So the great chemist besought the fanatics, patriots, orators, and provincial mayors of the Convention to preserve what they did not understand. In the first half of his apology there is scarcely an argument which might not appropriately be used to-day in defence of the endowment of scientific research by the state. The Academy of Science was an active body of state-supported professional research workers, a National Research Institute, and as such Lavoisier defended it.

In the latter half of the memorandum he emphasised the value of the Academy as an advisory body to the Government, and stressed in particular the importance of the Commission of Weights and Measures. The Convention, he knew, was genuinely interested in the question of satisfactory weights and measures, though bored with the rather long drawn out scientific preliminaries. Finally, he pointed out that the Academicians could hardly, in common decency, be left to starve. Having chosen science as a career, they had no other means of earning their bread.

Next day Lavoisier followed up the appeal with a further letter to Lakanal. He had heard, he said, that the Academy of Science was going to be turned into an amalgamated society of art and science. This was quite absurd. The spirit of the scientist and that of the artist were completely incompatible. The artist worked for gain—there was always a speculative element in his work. The tradition of science was that all discoveries should be immediately made public ; the idea of turning them to profit was rigorously excluded. Contact with artists would tend to destroy the disinterested spirit which reigned in the Academy of Science, a most precious possession which it had held from its very inception. (Those artists !—all his life he had thought little of them.)

On August 8th, 1793, the question of the various Academies came up before the Convention. The general feeling of the House was in favour of sweeping them all away as relics of the old *régime*. But one of the deputies, Grégoire, carefully briefed by Lavoisier, urged the preservation of the Academy of Science. His speech made a good impression. Unfortunately it was followed by a fiery oration from the painter David, who hated the very word Academy with the hatred of a profoundly original artist. He was specially concerned, he said, with the Academy of Painting and Sculpture, but all academies were tarred with the same brush. " In the name of justice, for the love of art, and especially for the love of youth, let us destroy, let us annihilate, these dismal Academies, which are incompatible with the reign of liberty." The Convention, carried away by such eloquence, immediately suppressed the Academies, and confiscated their property.

The business of winding up the affairs of the Academies was handed over to the Committee of Public Instruction. To this body Lavoisier now addressed himself. Another long memorandum was prepared. What was to happen about scientific work actually in hand, but not yet completed, on which public money had already been spent ? The work on weights and measures ? Vicq d'Azir had been occupied for some time with certain anatomical problems ; 6,000 livres had been spent, and 6,000 more would be needed to bring the investigation to a successful conclusion. Was all this work, and the money already spent, to be wasted ? A number of completed investigations awaited publication ; what was to be done about that ? Were the instruments of the astronomers, the property of the ci-devant Academy, to be torn from them ? As to the Academicians themselves, several were old and infirm men who had spent their lives in the service of science. Doubtless others would find work in other occupations, but once they were dispersed, it would take a very long time, fifty years even, to rebuild the scientific organisation it was wantonly proposed to destroy.

These arguments carried weight, as did the further suggestion that the Academy of Science should be merged into a " Free Society for the Advancement of Science." A few days later, on August 14th, the Convention passed a new decree which permitted the members of the dissolved Academy to continue to meet in the Louvre, and authorised the payment of their salaries. Lavoisier was delighted ; victory seemed at last assured. He immediately summoned his scientific colleagues to a meeting for Saturday, August 17th. But when the Academicians arrived at the Louvre, they found their rooms under the official seal of the Paris Directory, which had carried out the decree of August 8th abolishing all the Academies.

At this point Lavoisier gave in. That weary struggle—he could not begin it all over again ; if the Convention wished to continue its game of passing and annulling decrees, it could do so, he felt, without his participation. It would appear that the Committee of Public Instruction deliberately refrained from putting the later decree of the Convention, permitting the Academy of Science to continue its work, into operation. The instigator of this move was Fourcroy, who disliked Lavoisier personally, and wished to preserve nothing of the Academy and its activities except the Commission of Weights and Measures.

Lavoisier courteously thanked Lakanal for all the trouble he had taken. He did not, he said, think it advisable for the Academy to meet again under any conditions—to do so would probably offend the dominant parties in the Convention. Certain members of the Academy later took advantage of the decree of August 14th which permitted them to continue their work. But Lavoisier felt that he, personally, could do no more. *L'Académie Royale des Sciences*, founded in 1666 by the Grand Monarch, was defunct.

Marat did not live to see the downfall of the institution he so much detested, and the discomfiture of Lavoisier. A few weeks earlier a supercilious young lady from Normandy had thrust a carving knife into his heart.

CHAPTER XV

ARREST

In the very earliest days of the Revolution, even while the States General was still sitting, the Revenue Farm had been the object of fierce attacks. Of all the institutions which had flourished under the monarchy it was perhaps the most unpopular. That its transactions were essentially fraudulent was taken for granted. The Farmers themselves, who personified the mysterious power of wealth, occupied a prominent place in the public imagination. What did they do with all the money wrung from widows and orphans? What strange and evil transactions were carried out behind the scenes at their headquarters in the Rue de Grenelle-Saint Honoré? What luxurious orgies in their private palaces? There were whispers of corruption on an enormous scale. After the Revolution certain employees of the Farm, quick to take advantage of the trend of the times, came forward with horrifying exposures. " Could we but study the books of the Farm," wrote one, " what mysteries unknown to the State would be revealed?" The Farmers were careful to publish denials of all accusations of irregularity, but naturally these attracted less attention than the denunciations which prompted them.

In March, 1791, the *Ferme Générale* was dissolved by the Assembly, the odious *gabelle*, or salt tax, having been done away with some months previously. The task of winding up its affairs was entrusted to a Commission of six, entirely drawn from the ranks of the Farmers themselves. The Assembly at that date took a more realistic view of the personality of a *Fermier Général* than did the man in the street. Lavoisier was not included in the Committee, and severed all connection with the Farm from the date of its dissolution. Its suppression satisfied a section of the public, but there were many who wished to go further. The Farmers, it was urged, had been enriching themselves at the expense of honest citizens for years. They should be made to disgorge their disgracefully acquired wealth.

But in spite of virulent arraignments in the newspapers, in spite of the hatred with which the radical party in the Assembly regarded the still wealthy Farmers, no further steps against the Farm were taken for nearly two years. There were plenty of more exciting questions to absorb the attention of the Assembly and the proletariat. During this time the winding-up commission continued its work, but it was hampered by having to arrange for the sale of large supplies of salt and tobacco with which the company's warehouses were stocked. By June, 1793, it had not yet presented its report. During the interval the Farm, or what remained of it, had been attacked on several occasions by impatient deputies.

On June 5th an enraged patriot accused the Commission of deliberate procrastination. He urged that all money in possession of the Farm should be confiscated, and its books and papers put under seal. The Convention, amenable as ever to eloquence, immediately passed a decree to this effect. The Commission was thus accused of intentional delay, and at the same time entirely prevented from proceeding with its work of liquidation. In vain it pointed out the paradox to ministers with heads wobbling on their shoulders. The menace grew. Early in September an examination of the private papers of the individual *fermiers généraux* was ordered. Lavoisier's house in the Boulevard de la Madelaine was visited by two members of the revolutionary committee of the Section des Piques, who conducted a search which lasted two days. No incriminating material was discovered, and the officer in charge of the investigation expressed himself as entirely satisfied, but Lavoisier was astonished and alarmed. He had had nothing to do with the Revenue Farm for three years, he had in the interval played a leading part in the financial reorganisation of France, and had thought himself above suspicion in matters of finance. A packet of letters in

English and other languages[1] was taken away for examination by the Committee of General Security. Correspondence with *emigrés* was suspected. Lavoisier insisted on sealing the packet with his own seal, to minimise the risk of an enemy slipping in some compromising document.

[1] The packet of letters, which may still be studied in the *Achives Nationales*, is a very mixed collection, offering small satisfaction to investigators in search of treason. There is one from Franklin to Madame Lavoisier, dated "Philadelphia, Oct. 25th, 1786," which begins :—
"I have a long time been disabled from writing to my dear Friend by a severe fit of the gout, or I should sooner have returned my thanks for her very kind present of the Portrait, which she has herself done me the honour to make of me. It is allowed by those who have seen it to have great merit as a Portrait in every respect, but what particularly endears it to me is the Hand that drew it.
"Our English enemies, when they were in Possession of this City, and of my House, made a Prisoner of my Portrait, and carried it off with them, leaving that of its Companion, my Wife, by itself, a kind of Widow. You have replaced the Husband, and the Lady seems to smile, as well pleased."
And so on, in the same facetious strain. There is a letter from Dr. Gillan of 25 Devonshire Place, returning thanks for hospitality, and begging his late hostess to accept the works of Shakespeare in 20 volumes. Gillan had been an eye-witness of Lavoisier and Seguin's respiration experiments. Wedgwood replies to a request for some Staffordshire clay. Black writes very handsomely to affirm his conversion to the new chemical doctrines—a translation of his letter by Madame Lavoisier had already appeared in the "*Annales de Chimie.*" The packet also includes an extremely characteristic letter from Joseph Priestley :—

"Jan. 9th, 1792.

"DEAR SIR,
"I take the liberty to introduce to you Mr. Jones, who was lecturer in chemistry at the New College in Hackney, in which employment I now succeed him, and who is to be my successor in Birmingham. You will find him to be equally modest as sensible, and, as a philosopher, more inclined, I believe, to your system than to mine, but open, as we all ought to be, to conviction, as new facts present themselves to us.
"The late riots have interrupted my experiments near a whole year, but I am now refitting my apparatus, and about to resume my usual pursuits, and I shall not fail to give due attention to what you may advance in reply to my last memoir, a copy of which I sent you ; and for this purpose I shall be glad to be informed concerning them. Mr. Jones will convey your sentiments to me.
"In case of more riots, of which we are not without apprehension, I shall be glad to take refuge in your country, the liberties of which I hope will be established notwithstanding the present combination against you. I also hope the issue will be as favourable to science as to liberty.
"I am,
"Dear Sir,
"Yours sincerely,
"J. PRIESTLEY."

On the 24th of the same month, the seals were removed from the books of the Farm, and the Commission ordered to proceed with the liquidation. But two days later the affair of the Farm was again before the House. Dupin, who had held the post of Supernumerary General Controller in the Farm before its dissolution, proposed that the business of winding-up should be supervised by a revising committee of five, whose task it would be to detect fraud and denounce it. The members of the committee were promised rewards should they discover hidden sums which would enrich the Treasury; they were all old employees of the Farm and ready to enjoy the sensation of having their old masters in their power. Their president, Gaudot, had at the beginning of the Revolution been in prison charged with the embezzlement of 500,000 francs, and had regained his liberty during a mob attack on the prison in which he was confined. He hoped, it is said, to effect the quiet removal of certain entries, dangerous to himself, from the books of the Farm. The Convention decreed that the audit should be finished not later than April 1st, 1794.

From such an enquiry the *fermiers généraux* could scarcely hope to emerge unscathed. Lavoisier himself feared the confiscation of all his possessions, but, like Queen Elizabeth, he felt capable of earning a living if turned penniless into the street. If the worst happened, he told a friend, he would find work in a chemist's shop. Every day danger seemed to press a little closer. An old employee of the *Régie des Poudres* came forward with stories of irregularities under Lavoisier's directorship; it was a happy time for disgruntled subordinates with long memories. An anonymous letter accused him of correspondence with an *emigré*, Blizard, once architect to the Prince de Condé. The Committee of General Security ordered an enquiry by the police, and it was eventually decided that the charge was without foundation.

His father-in-law, Paulze, had actually been in correspondence with the Prince de Condé, had lent him large sums of money. There may have been some connection between this dangerous transaction and the anonymous charge against Lavoisier.

Things were moving fast in the capital that autumn. France, after a stormy trial of democracy, was reverting to despotism. The Second Committee of Public Safety, with Robespierre at its head, had come into being in July, and real power was passing into its hands, leaving the Convention enfeebled in all but eloquence. To enforce its will it had two formidable instruments : the Committee of General Security, in charge of the police organisation of the country, and the Revolutionary Tribunal (the Scourge of Vice), which was rapidly losing the character of a court of justice and becoming a summary court martial ready to despatch all defendants to the guillotine with as little fuss as possible. In April, on the occasion of the first capital conviction under the new stringent martial law, tribunal and spectators had wept without restraint. But the tears were soon dried. In October fifty were condemned to the guillotine, including Marie Antoinette, sustained to the end by an unshakeable conviction of majesty. The Girondin leaders, still dreaming impossible republican dreams, went singing to the scaffold. On November 12th, poor old Bailly, who had helped Lavoisier to devise the ingenious tests which discomforted Deslon in Franklin's house in Passy, was executed. In a perpetual fever of worry he had filled the post of Mayor of Paris for two years. He had ordered the National Guard to fire on the mob at the Champs de Mars in July, 1791, and now the mob had its revenge. The little red flag which he had waved to give the order was tied to the cart which took him to the scaffold and burnt before his eyes by the executioner.

The Convention had named April 1st, 1794, as the date by which the winding up of the Revenue Farm should be completed. But questions of finance were continually before the House, and the mere mention of the words *Ferme Générale* was enough to send certain deputies up in smoke. On November 14th further debate took place on the question of the liquidation of a number of financial organisations, including the Revenue Farm. A deputy named Bourdon burst out : " This is the hundredth time that we have discussed the accounts of the *fermiers généraux*. I demand that these bloodsuckers be arrested, and, failing the delivery of their accounts in one month, be dealt with according to the full rigour of the law." The Convention immediately ordered the arrest of all those who had put their names to the last contract of the *Ferme*.

Lavoisier was involved. He heard the news while on sentry-go at the Arsenal (strange as it seems, he was still a member of the National Guard). His mind moved quickly. To be arrested and imprisoned at such a time, when the Terror was already in full existence, was perilous in the extreme. Could he but avoid arrest, or suffer only nominal arrest, he would be able to continue working for the Commission of Weights and Measures and other public bodies, and, as a valuable and active public servant, he would be likely to receive more consideration than the other ex-Farmers. Once he was in gaol in the company of his business colleagues, the scientist and administrator would undergo a dangerous metamorphosis into the financier, the tax-gatherer ; his only hope was to cling to the character in which he had won distinction and honour. Surely it must be realised that he was not, had never been, a common money-grubber ? Meanwhile, the agents of the Committee of General Security were on his track, and he looked round desperately for a hiding place. The inefficiency of the republican police organisation gave him a few hours' respite, for the officer who set out to arrest him went first with his warrant to the old Arsenal laboratory, vacant for over a year.

A refuge suggested itself. He hurried to the Louvre. An old attendant of the Academy of Science, at great peril to himself, concealed him in the rooms which had once served the Academy as store rooms and lecture rooms. Here Lavoisier began composing and tearing up letters to various authorities, Exercising all his powers of self control, he at last finished a letter addressed to the Convention with which he was satisfied. In it he pointed out that he had severed all connection with the Farm three years previously, being subsequently appointed Commissioner of the National Treasury. It was well known, he added, and his published work proved it, that even when he had been a member of the Farm his main interest had been science and not finance. He was not a member of the winding-up committee, and therefore not responsible for the alleged delay in completing the audit; it was not just that he should be arrested under the law which ordered the imprisonment of the *fermiers généraux* until the accounts were made up. He was a National Commissioner of Weights and Measures, and had carried out his duties as such with zeal and some success.

This letter was sent by some unknown channel to the Committee of Public Instruction. He hoped that the Committee would espouse his cause and present the letter to the Convention. But he hoped too much. The Committee, with Guyton de Morveau at its head, disregarded his letter entirely.

The next day Lavoisier, having heard nothing further of his letter to the Convention, tried again. This time he wrote to the powerful Committee of General Security, which, he knew, had considerable liberty in the interpretation of the decrees of the Convention. The letter ran as follows :—

" Aux citoyens représentans du peuple composant le Comité de Sûreté générale de la Convention nationale.

" Citoyens représentans

" Lavoisier, de la ci-devant Académie des sciences, est chargé, par les décrets de la Convention nationale, de concourir à l'établissement des nouvelles mesures adoptées par la Convention nationale.

" D'un autre côté, un décret nouvellement rendu ordonne que les fermiers généraux seront renfermés dans une maison d'arrêt pour travailler à la reddition de leurs comptes ; il est prêt de s'y rendre, mais il croit auparavant devoir demander auquel de ces décrets il doit obéir.

" Le comité de sûreté générale concilieront l'exécution des deux décrets si, provisoirement, il ordonnoit que Lavoisier demeurera en état d'arrestation sous la garde de deux de ses frères sans-culottes. Il observe qu'il y a trois ans qu'il n'est plus fermier général et que sa personne et toute sa fortune garantissent sa responsabilité morale et physique.

" Ce sextidi frimaire, l'an 11 de la République une et indivisible.
" LAVOISIER."

This letter, written in such remarkable circumstances, is still preserved in the National Archives of France. It is firmly written in Lavoisier's rather beautiful unpretentious hand, with only one emendation. But that emendation shows the extreme care with which every word was meditated. He first wrote " *sous la garde de deux sansculottes*," and later added the words " *de ses frères*." The leader of French science claimed brotherhood with the riff-raff of the Paris slums. With full understanding of the minds of his fellow-countrymen he based his appeal on a point of law, suggesting to the Committee a loophole of escape from the Convention's decree of arrest. Such decrees, carrying the full force of law, were ineluctable, and a mere appeal for mercy would have been in the circumstances quite irrelevant.

It is not known by what means this letter was delivered to the Committee of General Security. That body certainly received it (for otherwise it could not have reached the Archives Nationales *viâ* the police records) and took no notice of it. For two days Lavoisier, in great distress of mind, lurked in the dusty rooms at the Louvre, surrounded by disused scientific apparatus, the very rooms in which he had moved as an acknowledged leader among his fellow scientists, and enjoyed the repeated triumphs of his life. Then, having heard no more of his appeal to the Committee of General Security, he gave himself up. He was imprisoned in the Port Libre prison on November 28th.

His father-in-law, Jacques Paulze, was arrested on the same day. Twenty-seven *fermiers généraux* were arrested at about this time as a result of the decree of the Convention. A month later eight more were imprisoned, but others remained at liberty till the middle of the following year. Fourteen seem to have escaped the notice of the Committee of General Security and their agents altogether. The incompetent manner in which the business of arrest was carried out is indicated by the following : a man named Lavalette was imprisoned in the capacity of *fermier général*, though he had never been a member of the *ferme* at any time ; the arrest of Baudon, from whom Lavoisier had bought his share in the *ferme*, was ordained. Baudon had been dead four years. Among the prisoners whom Lavoisier found in the Port Libre prison on his arrival were Saint-Amand, the Chief Director of the Farm, and Etienne Delahante, a *fermier-adjoint*, a man of about fifty years of age, who some years afterwards wrote a lively account of the imprisonment and trial of the *fermiers généraux*. The story of their adventures, as given here, is largely based on his memoirs. Delahante, and two other *fermiers-adjoints* imprisoned at the same time, hoped that, in virtue of their subordinate positions, they would soon be released.

The Farmers were linked together not only by long business intimacy, by membership of a closely-knit, powerful, and discreetly anonymous organisation ; they were, as a body, closely united by ties of blood. The Farm from its creation had tended to be a family concern. Sons had followed fathers into the charmed circle, nephews had followed uncles ; and what could be more natural than that rising young financiers should seek in marriage the well-doweried daughters of their seniors ? It was a sort of grotesque family reunion which took place at the Port Libre prison. Apart from Lavoisier, none of those arrested had achieved distinction in any but the business field, but the majority were men of culture and intelligence, representatives of families which had enjoyed wealth for several generations, and not financial adventurers. It is possible to retain doubts of their honesty, but not of their respectability.

The Port Libre prison was a transformed convent, and as such was a much more agreeable place to be confined in than the regular gaols of Paris, about which Lavoisier had so forcibly written a few years previously. The first storey was reserved for the rich, and it was here that the fallen financiers, after a few uncomfortable days in crowded rooms

in an annexe, were accommodated. They occupied the cells
of the departed *religieuses*, two in each cell. Lavoisier shared
with his father-in-law, and another ex-Farmer named
Deville, the largest of these, the only one, as it happened,
with a fire. Paulze, in his seventy-fifth year, had suffered
greatly from the cold during the first days of prison. The
prisoners took their simple meals in Lavoisier's room—they
still had plenty of money to buy the best food and drink, but
thought it politic to live frugally—and that room became
a sort of general meeting place for the discussion of plans
of defence. In such far from tranquil circumstances
Lavoisier began to write his already projected text-book of
chemistry.

Meanwhile his friends outside could do little for him.
The Bureau of Arts and Crafts, of which he had been
President until the day of his arrest, inserted the following
guarded note in its minutes.

" The Bureau considers that the *procès-verbal* should include
a reference to the esteem in which its members have always held
Citizen Lavoisier, and to the regret which they feel on learning
that he is no longer in a position to participate in their activities."

One would infer from the minute that the citizen had been
confined to his bed for a few weeks with muscular
rheumatism.

Madame Lavoisier did what she could on behalf of her
husband. She sought interviews with officials of State ;
she wrote sprightly letters—much too sprightly letters. One
of these, part of which still exists, was a protest to the
Comité de Sûreté Générale. She demanded to be allowed to
see her relations in prison. This request was granted, but
as the weeks passed and all efforts to obtain the release of the
prisoners proved fruitless, Marie began to show signs of
strain. In the middle of December her husband wrote to
calm her :

" You are giving yourself, my dearest, a great deal of trouble,
and a great deal of weariness of body and mind, and I cannot
help to share the burden with you. Do take care of your health.

If you lost that it would be the greatest misfortune. I am getting on in years, I have led a happy life ever since I can remember, and your affection has added every day to my happiness, and still adds to it. I hope at least to be remembered with respect and esteem. So my task is over, while you have still a long way to go. Don't spend yourself unnecessarily. Yesterday you seemed sad. Why was that? I myself am quite resigned to whatever may happen, and I will consider as gain everything which is not lost. But indeed we have not lost all hope of rejoining each other, and in the meantime I still have the sweet moments when you come and visit me."

Two public bodies made attempts to secure Lavoisier's liberty. The Committee of " *Assignats*," which he had been assisting in an advisory capacity, protested with considerable force to the Committee of General Security.

" All is ready for the manufacture of 5 décime pieces. The moulds are ready ; in 4 or 5 days 50,000 livres' worth can be turned out. But we must have balances to weigh these coins, new delicate balances which are extremely difficult to construct. Their manufacture is held up as a result of the arrest of Lavoisier. Whatever steps you may consider it appropriate to take in regard to this citizen, it is absolutely necessary that he should continue to work in his laboratory. If the charge against him is not grave, please arrange that his services should be immediately available in order that the work with which he has been entrusted may be continued. At the same time you can take what measures you please to ensure that he does not escape."

The omnipotent Committee did not respond ; it did not, however, take offence at the peremptory tone of the request. But a similar request from the Commission of Weights and Measures brought retribution on the heads of those who made it. Borda and Haüy, ci-devant Academicians, the latter a nonjuring priest, asked that Citizen Lavoisier should be allowed " to continue the important work which he had always carried out with so much zeal and activity." They added, with pardonable exaggeration, that the loss of Lavoisier would make it necessary to begin most of the work of the Commission all over again. The Committee of General Security treated the request with scant sympathy. A cold annotation was added to the letter : " *Le Comité de*

Sûreté Générale, considérant que le citoyen Lavoisier est porté sur la liste des ci-devant fermiers généraux, sous un état d'arrestation de decret de la Convention Nationale, passe à l'ordre de jour " ; and Borda and Haüy were immediately removed from the Commission, along with Laplace, Delambre, and others. Lavoisier's own name was struck off at the same time. It did not pay to force oneself on the attention of the Committee of General Security.

Meanwhile the news which reached the imprisoned Farmers from the outside world was not reassuring. On December 11th a deputy on the Convention alleged that the Revising Committee engaged in examining the books of the Farm would probably discover thefts amounting to 300,000,000 livres—a good round figure—which the robbers should be forced to repay. The Farmers had previously discussed the question of offering much less than one-hundredth of this sum to the Treasury as the price of their liberty, but this project had been abandoned since it was felt to involve an admission of guilt. Eventually, a letter was drafted to the Convention containing the request that the Farmers should be sent to their own headquarters, the Hotel des Fermes, where they undertook to remain until a full statement of accounts was prepared. Several advised against this move—Lavoisier, we may well imagine, was among this number. It was better, they urged, to make as little noise as possible and hope to be forgotten. But less wary members insisted, and the letter was sent. The result showed its unwisdom. The plea for transference to the headquarters of the Farm was granted, but at the same time, in order that the State should run no risk of finding the fabulous hoards of the Farmers spirited away by night, all their property was sequestered for the time being, and seals put on their houses. At one stroke the richest men in France were reduced to poverty.

Shortly afterwards Lavoisier had a brief glimpse of the outside world. Most of the active members of the Commission of Weights and Measures had been dismissed, but nevertheless the Committee of Public Instruction had orders to proceed with the work. It was therefore necessary to secure the instruments and records under seal in Lavoisier's house. The seals were raised in his presence, and he helped Guyton de Morveau and Fourcroy, members of the Committee of Public Instruction, to find what they wanted. It was a curious and probably painful meeting between three distinguished scientists. For the last time Fourcroy— timid, servile, quick-witted Fourcroy—saw the rival to whom he owed a great deal and repaid very little.

The day before Christmas, no longer a festival, the Farmers were taken from the Port Libre prison to the Hotel des Fermes in the rue de Grenelle-Saint-Honoré. Apparently some of them still possessed a little ready money, for on departure they made a donation of 4,000 livres to be spent for the benefit of poor prisoners in buying mattresses for the prison hospital. Just as they were leaving a fellow-prisoner went mad and stabbed himself.

CHAPTER XVI

LAST DAYS

THE Hotel des Fermes, hurriedly transformed into a prison by the addition of strong doors and iron window bars, lacked the amenities of home, and the financiers could no longer afford heavy expenditure on personal comfort. But at least they had a private prison to themselves, and work to do. The morning after their arrival they divided themselves up into committees and set to work on the accounts, with such industry—for some of them hoped for liberty on completion of the task—that, though the mass of documents was enormous, the audit was completed in a month. At the same time the Revising Committee of Five, under Gaudot, the ex-gaol-bird, was studying the affairs of the *Ferme*, and it was not difficult for the prisoners to obtain precise and highly disturbing information about the defalcations of which they were accused. In reply, they sent brief notes to the Committee, but later it was decided to draw up a lengthy memorandum destined to prove that all charges of dishonesty against them were groundless. Following the example of innumerable committees which had met in more encouraging circumstances, the Farmers entrusted the task of drafting the memorandum to Lavoisier.

There was much to justify. The Committee of Five framed its accusations of fraud under no less than nine heads, of which the most serious were the following : the Farmers were accused of having taken interest of 10 per cent. on the money which they had invested in the Farm, whereas the statutory limit was 5 per cent.; of persistent delay in paying the State the money owed, with the result that interest belonging by right to the State went into their own coffers ; and of having added excessive quantities of water to tobacco before selling it. The manufacture of tobacco had been a monopoly of the Farm, and consumers had grumbled for years at the quality of tobacco which it offered for sale. This last accusation, about which the ordinary citizen felt really strongly, was in fact the most dangerous which the Farmers had to meet. Lavoisier was at pains to refute it entirely in his memorandum. The addition of water, he pointed out, was a necessary part of the manufacturing process, and actually most of the water evaporated before the tobacco was weighed out for the purchaser. It had been the practice of the Farm to deliver one ounce in every seventeen free of charge, to make up for the water added in the factory. Finally, any intention on the part of the Farm to swindle the public with regard to tobacco was disproved by the fact that bad leaves had been invariably rejected, as much as one third of the raw material arriving in its factories having been habitually discarded as unfit for use. That the practice of the Farm in connection with the manufacture and sale of tobacco could be so effectively defended was largely due to Lavoisier himself. He had always been opposed to excessive *mouillage*,[1] and had indeed had sharp differences with his colleagues over this very question.

The amounts which the Farmers were accused of having stolen under the various heads were stated to the last livre. The grand total came to 107,819,033 livres.

The Farmers were, it seems, innocent of all the charges made against them by Gaudot's Committee. If they had indeed been guilty of fraud at the expense of the State, the Committee quite failed in its work of detection. Lavoisier's memorandum was an unanswerable reply to its report. Dupin, with report and memorandum before him, immediately realised this, for, thanks to his training as an employee of the Farm, he was well used to handling figures. Originally, it appears, he had been genuinely convinced that the

---

[1] According to a Government analysis made in 1785, each 100 lbs. of tobacco sold by the Farm at that date contained 5 lbs. of salt and 25 lbs. of water.

Farmers had been guilty of technical fraud, and a patriotic desire to enrich the funds of the State through the restitution of their fraudulent profits may have prompted his attack in the Convention. But Lavoisier and his colleagues had proved themselves much too clever for the blundering Committee of Five, and Dupin was placed in a quandary. It was too late to draw back. The Committee of Public Safety had heard of the alleged theft of over a hundred million livres, a sum large enough to be a genuine asset to the impoverished Treasury, and it had assumed that the money was actually in the possession of the Farmers. The easiest way of securing it was to execute the Farmers and confiscate their property. Hence Dupin, though he knew that no case of fraud against the Farmers had been proven, could not drop the matter. He hesitated to present his report, and immediately whispers circulated that he had been bribed by the financiers. A man who had voted against the death sentence on Louis Capet could not afford to be suspected of lack of zeal in the cause of the Republic. When at last he rose to accuse the Farmers in the Convention he had probably convinced himself, under the spur of peril, that, if innocent of overt fraud, they deserved death as the chief representatives of the rotten financial system under which France had groaned for many generations.

While the prisoners in the Hotel des Fermes laboured in the preparation of their defence, the Terror grew every day more formidable. The average citizen, it is true, found life under the despotic Committee of Public Safety less troubled than it had been during the earlier years of the Revolution ; he was tired of politics, riots, and massacres, and now that Paris was outwardly at peace, turned with relief to other interests. He sat in his favourite café discussing the latest play, the latest fête, and yawned as yet another cartload of bound prisoners passed on its way to the guillotine. As ever, the vast majority of the population was apathetic as regards affairs of State ; what really interested them was the price of victuals. But those who had had any close connection with the ancient *régime*, or with the middle class ascendency which followed it, those, indeed, who had any reason to fear denunciation by the ubiquitous spies of the Committee of General Security, lived in the shadow of fear. The Law of Suspects gave the revolutionary committees the widest powers of arbitrary arrest. To be " suspect of being suspect," as the saying went, was sufficient ground for seizure and imprisonment, and imprisonment, as the months passed, became more and more likely to mean death. Fouquier-Tinville, ex-police spy, Public Prosecutor and organising genius of the Revolutionary Tribunal, was proving himself a highly efficient man, a most valuable servant of the dominating political party. Unemployed and almost destitute, he had been given a job to do, and he intended to carry it out to the full satisfaction of his employers ; should he be accused of slackness, figures were available to prove the opposite. In December, 69 were condemned and beheaded by the Tribunal, in January 71, in February 73, in March 127, in April 257. In the early months of its existence the Tribunal had acquitted more prisoners than it condemned, but as the spring of 1794 advanced acquittals became increasingly uncommon. Fouquier-Tinville was able to rub his hands and remark with glee to his subordinates, whom he despotically ruled, " *Ça marche, n'est-ce pas ?* " He did not spare himself. He worked eighteen hours out of twenty-four, and soon began to feel the strain. But he was making good.

The Committee of Finance, presided over by Dupin, which examined the accusations against the *fermiers généraux*, did so in secret ; the prisoners were unable to learn the result of its deliberations. There were rumours that they were about to be freed. Meanwhile the arrest, trial and execution, early in April, of Danton and his friends, absorbed the attention of the authorities, Dupin frowned over the reports, and the financiers remained in suspense. Having completed their audit, they found themselves with plenty of time on their hands. Lavoisier himself, having prepared the case of the *Ferme Générale* to the best of his ability, began to do what he could in defence of his own life. Here he showed the same dogged energy, the same determination to leave nothing untried, that he had shown in support of the stricken Academy of Science. He obtained from the Bureau of Arts and Crafts a testimonial describing in general terms his services to that body and to science. He prompted two officials connected with the manufacture of gunpowder to demand his presence to assist in the audit of the accounts of the *Régie des Poudres*. From two ex-members of the Academy of Science, Cadet and Baumé, he obtained a certificate stating that he had always been opposed to the practice of adding excessive amounts of water to the tobacco sold by the Farm. Finally, he himself drew up an account of his public and private career with the following title : " Note on the services rendered to the Revolution by Lavoisier, late Commissioner of the National Treasury, member of the ci-devant Academy of Science, member of the Bureau of Arts and Crafts, cultivator in the district of Blois, in the departments of the Loire and the Cher." Even in prison he retained his life-long habit of continuous work from morning to evening. Surrounded by nervous, irritable and talkative colleagues, who discussed hour after hour their chances of survival, he wrote nearly two volumes of his projected " *Memoires de Chimie*," managed to convey the manuscript to a printer, and subsequently made some corrections to the proofs.[1] To add to the discomforts of confinement, the weather all that spring was abnormally hot, and the Hotel des Fermes, at first intended to house the Farmers alone, began to fill up with other prisoners.

In April it became apparent that the crisis was at hand. Dupin was at last about to present his report on the affairs of the Farm to the Convention. Even now a word in the right quarter might have secured preferential treatment for Lavoisier. The politicians of the day were doubtless as ignorant of science as those of our own time, but the Com-

---

[1] Lavoisier's prison writings were published privately by Madame Lavoisier in 1805. As might be expected, they are fragmentary and incomplete. In places sentences are left unfinished.

mittee of Public Safety included members capable of realising, somewhat vaguely it may be, that here was a man who deserved well of humanity. Dupin himself, it is said, was anxious that Lavoisier should be separated from the other *fermiers généraux*, and imprisoned elsewhere. But the word in the right quarter was never spoken. Certain of Lavoisier's old scientific colleagues—Fourcroy, Hassenfratz, Guyton de Morveau, Monge—occupied positions of influence, but these kept silence through fear, indifference, or, in the case of Fourcroy, fear and hostility combined. Marie Lavoisier, who, at considerable danger to herself, remained in Paris (most of the wives of the *fermiers généraux* had already left), was incapable of realising that she had one card to play, and one only : her husband's scientific achievements and his services to the State. Her father, with no possible claim to official gratitude, was in prison under the same charge; she was separated from the man who had guided her every action since childhood, and one need scarcely wonder that, in so dreadful an emergency, she was capable only of hysterical protests that the *fermiers généraux* were all entirely innocent. Dupin asked to see her ; he was ready to be kind to an attractive woman who should plead with tears for her husband's life. But Marie refused to play the correct part. " Lavoisier," she told Dupin, " would be dishonoured were he to allow his case to be separated from that of his companions. You want the lives of the *fermiers généraux* because you want their money. If they die, they die innocent." This irritated Dupin, guiltily aware of the slenderness of his case against the Farmers, and Lavoisier remained with the rest in the Hotel des Fermes.

On May 5th the blow fell. Dupin presented to the Convention a *résumé* of the report of the Committee of Five. Apparently he had by now forgotten his earlier scruples, and sought, by ingenious juggling with figures, to display the transactions of the *ferme générale* in the worst possible light. The Convention was immediately impressed by the professorial manner in which he handled his theme. He brought up the old accusation of intentional delay in completing the audit ; the Farmers, he declared, had procrastinated in the hope of an early return to the old *régime*. On one point he showed restraint : some of the Farmers, he remarked, had been opposed to the *mouillage* of tobacco—the Revolutionary Tribunal, before which the Farmers must plead their cause, could perhaps distinguish between these and the rest. It would seem that Dupin was here rather pitifully trying to avoid personal responsibility for the execution of Lavoisier. He knew that Lavoisier could prove that he had always been against excessive *mouillage*. If the Revolutionary Tribunal refused to make this the basis of an act of clemency, after the idea had been expressly suggested to it, his conscience and reputation were clear. Posterity would blame the Tribunal, not Dupin, for the death of the great scientist.

The Convention, without discussion, decreed that all the *fermiers généraux* should be tried by the Revolutionary Tribunal. This was sentence of death.

The decree was passed at four o'clock in the afternoon. A spectator who had been listening to Dupin's speech hurried to the Hotel des Fermes. The first person he saw there was Lavoisier, and to him he told the news. Lavoisier quickly passed it on to his fellow prisoners. With the knowledge that they had but a few more hours to live, the financiers began to burn their private papers and write farewell letters to relations and friends. Some of them contemplated suicide. Opium had previously been secured for this express purpose. It was suggested to Lavoisier that here was an easy mode of escape, but he rejected the proposal with scorn. He was far too vital a man to contemplate such an end, and perhaps he still hoped. Was it really possible, he may have asked himself, that the great Lavoisier should suffer a felon's death ?

After the Convention had passed its decree, Dupin arranged that no stranger should be allowed to enter the Hotel des Fermes. He did not expect that the decree would be put into execution for three or four days ; in actual fact it was sent to the Tribunal on the following day. But the remarkable efficiency of Fouquier-Tinville hastened the

trial of the *fermiers généraux*. Dupin began his speech early
in the afternoon. By seven o'clock that evening four large
closed carriages arrived at the Hotel des Fermes to
convey the prisoners to the Conciergerie. Fouquier-Tinville,
in contact with Dupin, had had the acts of accusation and
the order for removal ready many hours before Dupin
began his speech.

The formalities at the Hotel des Fermes occupied more
than an hour. Delahante and the two other *fermiers-adjoints*,
who still hoped to secure pardon by virtue of their minor
positions, found, to their dismay, that no distinction was
made between themselves and the others. It was already dark
when the cortège set out. The four carriages had to accom-
modate thirty-three prisoners, and the long journey across
the city, to the accompaniment of a troop of mounted
police, was not a pleasant one. They arrived at the Conciergerie at eleven o'clock, but further lengthy formalities
had to take place before they could be admitted. The
French nation, which had so triumphantly cast off the yoke
of monarchy, had not succeeded in lightening its load of
paperasserie. At last the formalities were completed, and
the Farmers were divided into two groups, one being accommodated in *cachots*, the other in the room in which Marie
Antoinette had passed her last hours. The night was cold
for May, and the prisoners had no coverings. There were
a few rough beds, but most of them spent the night on the
floor. Delahante tells how, when he and three of his colleagues were thrust into a *cachot* they found there three
prisoners from Châlon-sur-Saône, labouring desperately
over their defence by the light of a single candle, for they
were to appear before the Tribunal on the morrow. The
provincials greeted the newcomers politely but hurriedly,
and bent over their work again.

The Conciergerie was a hive of dark passages and darker
cells situated in the midst of the Palais de Justice. The
Revolutionary Tribunal sat in the same building ;
Fouquier-Tinville, passing from his rooms in the Tour
Bonbec to his offices, traversed a passage from which he

could see the prisoners' exercise yard. In 1794, the prison, scarcely fit to house human beings at all, was crowded with suspects of every age and sex from all corners of France. When Lavoisier had inspected it a few years previously he had found it damp, cold, airless, and evil smelling, and now its discomforts were many times greater. The sanitary reforms he had suggested—the washing of prisoners and their clothes, the supply of warm coverings, of sufficient water, the assurance of sufficient air space for each prisoner —had never been put into effect. He had stated, curiously enough, that the *cachots* were the least unsatisfactory part of the prison, being large and reasonably well ventilated, although their windows opened into a covered passage and not into the open air.

Those destined to appear before the Tribunal were usually transferred to the Conciergerie a few days before trial. From the prison a flight of steps and a corridor led into the centre of the Palais de Justice. In May, 1794, the whole building hummed with activity from morning to night ; the work of the Tribunal was continually expanding, and Fouquier-Tinville was forced to make frequent additions to his overburdened staff. There were preliminary examinations of the accused to be made, and a full record kept of question and answer, witnesses to be interrogated, acts of accusation and orders for transportation or execution to be completed. The transference of the property of the condemned to the State involved full legal registration. The executioners themselves were attached to the pay roll of the Tribunal ; important and irreplaceable functionaries, they needed careful handling, for they felt that continually increasing work deserved continually increasing wages. Sanson, arriving at noon to enquire how many carts were necessary to convey that day's batch of condemned to the guillotine, would be respectfully received by the Public Prosecutor himself.

The organisation of the whole concern was in Fouquier-Tinville's hands. He seemed to be everywhere at once— examining and annotating documents, informing judge and

FOUQUIER-TINVILLE.
Part of an engraving by Bouillon, " The Trial of Marie-Antoinette,"
1793.

[*To face p.* 176.

jury as to the correct verdict and punishment, urging his staff with ferocious geniality to greater efforts, bargaining with Sanson, appearing in court as prosecutor in cases which seemed important enough to demand it. An affectionate father and husband, he could spare time only for the briefest visits to his family in the Tour Bonbec ; he saw little of the young wife who in a few months time was to be the only friend left to him in the world. He would snatch a hasty meal in the Tribunal *buvette*, sitting at a table by himself, while prisoners from outlying prisons, eating what was probably to be their last meal at neighbouring tables under the eyes of the guard, stole fearful glances in his direction.

Not only had Fouquier-Tinville to supervise the organisation of the Tribunal ; he had to remain in the closest touch with his masters in the Committees of Public Safety and General Security. He had to keep himself fully informed with regard to the latest political upheaval. Eventually his job proved too much for him. At the start he had been determined that the letter of the law was to be fulfilled in every case, but as time went on and the pressure of work grew insupportable, the Tribunal lost much of its earlier efficiency. Names were misspelt, acts of accusation were left incomplete, prisoners were hastily condemned and executed in mistake for others. At his trial a few months later Fouquier-Tinville was to be faced by evidence of unpardonable carelessness on the part of himself and his subordinates.

After their first wretched night in the Conciergerie the prisoners fared slightly better. Delahante was distantly related to one of the judges of the Tribunal, by name Dobsen, a kindly and honourable man destined shortly to be removed from his position. Efforts were being made to secure the acquittal of the three *fermiers-adjoints*, and, meanwhile, Dobsen used his influence to improve the accommodation of the Farmers. On the following night half of them were put in less disagreeable quarters and provided with mattresses. A few blankets were sent to Delahante, which he distributed to his most intimate friends and the oldest of the Farmers ; they were full of fleas, but better than nothing. Paulze, who suffered readily from cold, was given one. Through these last days Lavoisier had the task of sustaining the old man and making him as comfortable as possible.

Early next morning the prisoners were searched and admitted one by one to a room in the building where the first part of the trial, the interrogation, took place. At this stage in the history of the Tribunal interrogations had been reduced to a brief formality. Lavoisier was examined by Dobsen. Having first been asked about his position in the Farm, he was then asked whether he had not been guilty of theft, exaction and fraud at the expense of the public. Retaining his life-long habit of scientific accuracy, he replied that he had known abuses to occur, but that it had been his practice to report these to the Ministry of Finance, particularly in the case of tobacco. He was in a position, he added, to prove this by fully authenticated documents. Finally, the examining judge asked him whether he had chosen counsel for his defence ; he replied in the negative, and one was allocated to him. The *procès-verbal* of the interrogation was read over to him, and signed by Dobsen, Fouquier-Tinville, a clerk, and himself. The interview, in all probability, was conducted with frigid politeness throughout. Delahante, who was examined, not by his relative Dobsen, but by a judge named Cellier, expressly records the courtesy and even geniality which the examiner displayed towards him. This may have been partly due to his relationship with Dobsen, but there is no reason to suppose that the senior members of the *ferme* were roughly interrogated.

Before the examination the prisoners had been deprived of what money remained to them. When taken back to the Conciergerie they anticipated nothing better to eat than the rough food doled out to common prisoners. But some unknown friend (perhaps Dobsen) had given orders that they were to be supplied with a good meal, including *vins de choix*. Experienced and appreciative diners, the financiers enjoyed one last excellent dinner.

The short period which the *fermiers généraux* spent in the Conciergerie was marked by an unusual incident. The *Lycée des Arts*, with the recent foundation of which Lavoisier had been connected, sent a deputation to the prison to present him a token of its admiration for his genius. Apparently the deputation crowned him, or at least arrived with the intention of crowning him, with a laurel wreath. At that period of the Revolution pseudo-classical customs and fashions were all the rage. One may surmise that Lavoisier, oppressed by the now rapidly darkening shadow of death, received the deputation with scant patience. His friends and admirers had accomplished nothing for him, and so hysterical and useless a gesture can have made no appeal to his well-balanced and matter-of-fact mind.

He wrote, during these last hours, a calm and considered letter to his cousin, Augey de Villers :—

" J'ai obtenu une carrière passablement longue, surtout fort heureuse, et je crois que ma mémoire sera accompagnée de quelques regrets, peut-être de quelque gloire. Qu'aurais-je pu désirer de plus ? Les événemens dans lesquels je me trouve enveloppé vont probablement m'éviter les inconvéniens de la vieillesse. Je mourrai tout entier, c'est encore un avantage que je dois compter au nombre de ceux dont j'ai joui. Si j'éprouve quelques sentimens pénibles, c'est de n'avoir pas fait plus pour ma famille ; c'est d'être dénué de tout et de ne pouvoir lui donner ni à elle ni à vous aucun gage de mon attachement et de ma reconnaissance.

" Il est donc vrai que l'exercice de toutes les vertus sociales, des services importans rendus à la patrie, une carrière utilement employée pour le progrès des arts et des connaissances humaines, ne suffisent pas pour préserver d'une fin sinistre et pour éviter de périr en coupable !

" Je vous écris aujourd'hui, parce que demain il ne me serait peut-être plus permis de le faire, et que c'est une douce consolation pour moi de m'occuper de vous et des personnes qui me sont chères dans ces derniers momens. Ne m'oubliez pas auprès de ceux qui s'intéressent à moi, que cette lettre leur soit commune. C'est vraisemblablement la dernière que je vous écrirai.

" LAVOISIER."

It is a fine grim pagan letter of farewell, devoid of recrimination, rhetoric, and all false sentiment, the letter of a man who lived and died in the sharply-defined world of the scientific humanist. Did he perhaps write too from the Conciergerie to Marie, a little more intimately, a little less reasonably ? No letter remains.

Late that evening a clerk from the Tribunal brought the Farmers their acts of accusation. They were called singly by name, and to each was handed a paper setting forth the charge. This meant that trial was to take place on the following day. Prisoners in the Conciergerie, having read their acts of accusation, often experienced a sense of relief, because they found that the charge proffered against them was nebulous, irrelevant, or quite absurd, and they felt sure that refutation on the morrow would be easy. The Farmers experienced no such illusory consolation, for their acts of accusation, written in close fine handwriting on both sides of a single sheet of paper, proved quite illegible in the growing dusk of the prison. With the knowledge that they were to be tried for their lives in a few hours, they settled down to obtain what sleep they could. Delahante remained wide awake till morning, but three elderly Farmers who shared his cell slept peacefully all through the night.

CHAPTER XVII

THE GUILLOTINE

I⊤ was scarcely light on the morning of May 8th when the Farmers were roused and told to dress themselves. Quarter of an hour later they were taken into a corridor leading to the record office of the prison and ranged along the wall on one side. There were thirty-two of them. One by one they were called into the office and thoroughly searched, all their valuables, money, watches, rings, etc., being taken from them. Delahante says he was stripped of everything except his handkerchief and snuff box. While the search was proceeding a man in black suddenly appeared and called for M. Verdun, one of the senior members of the Farm. M. Verdun was detached from the rest and disappeared into the inner parts of the prison. He had been a friend of Robespierre, who had ordered Fouquier-Tinville to remove his name from the general act of accusation against the Farmers.

Stripped of their belongings, the Farmers were told to follow a police officer, who led them along a dark corridor and through a low door, guarded by a heavy iron grille, and so suddenly out into the busy humming hive of the Palais de Justice. In a room adjacent to the Salle de la Liberté, where the trial was to be held, they were visited by their defending counsel, of whom there were four. It may be presumed that Lavoisier had with him the various certificates which he had laboriously prepared and collected during his stay in prison, and he may have attempted to explain these to one of the lawyers. Actually, the defending counsel assigned to him the day before, Sézilles, did not appear at the trial. The time allowed for the preparation of the defence was ludicrously short, for in a quarter of an hour the lawyers were told to withdraw, since the Tribunal was about to sit. In the hurry and press, Delahante could establish no contact at all with his defending counsel, and had to content himself with handing him a note explaining his position as *fermier-adjoint*.

At the door of the room a clerk from the Tribunal began to call out names. The first to be summoned was Sanlot, one of the *adjoints*. Delahante was seized with sudden hope ; perhaps the *adjoints* were to be called first and tried separately from the others ? He hurried over to the clerk and asked whether he was wanted too. But the clerk told him to wait his turn, and he listened in despair to other names being called, his own being twenty-seventh on the list. All hope of escape now left him.

In the great Salle de la Liberté the stage was fully set. On a dais sat the three judges, wearing black silk coats crossed slantwise by a tricolour ribbon to which was attached a medal bearing the words " *la loi*," and black caps, raised in front, surmounted by a panache of three black plumes— a theatrical ensemble which had disgusted conservative members of the bar on its introduction in 1791. Each judge had a table to himself, on which was a carafe of water and a tumbler. To the right of and a little behind the judges stood the Substitute Public Prosecutor, Liendon. Fouquier-Tinville did not appear in court that day. The prisoners were placed on a series of steps ranged along one wall, facing, not the judges' tables, but the seats of the jury ; their hands were free, as the law ordained, but they were closely guarded by slatternly soldiers with fixed bayonets. In the body of the court sat the four lawyers entrusted with the defence. The large part of the hall, which, partitioned off from the court itself, was open to the public, was closely filled with a keenly interested crowd.

The presiding judge was Pierre-André Coffinhal, a huge black-eyed yellow-faced young man (he was thirty-one) with a penetrating voice. There were balanced and kindly men to be found among the officials of the Revolutionary Tribunal ; men who at great personal risk strove to mitigate its barbarities ; Coffinhal was not among that number. He had had an adventurous career and followed many trades, including that of the law, but he was primarily an orator and politician, calling himself, in accordance with the fashion of the times, Mucius Scævola Coffinhal. He was Vice-President of the Paris Commune. Scarcely less malignantly disposed toward prisoners than his colleague, the redoubtable Dumas, he dealt with his victims in a brutal and sarcastic manner which delighted the baser elements in his large audiences. Many of his sayings—such as his favourite phrase " *Tais toi, tu n'as pas la parole,*" and his remark to a fencing master he had just condemned to death, " Well, old cock, parry that thrust if you can "—were gleefully quoted throughout revolutionary Paris. Robespierre himself had objected to his young colleague's emotional violence : " You destroy me, you destroy yourself, you destroy the Republic," he had said. Like many members of the Tribunal, Coffinhal was overstrained, and was seeking relief from tension in the brandy bottle.

The jury of each of the four sections of the Tribunal consisted of fourteen permanent officials, chosen for their devotion to the dominant party, belonging for the most part to the class of small tradesmen, and glad enough to have the chance of earning eighteen francs a day. The fine oath which the law demanded of them—to examine with the most scrupulous attention all charges against the accused, to be swayed neither by hatred, fear, nor affection, to give all decisions after a careful hearing of the cases for the prosecution and defence, in accordance with the dictates of conscience and inner conviction, impartially and firmly as befits a free man—had little influence over minds distorted by fanaticism. The official record of the trial of the *fermiers généraux* states that twelve jurymen were present. Delahante, who even at this desperate moment did not lose interest in his surroundings, noticed only seven.

The trial was opened by Coffinhal, who questioned the accused with regard to their connection with the Farm and their knowledge of abuses—a very similar interrogation to that of the previous day—and further asked each whether he was of noble rank, and what he had done since the Revolution. Some of the replies were derisively interpreted by judges and jury to the disadvantage of the accused. Judges and jury had pen and paper before them, and all appeared to be busily writing, but to Delahante it seemed unlikely that they were really engaged in noting the pros and cons of the case. After about an hour and a half of this, there was a brief interval of twenty minutes, during which the officials of the Tribunal chatted and took their ease. Then Coffinhal reopened the proceedings by announcing that the act of accusation was about to be read ; he recommended the accused to follow the reading with the closest attention. The basis of the act was three of the charges put forward by Gaudot's committee : the taking of excessive interest, delay in paying funds into the Treasury, and the addition of excessive quantities of water to tobacco manufactured and sold, thereby defrauding the public, and endangering its health by the sale of an article of bad quality. A general formula was added to the effect that these things had been done for hate of the Republic, and to further the designs of the enemies of the State.

When the Act had been read by the Clerk of the Court, the Public Prosecutor, Liendon, arose to put a question. No one answered, the question not being understood. Coffinhal asked Sanlot to reply, an unfortunate choice from the former's point of view, for Sanlot immediately remarked that he was only an *adjoint* and had had nothing to do with the Farm for ten years. The President thereupon turned to Delaage, a man seventy years old, saying that one who had been so long a member of the Farm must know all about everything. Old Delaage, put about by Coffinhal's manner, stammered that he had not understood the question and that replies to all accusations were to be found in the justificatory memorandum—the only reference to that document to be made throughout the trial.

" Let us see," Coffinhal said, " whether Monsieur de Saint-Amand, who ruled the Farm with a rod of iron, will not find himself in a better position to explain."

But Saint-Amand had not understood the question either. He asked the Public Prosecutor to repeat it. Liendon, however, did not do so, and asked another instead. Had it not been the practice of the Farmers, when arranging a new contract with the Government, to produce a false balance sheet of the old one, so that the deal should be to their advantage? To this Saint-Amand readily and fluently replied that the figures on which the price of each new contract depended were prepared by the Treasury and not in the offices of the Farm, explaining in detail the customary procedure. The aptness of his statement incensed Coffinhal; very few prisoners succeeded in scoring at the expense of the Tribunal. He interrupted the speaker violently, shouting that the Farmers were trying to gain time. He would have them understand that such tactics would not influence the judgment of the Court. When Saint-Amand quietly pointed out that it was difficult to reply to such a question in a single sentence, the President declared that questions must be answered by yes or no. Up to this point some of the Farmers may have retained hopes of a genuine trial; it now became obvious that they were to be condemned without a hearing.

The course of proceedings was suddenly interrupted. During the passage between Coffinhal and Saint-Amand a folded piece of paper had been passed to Liendon, who now rose to read it to the court. It was a decree of the Convention. Three of the accused, the *fermiers-adjoints* Delahante, Sanlot, and the younger Delaage de Bellefraye, were placed *hors de débats*; they were to be immediately returned to their prison in the Hotel des Fermes. The eleventh hour reprieve was due to the good offices of Dobsen, who, having pleaded in vain with Fouquier-Tinville, managed to secure the assistance of Dupin himself. That very morning Dupin had obtained from the Committee of General Security a report emphasising the *adjoints'* lack of responsibility for the policy of the *Ferme*, had hurried to the Convention with it, and obtained without discussion the decree which saved them. Unhappy about the whole affair, Dupin had in all probability welcomed the opportunity of reducing the number of victims.

The three *adjoints* were escorted into an adjoining room. Delahante staggered out of court and sank on a bench, feeling very sick. Only by degrees, with the kind assistance of a friendly gendarme who brought him a glass of water, and offered to pay for wine out of his own pocket, was he roused from a state of collapse. He had not slept a moment during the three previous nights. During the rest of the day, treated by all with the careful kindness accorded to castaways who have been rescued from death by a miracle, he and his two friends were quite incapable of further interest in the fate of their colleagues. With his departure from the Salle de la Liberté, his lively and vivid narrative of the trial naturally comes to an end, and for the rest of the proceedings it is necessary to rely on the official report.

Liendon, having put a few more questions, launched himself into the speech for the prosecution—a diatribe full of sound and fury. In extravagant language he recapitulated the already familiar charges. He gave an eloquent account of the exactions and thefts of the *fermiers généraux*, painting a hideous picture of their sly treachery and greed. " The crimes of these vampires," he declared in his peroration, " cry aloud for vengeance. The wickedness of these beings is indelibly graven on the public mind, for, indeed, all the ills which have afflicted France during recent years must be laid to their charge."

After this forensic masterpiece it was the turn of the counsel for the defence—for even at this juncture in the history of the Tribunal the forms of law were still observed. A few weeks later, by Robespierre's infamous law of Prairial, prisoners were to be deprived of all means of defence. The four defending counsel could, of course, do nothing for the Farmers as a body, but special pleas were made for certain individuals. At this point the name of Lavoisier was brought to the notice of the court. It was all happening exactly as he had feared—the discoverer of the fundamental laws of chemistry had become *fermier général* number 5, a mere member of a gang of financiers accused of defrauding the State. But now the scientist was to reappear for one last time.

The physician Hallé, a member of the Bureau of Arts and Crafts, managed to bring to the notice of the Tribunal the testimonial to Lavoisier's services to France as scientist and administrator which the Bureau had drawn up. The Tribunal refused to take note of it, and Lavoisier's other defensive documents were not put in evidence. But a further plea was made, either by Lavoisier himself or by counsel—a plea of a kind never heard before in the Salle de la Liberté, which must indeed have struck a strange note in that *milieu* of fear, fanaticism and hysteria. Citizen Lavoisier was engaged on certain experiments on transpiration, which promised, when finished, to be of great value to humanity. Would the Tribunal defer sentence for two weeks to allow him to finish this work?

Coffinhal, impatient to make an end, thereupon spoke these famous words : " *La République n'a pas besoin de savants ; il faut que la justice suive son cours.*" [1]

So much for science. It was now the President's task to sum up, and direct the jury in their verdict. While there was no doubt in his mind or in the minds of the jury that the Farmers were guilty, and carts to convey them to the guillotine were actually waiting in the courtyard of the prison, the matter had to be put on a legal footing. Here a difficulty arose. The offences of which the Farmers were accused had been committed before the Revolution, and the Tribunal had no legal power to deal with offences committed before

[1] There is no documentary evidence of Lavoisier's request and Coffinhal's reply, but the story was being told within a few months of the trial. Coffinhal's remark is quite in character and in tune with his behaviour during the rest of the trial. Carlyle's version is as follows :—

" The Spring sends its green leaves and bright weather, bright May, brighter than ever : Death pauses not. Lavoisier, famed Chemist, shall die and not live : Chemist Lavoisier was Farmer-General Lavoisier too, and now ' all the Farmers-General are arrested ' ; all, and shall give an account of their moneys and incomings ; and die for ' putting water in the tobacco ' they sold. Lavoisier begged a fortnight more of life, to finish some experiments : but ' the Republic does not need such ; the axe must do its work.' "

the Revolution. It was necessary to find a form of words which would bring such crimes under its jurisdiction. Coffinhal, in putting his questions to the jury, was more than equal to the occasion. Possibly he may have been prompted by Fouquier-Tinville. Had there, he began, existed a plot against the French people to the advantage of its enemies ?— a general formula in daily use in the Tribunal. He proceeded to define the plot, citing once again the various accusations against the Farmers, and adding one of his own —had they not mixed with tobacco not only water but certain ingredients deterimental to the health of the public ? Had not such depredations, he continued, deprived the nation of money necessary to carry on the war against despots, the money being handed over to the despots themselves. This last was a somewhat wild flight of fancy, but the general effect of the speech was to show that even an ancient crime might weaken the Republic, and so be punishable by the Revolutionary Tribunal.

The jury retired to their room for a brief interval, during which the prisoners were taken back into the Conciergerie. Soon they were brought into court again to hear verdict and sentence. For many of the habitués of the court this was the great moment of the day. Spectators were inclined to lose interest during the most eloquent speeches for the prosecution, and leave the building for strolls in the vicinity, but when the hour of sentence drew near they would once more throng into the court rooms. With keen interest connoisseurs would note how the victims received their sentences of death. Some would affect indifference, and attempt to crack a joke, others would pale and faint, others again grow uselessly violent. Many wept. In the early days of the Tribunal there had been one dramatic suicide, but later the careful preliminary search made it difficult for prisoners to secrete knives or poison about their persons. Altogether it was excellent entertainment for citizens in the strange mood of the Terror, a mood which was to pass as suddenly as it had come, leaving its victims to wonder at themselves, as many of those who lived through the Great

War later wondered to recall their behaviour while the fight was on.

The jurymen, questioned one by one, beginning with the youngest, were unanimous in their verdict : guilty. It only remained to pass sentence. Coffinhal read out the names of the prisoners one by one, declared they had been proved guilty of plotting against France, and condemned them all to death, the sentence to be carried out within twenty-four hours. The law which made such plotting a capital offence, a law framed when the defeat and invasion of France seemed imminent, the mandate for the activities of the Tribunal, was given its daily reading.

" All plotting, all communication with the enemies of France which may result in facilitating an invasion of French territory, or in giving them the possession of cities, fortresses, ports, ships, magazines or arsenals belonging to France, or in adding to their resources with respect to soldiers, money, goods, or munitions, or in assisting in any way the progress of their invasion of French territory, or their camapign against the naval or military forces of France, or in undermining the loyalty of her officers, soldiers, or other citizens, will be punished by death."

All the property of the condemned was declared forfeit to the Republic.

The afternoon being now well advanced, a certain haste crept into the proceedings. The form recording judgment was signed by Coffinhal and his two fellow judges, but not, as the law demanded, by the members of the jury also—a legal omission which would scarcely have occurred had Fouquier-Tinville himself been present in court. One may find further evidence of hurry and carelessness in the official Bulletin of the Tribunal, published on the morrow : a number of names are mis-spelt, Lavoisier being given as Laroisière.

No account remains of how the Farmers received their death sentence. We may surmise that men with a life-long habit of reticence did not provide the best entertainment. They were immediately hurried out of the Palais de Justice into the Conciergerie, where, in a room devoted to that purpose, two of Sanson's assistants cut off their hair at the neck, and bound their hands. Should any of the condemned have required a priest, a priest was at his disposal, for it was a rigid rule of the Tribunal that a list of those about to be executed should be immediately transmitted to the two prison chaplains. Meanwhile the clerks drew up twenty-eight individual orders of discharge from prison, or, more probably, produced documents prepared at ease during the course of the day.

Formalities were soon complete, and the prisoners were taken down to the courtyard of the Palais de Justice, where the *charrettes* awaited them. Here they were joined by Sanson—little, round, fat, dapper Sanson, with carefully combed hair and an elegant coat and a hat in the latest English fashion, who, with seven assistants at his command, had reached a position in which he left dirty work to others. Just before 4 o'clock the little company of elderly business men,[1] closely guarded by soldiers with fixed bayonets, set out on its last journey. It was a warm, still afternoon, and even in the heart of Paris the air must have been full of the sweetness and freshness of early summer.

We must not suppose that there was any great excitement among the populace as the carts rumbled out of the courtyard of the Palais de Justice, on to the Quai de l'Horloge, across the Pont Neuf, and on into the shadow of the narrow Rue de la Monnaie. Such a spectacle could not but arouse interest, could not be entirely staled by daily repetition. There were those who made it their habit to jeer as the dismal daily procession of carts passed by. But a city which had seen within a few months the execution of the King and Queen, of Bailly, of the Dantonists, would be unlikely to display much emotion at the sight of twenty-eight tax-gatherers being driven to the guillotine. The Farmers were personally unknown to the public, the Farm itself, with its

---

[1] The average age of the twenty-eight condemned farmers was fifty-eight, four were over seventy, the oldest being seventy-six, and the youngest thirty-four. Lavoisier was fifty years and eight months old.

legends of colossal fraud and extravagance, was ancient history. No one took the trouble to observe and record the behaviour of the financiers on their way to execution, as the behaviour of more famous victims was observed and recorded. A single incident, however, remains. At one point on the route the carts were held up by the press in a narrow street, and old Papillon d'Auteroche, looking out over the crowd, remarked that he thought little of his heirs. It was a fine piece of Gallic wit, in the best tradition of the tumbril ; it amused Sanson, and so was preserved. But for the most part the Farmers, it seems, remained silent, having, indeed, nothing to say to each other. What were Lavoisier's thoughts as the carts advanced steadily, through streets familiar to him since childhood, towards the Place de la Revolution ? Was there nothing but blind terror of the approaching agony and end ? Alive in every cell, filled with eager interest in every aspect of the material world, and with no belief in any other, he must have shrunk from death with peculiar intensity. Or did he perhaps find consolation and repose in the contemplation of work well done, of truths established which would remain truths whatever else crumbled, a memorial to his name throughout succeeding generations ?

The final scene in the Place de la Revolution was soon over. The bound prisoners were helped from the carts, placed standing with their backs to the scaffold, and dealt with one by one by Sanson and his assistants. A motley crowd watched and commented on the familiar spectacle, moved by strange sadistic impulses as the great knife clattered down, the heads fell, and the blood spurted. There was so much blood. The ingenious death-machine of the Republic rapidly and efficiently performed its work.

Lavoisier was the fourth to die. His father-in-law was executed before him. Heads and bodies were thrown into a common grave in the cemetery des Errancis. In a short time the newsboys could be heard shouting, " *Grand jugement du Tribunal Révolutionnaire qui condamne vingt-huit ci-devant fermiers généraux à la peine de mort.*" In this manner the death of Antoine-Laurent Lavoisier was announced to the world.

At midnight one of the gaolers at the Hotel des Fermes came into the room where Delahante and the other two *adjoints* were confined, and told them that their colleagues were all dead. He assured them that they had died with courage and resignation, and that the crowd in the great square, far from railing at them, had seemed to feel pity. Delahante, with every nerve of his body on edge, found himself crying bitterly.

CHAPTER XVIII

RESTITUTION

When Lavoisier died Robespierre had still eleven weeks to live and the Terror eleven weeks to run. For the time being his name passed almost completely into oblivion, since those of his friends who were left had much else to think about. The day after the execution Lagrange remarked bitterly to Delambre that it took only an instant to remove his head and it might take a hundred years to produce another like it. But less irreplaceable heads were falling fast ; and it was no time to compose *éloges* on the dead, or seek to revenge them.

Marie Lavoisier, having lost father and husband in a single day, retired to the desolate house in the Boulevard de la Madeleine, which now no longer belonged to her. There she remained, harassed by officials carrying out the preliminaries of the decree of confiscation, until June 14th, when the Committee of General Security ordered her arrest. This was apparently on general principles ; no specific charge was made against her, a fact which she forcibly pointed out to the local revolutionary committee. The police officer who filled in the form recording her arrest noted that " *la veuve Lavoisier* " had had no life or opinions her own apart from those of her husband.

It was a dangerous moment to be in prison, for the Terror had risen to its climax. The gaols were full of spies ready to report imaginary conspiracies. Nearly two hundred victims, deprived of all defence, were being sent to the guillotine every week. There were thousands waiting to be tried, and the capacity of the Tribunal and the guillotine to deal with prisoners, for all Fouquier-Tinville's slave driving, was limited, but since no prisoner knew when his turn would come, all lived in daily expectation of the end. The selection of victims lay with the Committee of General Security and Fouquier-Tinville. At first selection had been a serious and considered matter, and only those genuinely suspected of anti-revolutionary principles or activities were chosen for trial, but as time went on one decapitated head became as good as another; the important thing was to supply the guillotine its daily quota of victims. Fouquier-Tinville considered forty a nice round number, well within the scope of his organisation. The random nature of his methods of selection soon became obvious, and the clerks of the Committee of General Security increased their incomes by taking bribes from friends of prisoners in return for the small service of placing particular dossiers at the bottom of the files of prisoners' papers, where they would not strike the eye of the Public Prosecutor. Delahante and his friends, still in gaol and therefore still in danger, tried to comfort themselves with mathematical calculations of their chances of survival, calculations rendered difficult by the existence of one unknown quantity—no one knew how long the Terror would last, though all felt that it must soon end.

Marie Lavoisier escaped. Danger passed with the *coup d'état* of the 9th Thermidor and the execution of Robespierre; she was eventually set free on August 17th. Delahante and the two other *adjoints* were released at about the same time. Marie was completely penniless. Not only had her husband's and father's money and property been confiscated, but a tiny private income of 2,000 francs was filched from her by a new ruling of the Convention, which rendered any gifts made by the Farmers to their relatives since 1775 liable to confiscation. She was saved from destitution by an old servant who gave her a roof, and food to eat.

But the tide of reaction was rising fast. The Terror over, France was seeking scapegoats to expiate its horrors. A few days after the fall of Robespierre, Fouquier-Tinville and most of his fellow officials at the Revolutionary Tribunal were deprived of their posts and committed to prison. Mucius Scaevola Coffinhal, threatened with arrest during the raid by the agents of the Convention on the Hotel de Ville on the 9th Thermidor, escaped and remained some days in hiding. A decree of the Convention placed him *hors la loi*— an outlaw liable to summary execution on capture, only evidence of identification being necessary. Disguised as a ferryman, he took refuge on the Ile des Cygnes on the Seine, where he remained for a week without food or shelter. The magnificent weather of spring and early summer had broken, and the rain fell incessantly. Driven at last to seek food in the city, he was betrayed by a friend from whom he asked help, arrested, and dragged to the Conciergerie, his great body wasted by privation and exposure. He shouted for food. No one could imagine, he said, what tortures he had gone through. Death would be a positive pleasure in comparison. Next day he was taken before a police tribunal, formally identified, and forthwith despatched to the guillotine. As he passed through the streets it was pouring with rain, and citizens poked him in the ribs with their umbrellas, shouting " Ha, Coffinhal, parry that thrust if you can." As he mounted the steps of the scaffold, the mob, with fearful humour, bawled the phrase so often on his lips, " *Coffinhal, Coffinhal, tu n'as pas la parole.*"

Fouquier-Tinville passed to his death with more ceremony and delay. From the moment of his arrest it had been a difficult matter to find a suitable place in which to imprison the most hated man in France. As soon as his presence was known his fellow prisoners would gather to shriek invective, to threaten his life. The very gaolers, not in general over-sensitive men, would shrink away from the Monster's presence. At last a refuge was found for him in the quiet Prison de l'Archevêché, where during the Terror women condemned to death and found pregnant by the doctors had been sent to await labour, and from whence, their labour scarcely over, they had been despatched to execution, for the Tribunal did not allow such prisoners to be forgotten. From prison the Monster wrote frequently to his wife : he was not sleeping very well and his appetite was poor, but she could continue to send him whatever food she thought best. She knew that he had never been pernickety about his food. He had specially liked the spinach and eaten it almost immediately. He would like a little cheese. As for the chicken, it would last two days. Sometimes, rising above domesticities, he would assure her of his love for her, and voice bitter fears for her future and the children's. Let her not be too sorry when he was gone, and try to forget the little quarrels they had sometimes had, which had been due solely to his nerves. He had never really ceased to love her.

At his protracted trial certain facts came out about the condemnation of the *fermiers généraux*. He was asked to explain why the general act of accusation against the *fermiers généraux*, which had led to their rapid removal to the Conciergerie, was dated the 16th Floréal, the very day on which Dupin presented his report to the Convention. The Convention's decree which ordered their trial by the Revolutionary Tribunal had not been officially registered until two days later. Fouquier answered that he had heard privately of the matter from the Committee of General Security, but the Prosecutor showed that he had not been near the Committee during the daytime on the 16th Floréal. He was further questioned about the release of Robespierre's friend, Verdun, an illegality at which he had connived. Finally, the Prosecutor asked why the form recording verdict and sentence bore only one signature, that of Coffinhal, and not the signatures of the jury, to which Fouquier rightly replied that the omission was Coffinhal's fault and not his own. He might have added such negligence outraged him as much as it outraged his judges.

But he had to meet more serious charges than those of a little shuffling with charge sheets, a little carelessness in drawing up acts of condemnation. The affair of the *fermiers généraux* did not long occupy the attention of the court. Game to the last, snarling abuse at his accusers, he was gradually overwhelmed by the weight of evidence piled up against him, evidence which filled France with shame and horror. When at length the whole story was told, and the late Public Prosecutor was in his turn jolted along the route to the scaffold, thousands lined the streets to howl at the man whom they held to be the principal agent of the Terror. He glowered through tired, red-rimmed eyes and cursed them for *canaille*. At the request of the crowd, the executioner held his severed head aloft for some minutes, turning it this way and that for their rapturous contemplation. So died a rather stupid farmer turned bureaucrat who lacked imagination and therefore lacked pity.[1]

The confiscation of the property of Lavoisier and his colleagues continued for some months after the Terror had ceased. His scientific apparatus and collections were assigned to various institutions and museums, and an inventory was made of the furniture of the house in the Rue de la Madeleine. In December, 1794, the destitute widows and children of the executed Farmers petitioned the Convention for a return of their properties; the Convention listened sympathetically, but, fearing to create a precedent, did nothing for the time being. The next summer, however, brought full restitution. First the Convention decreed the restoration of the personal property of the Farmers, and shortly afterwards their landed property also was handed back to their heirs. The proposer of the decree which legalised the latter transaction was none other than Dupin, the man whose activities had led to the Farmers' arrest and execution. His action may have been due to remorse, for the bloody issue of the affair undoubtedly weighed a little on his conscience, but it may, on the other hand, have been simply an attempt at placation, for the widows and children of the Farmers, led by Madame Lavoisier herself, and

---

[1] Thus Carlyle: "Remarkable Fouquier; once but as other Attorneys and Law-beagles, which hunt ravenous on this Earth, a well-known phasis of human nature; and now thou art and remainest the most remarkable Attorney that ever lived and hunted in the Upper Air! For, in the terrestrial Course of Time, there was to be an *Avatar* of Attorneyism; the Heavens had said, Let there be an Incarnation, not divine, of the venatory Attorney-spirit which keeps its eye on the bond only; and lo, this was it; and they have attorneyed it in its turn. Vanish then, thou rat-eyed Incarnation of Attorneyism; who at bottom wert but as other Attorneys, and too hungry sons of Adam!"

supported by a number of prominent lawyers, were hard on his track. If this was his purpose, he failed. The widows and children, undeterred by his efforts on their behalf, published a virulent pamphlet denouncing his conduct in connection with the affair of the Farm, which had an enormous circulation. A deputy presented the pamphlet to the Convention, and another, arraigning Dupin as assassin and thief, demanded his arrest on a variety of charges. He was expelled from the Convention and arrested, but regained his liberty shortly afterwards as a result of the general amnesty in October, 1795. He thereupon retired to the country, where he obtained a minor position under the newly-established state revenue authorities, and survived until 1820.

The vindication of the Farmers seemed complete when a few years after their execution an official statement was issued to the effect that the *Ferme*, far from owing 107 million livres to the State, was actually at the time of its dissolution owed 8 million. Neither calculation need be taken seriously. The real truth seems to be that the Farmers administered an iniquitous and extraordinarily complicated system with reasonable honesty. Their legal profits were large enough to make fraud unnecessary. They were executed as representatives of that system, as wealthy men whose riches the revolutionary leaders coveted, and not for cooking their accounts. Dupin was a catspaw, far less responsible for the death of his late employers than he or Marie Lavoisier imagined. Even if he had entirely refrained from making his accusations, the *fermiers généraux* could never have escaped the Terror. Some charge would have been trumped up, or, had they survived until after the Law of Prairial was passed, Fouquier-Tinville would have sent them to the guillotine without any legal preliminaries. Like many other well-meaning and personally innocent people, they were destroyed by great forces of hatred engendered during long years of oppression and misrule.

Marie Lavoisier thus found herself restored to wealth and position, the widow of a man unjustly condemned. All now agreed in bewailing the tragedy of his undeserved and premature death, which some were beginning to call the greatest crime of the revolution. Robert Kerr expressed the general sentiment when he wrote as follows in a postscript to the third edition of his translation of the " *Traité Élémentaire de Chimie* " :—

" The Philosophical World has now infinitely to deplore the tragical and untimely death of the great LAVOISIER ; who has left a rare example of splendid talents and great wealth, at the same time immersed in numerous and important public employments, which he executed with diligent intelligence, and devoting his princely fortune and vast abilities, to the sedulous cultivation, and most successful improvement, of the sciences. If the sanguinary tyranny of the monster Robespierre had committed only that outrage against eternal Justice, a succeeding age of the most perfect government would scarcely have sufficed to France and to the world to repair the prodigious injury that loss had produced to chemistry, and to all the sciences and economical arts with which it is connected."

In August, 1796, the *Lycée des Arts* arranged a magnificent funeral ceremony in his honour, unfortunately having to dispense with the remains, since these lay inextricably mingled with quite a number of other remains in the Errancis cemetery. Above the entrance to the *Lycée*, hung in great letters the words " *À l'immortel Lavoisier.*" Within, in the great hall, the windows were darkened with black tapestries hung with wreaths and ermine ; twenty funeral lamps, and an immense chandelier decorated with flowers and cypress branches, illuminated the scene. Every pillar supported a shield with inscriptions briefly naming Lavoisier's scientific discoveries. The thousands who attended the funeral ceremony—the men in black, the women in white, but crowned with roses—were rewarded by an excellent entertainment. A curtain which hid one end of the hall was slowly drawn back, to reveal a tomb surmounted by a statue of liberty. A choir of one hundred voices, grouped around the tomb, sang a long and doleful cantata, of which the final verse was as follows :—

" Des utiles talens consacrons les bienfaits.
Ouvrons à Lavoisier les fastes de l'histoire.
Pour consacrer son génie à jamais,
Qu'un monument s'élève à sa mémoire."

Obediently, as the last verse ended, there appeared from aloft, through the agency of a mechanism invisible in the dim light, a large bust of Lavoisier on a pedestal, the head crowned with a wreath. So the *Lycée des Arts* did honour to the memory of the supercilious and clear-headed Lavoisier. It was this body which had tried to crown him with a laurel wreath on the eve of his execution.

The *éloge* was pronounced by Fourcroy, a somewhat embarrassing choice, though Fourcroy was now considered the most distinguished chemist in France. He had been the second most distinguished. In the course of his speech he indirectly excused himself for having made no attempt to save Lavoisier from death.

" Throw yourselves back," he cried, " into those terrible times when the Terror cleft asunder even the closest friends, when barriers separated even the members of the same household, when one little word, one tiny mark of solicitude for the unhappy ones descending the pathway of death before you, were crimes and conspiracies."

Fourcroy had undoubtedly behaved meanly towards Lavoisier on many occasions before the Terror, but we need scarcely blame him for his desertion of his former colleague during those grim months whose atmosphere he so aptly describes. Men are men. The Terror was the Terror. But Marie Lavoisier never forgave him, nor did she forgive Monge, or Hassenfratz, or any of her husband's scientific colleagues who had held office under Robespierre. As in the old days, her house became once more a meeting-place for scientists, but certain men were never invited. We may imagine that her friends were cautious in their references to Lavoisier, for any slur on his memory, indeed any suggestion that he had not achieved perfection in every action of his life, was hotly and bitterly resented.

So wealthy and attractive a widow probably received

frequent offers of marriage from the members of her distinguished but generally impecunious entourage. It is said
that Sir Charles Blagden, the Secretary of the Royal Society,
who spent much of his time in Paris, wished to marry her.
Brougham says that Blagden, " having received a considerable annuity from Cavendish, upon condition that he gave
up his profession and devoted himself to philosophy,
complied with the former portion of this condition, devoting
himself to the hopeless pursuit of a larger income in the
person of Lavoisier's widow, who preferred Count Rumford."
Brougham was, of course, simply repeating here the tittle-
tattle of Royal Society soirées. The man whom Marie
Lavoisier chose as her second husband, Benjamin Thomson,
Count Rumford, was a more interesting character than
the cautious and prosy Blagden. Thomson was a talented
adventurer who settled in Paris in 1801 after a remarkable
career. Though coming of a family which had lived in
the New World for several generations, he had served as a
" loyalist " in the American War of Independence, and the
greater part of his life had been spent in Europe. Having
entered the service of Prince Maximilian of Bavaria, he ran
that potentate's kingdom for a number of years with considerable ability, originality and success, in return for which
the title of Count of the Holy Roman Empire was bestowed
upon him. He chose the name of Rumford because it was
the name of his first wife's home town in New Hampshire ;
she had been a minister's daughter there. His very real
scientific gifts had been for the most part devoted to the field
of applied rather than pure science. He is said to be the
inventor of steam heating ; he studied the cause of smoking
in chimneys, an intolerable nuisance in that epoch, and
established principles of chimney construction which soon
came into general use ; he had, like Lavoisier, carried out
many investigations on guns and gunpowder. His most
famous experiment was one in which he used the heat
generated by friction during the boring of a cannon to boil
water, thereby showing that " work " can be converted
into heat, and incidentally helping to establish the principle

of the conservation of energy. In 1796 he had presented £1,000 to the Royal Society to establish the Rumford Medal, of which he himself was the first recipient ; a few years later, in conjunction with Sir Joseph Banks, he founded the Royal Institution in Albemarle Street. Apart from his scientific achievements, the Count was internationally famous as a philanthropist. He had dealt with the beggars of Bavaria by forcibly housing them in institutions where they were made to work, with what enthusiasm history does not record, for the benefit of the state. His philanthropy, it was noted, did not spring from a large-hearted pity of the poor in their misery. " He spoke of charity," wrote de Candolle, " as a sort of discipline. The poor he considered vagabonds, and he thought that those who dispensed alms should be punished. Enthusiastic about charitable organisations, he acknowledged freely that he had no love for his fellow men."

Marie's marriage to this not quite satisfactory imitation of Lavoisier was a complete failure. He was a handsome man, and at the outset she seems to have been genuinely in love ; she settled a very large sum on him in their marriage contract. He, for his part, was delighted with his capture. During the courtship he described Marie in a letter to his daughter in the following terms :—

" I shall withhold this information from you no longer. I really do think of marrying, though I am not yet absolutely determined on matrimony. I made the acquaintance of this very amiable woman in Paris, who, I believe, would have no objection to having me for a husband, and who in all respects would be a proper match for me. She is a widow, without children, never having had any ; is about my own age, enjoys good health, is very pleasant in society, has a handsome fortune at her own disposal, enjoys a most respectable reputation, keeps a good house, which is frequented by all the first Philosophers and men of eminence in the science and literature of the age, or rather of Paris. And what is more than all the rest, is goodness itself. . . . She is very clever (according to the English signification of the word) ; in short, she is another Lady Palmerston. She has been very handsome in her day, and even now, at forty-six or forty-eight, is not bad-looking ; of a middling size, but rather *embon-*

point than thin. She has a great deal of vivacity, and writes incomparably well."

But the truth is that the Count, though a widower and temporarily enthusiastic about the prospect of regaining the married state, was one of nature's bachelors. He was set in his habits, and liked things in the house to be done his way ; he was highly particular, for example, about proper waiting at table. He preferred to spend his evenings with a book or with one or two intimate friends, who would listen to what he had to say without interrupting. He was inclined to be a little opinionated, and a tendency to chronic dyspepsia made him crotchety, so that he did not shine at the large and animated parties which Marie liked to give two or three times a week. American by upbringing, he liked to state his opinions with due deliberation, and give the other fellow his chance. Marie's distinguished Parisian friends scarcely allowed each other to finish a sentence. Bitter quarrels arose over her delight in frequent and lavish hospitality, with its consequent disruption of domestic tranquillity.

This was the ostensible cause of most of their differences, but probably these had deeper roots. Rumford profoundly disappointed Marie. Doubtless she had hoped, in his company, to recall the eager happinesses of her young womanhood, to enjoy once more the opportunity of devoting her excellent brain to the service of science—had hoped, indeed, that her second marriage would be a replica of her first. But Lavoisiers are uncommon ; the Count was not in that particular class ; he could not guide and inspire her as Antoine had done. He, for his part, may have soon tired of comparisons, spoken or implied, for he was not a modest man. His wife's insistence that she should be called Madame Lavoisier de Rumford (she had a clause to that effect inserted in the marriage contract) pained and angered him. " I regard it as an obligation," she had written, " as a point of religion, not to drop the name of Lavoisier."

" Peace," wrote the Count to his daughter a few months after his wedding, " dwells no longer in my habitation."

His daughter, to whom alone he laid bare his troubles, was soon to hear worse. " I have the misfortune to be married to one of the most imperious, tyrannical, unfeeling women that ever existed " ; " A female dragon " ; " never were there two more distinct beings than this woman (for I cannot call her a lady) before and after marriage "—remarks of this nature grew more and more frequent in his correspondence. As mutual hostility grew, ludicrous and undignified tiffs began to be of common occurrence. The Count, in a letter to his only sympathiser, describes one such scene as follows :

" A large party had been invited, which I neither like nor approve of ; and invited for the sole purpose of vexing me. Our house being in the centre of the garden, which is walled around and has iron gates, I put on my hat, walked down to the porter's lodge, and gave him order to let no one in at his peril. I locked the gates and took away the keys. Madame came down. When the company arrived she talked with them, she on one side, they on the other side of the brick wall. After that, she went and poured boiling water on some of my flowers ! "

It was a cruel retort, for the Count thought a great deal of his flowers. But clearly encounters of this nature, however temporarily exhilarating to the protagonists, were incompatible with civilised existence. After four years of quarrels, the Count and Countess agreed, amicably enough at the end, to see no more of each other. Freedom from a situation grown intolerable brought delight to both : " I find myself relieved from an almost unsupportable burden," wrote Rumford. " Oh happy, thrice happy, am I to be my own man again ! "

Marie, for her part, settled down to live out her remaining years in comfort and busy placidity with her chosen friends and her memories for company. She lived until 1832, being seventy-eight when she died. She remained a great figure in the scientific and intellectual life of Paris, a relic of a bygone age. Her salon was described as the last eighteenth-century salon in France. Ideals of womanhood were changing ; old freedoms were passing, and crochet work and romantic love and boudoirs coming into fashion. But she had lived in the great world on an equality with men ; she had worked with Lavoisier and Lavoisier's friends as one of themselves, and as hard and well as any of them. To the end of her days she treated her male friends with a free and easy camaraderie which must have shocked the rising generation. For the pleasure of her circle she was accustomed to comment on contemporary life with wit and intelligence, but as old age closed in on her, the changing, scurrying scene of the nineteenth century must have grown dim and meaningless compared with her memories of great strenuous days at the Arsenal, the days of her real life, so long past, when she and her husband had shared the joy of labour and achievement, and every hour had been filled with high purpose and eager effort.

CHAPTER XIX

DEATH OF TWO PHILOSOPHERS

THE place eventually chosen by the Priestleys as their home in America was Northumberland, a small township in Pennsylvania, about 130 miles inland from Philadelphia. Their sons had settled in the neighbourhood. They found the port of disembarkation, New York, delightful, their reception being all that could be desired ; Priestley was very much struck by the prosperous appearance of the citizens, and the absence of beggars. But Philadelphia, then the capital, was far less attractive ; it was grossly expensive by English standards, the blinding heat of its summer made it unhealthy, and it was full of smug and wealthy Quakers who did not meet with the approval of the emigrants. Mrs. Priestley, a woman of quick aversions, could not stand them and their city. The Priestleys therefore decided, in spite of certain offers and opportunities of employment in Philadelphia, to make their home in a cheaper and healthier place.

Northumberland at that date was the back of beyond, for civilisation in America was as yet scarcely more than coastal. It took the Priestleys five strenuous and exhausting days to cover the short distance which separated it from the capital. The inns, to those used to English amenities, were frightful. But when at last the travellers reached the little township, set in a lake-studded woodland landscape, they were well-pleased with the place. Mrs. Priestley, feeling that here at last they were out of reach of mobs, was perhaps the more enthusiastic of the two. Her husband liked the place well, but he anticipated difficulties in obtaining books and scientific instruments and observed a certain lack of congenial society. But after a few weeks' stay he was so well satisfied that he refused, though with some hesitation, the offer of the post of Professor of Chemistry in the University of Pennsylvania, which attracted less because it involved a return to scientific pursuits, than because it involved residence in Philadelphia and the opportunity of founding a Unitarian congregation. Some months later, in a letter to a friend in England, he referred to his refusal of the post in the following terms :

" As to the chemical lectureship, I am now convinced I could not have acquitted myself in it to proper advantage. I had no difficulty in giving a general course of chemistry at Hackney, lecturing only once a week ; but to give a lecture every day for four months, and to enter so particularly into the subject, as a course of lectures in a medical university requires, I was not prepared for ; and my engagements there would not, at my time of life, have permitted me to make the necessary preparation for it, if I could have done it at all. For, though I have made discoveries in some branches of chemistry, I never gave much attention to the common routine of it, and know but little of the common processes. On the whole, I am satisfied that I can never appear at Philadelphia as a Unitarian preacher, if I have anything else to attend to ; and to this object I am determined to devote my time, and all my resources, whenever I get into a settled way of living."

As Priestley grew old, his thoughts centred more and more on religion, and his strangely irrelevant pastime of scientific research lost some of its interest for him. " No discovery in philosophy," he wrote in the preface to his last scientific pamphlet, " bears any proportion in real value to that of *bringing life and immortality to light*, which is completely effected in the gospels, and nowhere else. None of our experiments, or observations of the course of nature, could have given us the least glimpse of this. Without a view to our future situation, all our pursuits appear to me to have little in them that is interesting, especially in the decline of life, and the near prospect of death, which, if it put a period to our existence, involves everything in everlasting darkness, leaving us uncertain whether even the world itself and the whole race of man, as well as all other animals, may not be doomed to destruction." Or, again, " My philosophical friends must excuse if, without neglecting natural science, I give a decided preference to theological studies, and here, as in Europe, I give the greatest part of my time to them. They are unquestionably of unspeakably more importance to men, as beings destined for immortality, and I apply myself with so great satisfaction to the study of nature, not so much on account of the advantage we derive from it at present, though this is very considerable, as from its being a delightful field of speculation barely opening to us here, to be resumed with greater advantage in a future state."

During their first year in Northumberland the Priestleys lived uncomfortably in their son Harry's house. The Doctor had rather more time than he liked on his hands, and, as a consequence, found himself a little home-sick, though he liked the climate and felt reasonably strong. His chief lack was friends. His front teeth began to fall out, a loss which he feared would not improve his pulpit manner, and he had to give up his wig, there being no one in the township capable of dressing it. He received one invitation to preach in the Presbyterian chapel in the town, but this was not repeated, and he had to content himself with reading a sermon to his own household on Sundays. " My great consolation," he wrote to his friend Lindsay in a despondent moment, " is in the consideration of an over-ruling Providence, which has fixed me here, and I hope for some good purpose, and whether more or less pleasing to myself, is of no great consequence, considering the short time I have to live."

Soon, however, the building of a house provided him with a new interest in life. He bought, for £100, 11 acres of ground from which there was a delightful view over the Susquehanna river and the township, and on this site the building was begun, no simple undertaking in so remote an outpost, where the necessary skilled labour was lacking. Slowly, however, the house progressed. The steady rise in the cost of living frightened him, dependent as he was on a fixed income provided by friends in England, but he hoped

PRIESTLEY'S HOUSE IN NORTHUMBERLAND, PENNSYLVANIA.

[To face p. 208.

that he and his sons would soon be able to supply themselves with the necessities of life by their own labours. His youngest son, Harry, was growing into an extremely able and energetic farmer. " He is the wonder of the place," his father wrote, " and, I hope, will not fail to do well." He himself occasionally assisted the young men in the work of their farms. " Even I," he wrote, " sometimes take my axe or my mattock and work, as long as I can, along with them."

During the second winter of Priestley's residence in America, Harry died suddenly. The young man had been accustomed to work hard in all weathers, and he contracted a chill of which the local doctor and his parents at first made light, but which progressed rapidly to a fatal end. Priestley was staggered by the blow, for Harry was his favourite son, the only one of his sons, he had thought, whose character at all resembled his own. With obvious difficulty he tried to resign himself to the curious arrangements of Providence, and to find consolation in the hope that he would soon meet his son again. At the same time, his natural common sense, never quite obscured by religious fatalism, led him to blame the doctor for making a tardy diagnosis.

That same year Priestley and his wife were saddened by quarrels which took place between them and William, the second son, to which no reference is made in the Doctor's correspondence, for he had the middle-class pride which keeps such things a family secret. He himself was able to shake off depression in the excitement of delivering a series of sermons on the " Evidences of Christianity " in Phila-delphia, which were attended by crowded congregations, the Vice-President, Adams, being among his regular auditors. He was honoured by occasional invitations to the house of George Washington. He had great hopes of founding a society of Unitarians in Philadelphia, and wrote to friends in England to be on the look-out for a suitable minister. He sent two scientific contributions to the " Transactions " of the Philosophic Society of Philadelphia. But when, after a period of happy activity, he returned to Northumberland, he suffered an irreparable loss in the death of his wife, his companion for thirty-four years. She had liked living in America, for the inconveniences of frontier life had not daunted so competent a housewife. All that year she had been busy with the planning of the new house, but died of an obscure fever (probably enteric) before it was ready. " I never stood in more need of friendship than I do now," he wrote to Lindsay. " She, as well as myself," he says in the same letter, " was much affected by the death of Harry. Though it is now near nine months since he died, he has never been long out of my thoughts ; but this will affect me much more." Mrs. Priestley had indeed supplied him with more than companionship ; she had excelled him in common sense, and he had learned to rely on her wisdom in practical affairs. The consolations of religion were once more summoned to his aid, he returned after an interval to his varied intellectual activities, but during the declining years of his life it is often difficult to see him otherwise than as a lonely and rather foolish old man.

He became immersed in that strange occupation which before the days of bridge and crossword puzzles so often captured the English mind—the study and interpretation of the prophetic books of the Bible. His letters to his friends now begin to abound in obscure references to the Woman in the Wilderness, the Restoration of the Jews, the Personal Reappearance of Jesus, the Millennium. He read the newspapers with the book of Daniel open before him. The fall of the papal power seemed a highly significant incident. When news arrived of Napoleon's Egyptian expedition, he wrote that " something favourable is promised to Egypt in the *latter days*, which I think are at hand, but I do not presume to say that Buonaparte is the deliverer there promised them." Though he had little doubt that " the great prophecies relating to the permanent and happy state of the world, were in the way of fulfilment " he feared that " the preceding time of calamity might be of long continuance." Of all the minor prophets, he found Zechariah the most difficult and obscure. When certain of his English friends gently protested at the extravagance of his prophetic deductions, Priestley, in a rare mood of self-criticism, became apologetic :

" I find a great disadvantage," he wrote, " in being alone, having no person whatever to confer with on any subject of this kind . . . and my solitary speculations may lead me astray, farther than I can be aware of myself ; and for this there is not perhaps any remedy, and therefore my friends must bear with me. They should, however, consider that they are not infallible, any more than myself ; and to many of us the time is not far distant when we shall see more clearly than we do at present."

Later his mind turned to speculations on the future state. He wrote to Belsham, who had received with a certain scepticism some of his interpretations of Daniel, that he hoped to hear Daniel himself giving the critic a gentle reproof for his obduracy.

" But considering," he added, " the great number that are to be raised, I sometimes think that our chance of having any interview with persons who have lived in a period and a country very remote from us, cannot be great, and that we shall have something else to do than converse with one another."

Hopes of seeing a Unitarian Society founded on American soil were not fulfilled. A second series of addresses, on the " Evidences of Christianity," delivered in Philadelphia the year after his wife's death, turned out a failure ; towards the end he found himself preaching to empty benches. The simple wearing off of novelty, possibly assisted by the increasing toothlessness of the lecturer, may be held to blame. He managed to collect a few faithful followers, and a beginning was made towards the foundation of a Society, but in 1796 several of the keenest Unitarians died of yellow fever, and the whole project was abandoned. He preached every Sunday in his own house in Northumberland, but here also he made little headway, for the majority of his neighbours, of Scotch and Northern Irish origin, were staunch Presbyterians. So at last we find him falling back on the metaphors which solace unsuccessful missionary endeavour : seed had been sown ; a little leaven might leaven the whole mass.

During his years in America Priestley did not meddle to

any considerable extent with politics on either side of the Atlantic. He was called a " hoary old traitor " by Cobbett on the somewhat slender ground that a letter addressed to him from a friend in Paris, and intercepted, contained phrases derogatory to England. Actually his patriotism was so strong that to the end he never became an American citizen ; no exile, no persecution, could weaken the links which bound so insular an Englishman to his home. But his interest in English affairs, though intense, was passive. In America his reputation as a political firebrand made him suspect, but on the whole he gave the authorities little cause for alarm. A book published in 1798, entitled " Letters to the Inhabitants of Northumberland," which included a statement of his political and religious principles, caused offence, and brought abuse on his head from many quarters, but the authorities took no action. In the same year he was in some danger of deportation as an undesirable alien. War between France and America seemed imminent ; feeling in America was running high, the newspapers, Priestley noted, being filled with abuse of France " more violent and coarse than in any English newspaper whatever." He himself was a known French sympathiser ; he was indeed actually a French citizen. Certain politicians were anxious that the new " Aliens Act," a measure passed under threat of war, should be first tried out on Joseph Priestley. But President Adams himself, who had met and liked Priestley in Philadelphia, intervened. " I do not think it wise," he wrote, " to execute the alien law against poor Priestley at present. He is weak as water, as unstable as Reuben or the wind. His influence is not an atom in the world." So the old man remained unmolested. Actually, the " Aliens Act " was never enforced against anyone, for in such matters the eighteenth century was much more civilised than the twentieth.

At one period Priestley played with the idea of returning to Europe to take up residence in France. He happened to possess a little money in the French Funds, probably of nominal value, which he imagined might provide an income were he living in France ; further, Talleyrand, whom he must have met in Philadelphia in 1794, had promised to give him what help he could, should he decide to take practical advantage of his French citizenship. " The last thing M. Talleyrand said to me," wrote Priestley, " was that he expected to see me in France." Fortunately Priestley did not find himself in the position of having to rely on Talleyrand's casual promise of patronage. The projected journey was vetoed by his family, it being obvious that the old man would not survive another uprooting.

In Northumberland there was not a single person of education on whom Priestley could sharpen his wits ; apart from infrequent letters from English friends, he was entirely deprived of friendly, common-sense criticism, so essential to his creative but undisciplined mind. Out of contact with scientific research, he continued to make investigations which filled him with complete satisfaction, but were considerably less valuable than he supposed. His fine discoveries had been incorporated into the body of scientific knowledge—we have seen how much Lavoisier owed to him—but now advancing research had left him far behind. In 1798 he wrote to Lindsay that he had been very busy in his laboratory, having " made as many original experiments this summer as I almost ever did in the same time." Again, in 1800 : " I send along with this an account of a course of experiments of as much importance as almost any that I have ever made . . . I was never more busy or more successful in this way, when I was in England ; and I am very thankful to a kind Providence for the means and the leisure for these pursuits, which, next to theological studies, interest me most. Indeed, there is a natural alliance between them, as there must be between the word and the works of God." He still studied problems which chemists in general regarded as long since solved—the composition of water, the nature of combustion, the question of the identity of " phlogiston " and " inflammable air." His last scientific paper, entitled " The Doctrine of Phlogiston established, and that of the Composition of Water refuted," was almost completely ignored by the scientific world, for such a position was no longer worth the compliment of attack. The new chemistry was being taught in all the schools. It was as though a physicist, having won fame by valuable observations on the atom in 1900, should in 1933 persist in publishing refutations of the Quantum Theory. But Priestley was still capable of original discovery, for in 1799 he isolated the gas now known as carbon monoxide, by passing steam over glowing charcoal.

We need not, indeed, paint a very gloomy picture of Priestley's declining years. He lived agreeably with his eldest son, now a middle-aged man with a growing family of his own, in the new house at Northumberland. He had always been fond of children. He had plenty to occupy his time : gardening, tinkering in the laboratory, writing works of theology. Whatever else might fail him, theology remained. His output of works on theological subjects did not diminish with advancing years. In Northumberland he continued his " History of the Church "; he wrote pamphlets with such titles as " Jesus and Socrates Compared " ; " A Comparison of the Institution of Moses with those of the Hindoos and other Ancient Nations, with Remarks on M. Dupin's ' Origin of all Religions ' "; " On the Allegorizing Talents of M. Boulanger "; "The Laws and Institutions of Moses Methodized and an Address to the Jews on the present state of the World, and the Prophecies relating to it " ; "An Inquiry into the Knowledge of the Ancient Hebrews concerning a Future State", " The Doctrines of Heathen Philosophy, compared to those of Revelation"; "A Letter to an Anti-pædobaptist." His religious pamphlets were written to instruct and not for profit. " I do not think," he wrote, " I can employ my time, or any money I can spare, to better purpose than in printing what I have prepared for public use."

During the last years of his life Priestley was flattered by the friendship of that great and cultured gentleman, Thomas Jefferson, who became President of the Republic in 1801. Jefferson had a taste for science, and must have been familiar with Priestley's discoveries. Priestley wrote frequently to the President, sent him copies of his pamphlets, and obtained permission to dedicate to him his Church History. In return Jefferson wrote long letters in the most dignified English, filled with kindly and tactful references to Priestley's character and career, copies of which the recipient proudly sent to his friends in England. " Accept my affectionate salutations, and assurance of great esteem and respect "—it was gratifying in the highest degree to be so addressed by the head of the State. Jefferson apologised on behalf of America for anything that might have been lacking in his reception. He discussed at considerable length theological questions raised by Priestley in his works—in those far off days in America even the President had leisure and inclination for intellectual pursuits. But though Jefferson took Priestley with reasonable seriousness as a political and religious thinker, his main motives in corresponding with him seem to have been kindness and good manners. He wished to show that the New World could surpass the Old in courtesy to a distinguished man of science. His letters meant a great deal to the old man, who for almost the first time in his life found himself on good terms with authority.

With the dawn of the new century Priestley, now approaching his seventieth year, began to fail in health. During a visit to Philadelphia he was attacked by a complaint which the doctors called " bilious fever with pleurisy," from which his recovery was incomplete. He would certainly have died, he wrote, if Dr. Rush had not bled him seven times. From that time he began to go slowly down hill. He suffered from constant indigestion, and took to living on slops ; he was troubled with deafness and bought an ear trumpet. As a result of increasing disabilities, work in the garden and laboratory had to be largely abandoned, more time being spent in reading and writing, so that there was no decrease in his literary output. Towards the end of 1803 it became obvious, both to Priestley and his family, that death was near. His feet began to swell, his stomach troubles became more distressing, his bodily weakness more pronounced. He could no longer conduct service in his house on Sundays. Unwillingly, he allowed his son to perform little domestic offices for him, such as laying his fire and helping him to bed. He took the precaution of re-writing every day in long-hand what he had written in short-hand the day before.

On January 31st his little granddaughter came to ask him for a five-cent piece, long promised. He gave her the money, but suddenly found himself unable to speak to her. Later he recovered his speech, seemed to rally, and chatted cheerfully with callers. This lasted some days. He read a little, corrected proofs, gave instructions about the printing of his manuscripts, and in conversation with his son dwelt on " the peculiarly happy situation in which it had pleased the Divine Being to place him in life." He was grateful, he said, to be allowed to die quietly in his family, without pain, with every convenience and comfort he could wish for.

On Sunday evening he felt himself sinking. When the children came to his room to say goodnight, he said : " I am going to sleep as well as you ; for death is only a good long sleep in the grave, and we shall meet again." The next morning he was very weak, but he managed to dictate clearly certain alterations which he wished to be made to one of his pamphlets. When his son read over to him what had been dictated, he said, " That is right. I have now done." After which he lingered for about half an hour, passing insensibly from weakness and coma into death.

*　　*　　*　　*　　*

The passage of time seemed to have little effect on the Honourable Henry Cavendish. To his acquaintances in the Royal Society—he had no others—it seemed that thirty years had brought no change. They had never known him young. Revolutions might come and pass, a new era dawn, a great conqueror shake the foundations of Europe, but Cavendish had no concern in such matters. In 1808, as in 1778, at the age of seventy-seven as at forty-seven, he continued to drive in the seclusion of his carriage from Clapham to Somerset House, from Somerset House to Sir Joseph Banks' house in Soho Square, to join timidly in the talk provided it was strictly scientific, to fly precipitately from undesired acquaintanceships. He seemed a permanent feature at the meetings of the Royal Society, like the portrait of Newton, but a feature best studied by newly-elected members from a distance. To his neighbours in Clapham, he was now more than a wizard ; he was an immortal wizard. But though he had all his life thrust from him the experiences and adventures of common humanity, he had to die like other men. One evening in March, 1810, he came home from a meeting of the Royal Society and went silently to bed. The next morning he did not get up, and his servant noticed blood on his under-linen, but dared not ask his master what ailed him. Cavendish remained in bed, with little appearance of suffering, for two days, seeing no one except his servant ; on the third he suddenly summoned the man and told him he was going to die. He gave precise orders : when he was dead, but not on any account before, the man was to go to Lord George Cavendish and tell him of the event. Then he told the man to go away and not return for some hours, since he had something particular to think about and did not wish to be disturbed by anyone. When the servant, anxious and alarmed, crept quietly into the room before the specified time, Cavendish snarled at him to go away. When next he summoned up courage to return he found his master dead.

BIBLIOGRAPHY

LAVOISIER

E. Grimaux. " Lavoisier." Paris. 1888.
A very complete and painstaking piece of work, the chief source of information about Lavoisier's private life.

M. Berthelot : " La Révolution Chimique, Lavoisier." Paris. 1890.
A book mainly devoted to the scientific side of Lavoisier's career ; it contains his laboratory registers.

J. A. Cochrane : " Lavoisier." London. 1931.
The only complete biography of Lavoisier in English.

Shorter accounts of Lavoisier's career, or of certain aspects of his career, are to be found in the following :—

Henry, Lord Brougham. " Lives of Men of Letters and Science who flourished in the time of George III." Vol. II. London. 1845.
Brougham's account of Lavoisier is extremely inaccurate and unsympathetic. His chapters on Black, Priestley, and Cavendish also contain extended references to Lavoisier in the same strain.

T. E. Thorpe. " Essays on Historical Chemistry." 1893. No. V. " Antoine Laurent Lavoisier," based on Grimaux, and No. VI., " Priestley, Cavendish, Lavoisier, and *La Révolution Chimique*," a reply to Berthelot's claim that Lavoisier was the virtual discoverer of oxygen and of the chemical composition of water.

Numerous shorter accounts of Lavoisier and his work are to be found in various encyclopedias, histories of chemistry and science, and scattered through the scientific journals of the last hundred years.

The following works also contain information about Lavoisier and his wife :—

J. B. DELAMBRE and P. F. A. MÉCHAIN. " Base du Système Métrique," 1806.

A. DELAHANTE. " Une famille de Finance au XVIIIme Siècle." Paris. 1881.

Contains E. M. Delahante's account of the arrest and trial of the Farmers General.

GRAHAM LUSK. " Nutrition." Clio Medica History of Medicine Series. New York. 1933.

J. B. BIOT. " Essai sur l'histoire générale des Sciences pendant la Révolution." Paris. 1803.

G. POUCHET. " Les Sciences pendant la Terreur." Paris. 1896.

G. ELLIS. " Count Rumford." Two vols. Boston. 1870.

The second volume gives an account of the Rumford-Lavoisier marriage, and part of Guizot's memoir of Countess Rumford (from " Mémoires pour servir à l'Histoire de mon Temps." Paris. 1858) is included.

WORKS OF LAVOISIER. " *Les Œuvres de Lavoisier, publiées par les soins du Ministre de l'Instruction Publique.*" 6 vols.

These volumes, published at intervals during the latter half of the nineteenth century, contain Lavoisier's two main works—the " Opuscules Physiques et Chimiques," and the " Traité Élémentaire de Chimie " ; his scientific papers ; reports to the Academy, etc. ; and a number of letters of an official nature, such as his correspondence with Lakanal about the Academy of Science in 1792–3.

ROBERT KERR. "Elements of Chemistry in a New Systematic Order containing all the Modern Discoveries, by Mr. Lavoisier, Member of the Academies and Societies of Paris, London, Orleans, Bologna, Basel, Philadelphia, Haarlem, Manchester, etc., etc." 2 vols. First Edition. Edinburgh. 1793.

A most elegant translation.

PRIESTLEY

R. M. Caven. " Joseph Priestley." Booklet published by the Institute of Great Britain and Ireland. London. 1933.

Dictionary of National Biography. Art. " Joseph Priestley."

Anne Holt. " Joseph Priestley." Oxford. 1931.

A biography which stresses the theological aspects of Priestley's career.

Joseph Rutt. " The Theological and Miscellaneous Works of Joseph Priestley, LL.D., F.R.S., etc., with notes by J. T. Rutt." Vol. 1. Parts 1 and 2. London. 1817–1832.

Vol. 1. Parts 1 and 2 contain a great deal of Priestley's non-scientific correspondence, his own memoirs, and an account by his son of his last days and death.

T. E. Thorpe. " Joseph Priestley." English Men of Science Series. London. 1906.

Thorpe's " Essays on Historical Chemistry " (1893) contains a chapter on Priestley.

CAVENDISH

Dictionary of National Biography. Art. " Hon. Henry Cavendish."

G. Wilson. " The Life of the Honourable Henry Cavendish, including Abstracts of his more important Scientific Papers." London. 1851.

Contains almost all the scanty information available about Cavendish's private life. Accounts of Cavendish, in monographs, histories of chemistry, etc., add nothing to Wilson's work, on which, indeed, they are all based.

HISTORICAL

It does not seem necessary to give a list of the various historical works which provided material for the preparation of this book. Special acknowledgement may, however, be made of a few which proved exceptionally useful. Such were R. P. Perken's " France under Louis XV," H. Belloc's, H. M. Steven's and J. M. Whetham's various books on the French Revolution, two books by G. Lenotre, " La Guillotine " and " Le Tribunal Révolutionnaire," and Anatole France's fine romance of the terror, " Les Dieux ont soif."

INDEX

Academy of Science, 10–12, 23, 24, 93, 145–154
Adams, John, 209, 212
Agriculture, Lavoisier and, 91–93
Air, composition of, 68–70
Alaterre, Julien, 13
Alexander, Mr., 37
Animal heat, Lavoisier's experiments on, 103–113
Animal magnetism, 95–101
Aristotle, 43, 44, 46, 103
Arnold, Thomas, 122
Arsenal, 22, 88
Artois, Comte d', 124
Ashworth, Dr. Caleb, 36
Augey de Villers, 179

Bailly, Jean Sylvain, 96, 116, 117, 119, 125, 159
Banks, Sir Joseph, 75, 217
Baudon, 14, 163
Baumé, 172
Beauharnais, Vicomte de, 115
Belloc, Hilaire, 13
Belsham, Thomas, 211
Bergman, Olaf, 84
Berigard of Pisa, 45
Black, Joseph, 48, 49, 105, 157
Blagden, Sir Charles, 82–85, 201
Blizard, 158
Borda, 165, 166
Boulton, Matthew, 128
Bourdon, 160
Boyle, Robert, 46, 47, 86
Brougham, Lord, 49 n, 67, 77, 127, 201
Brunswick, Duke of, 143
Buckle, Henry Thomas, 26
Bucquet, 69
Buffon, 11
Burgundy, Duke of, 16
Burke, Edmund, 131, 133

Cadet, 66 n, 172
Canton, 52
Carlyle, Thomas, 187 n, 197 n

Cavendish, Lady Anne, 71
Cavendish, Lord George, 217
Cavendish, Hon. Henry, ancestry and birth, 71 ; education, 72 ; travels in France, 72 ; wealth and eccentricities, 73–76 ; life at Clapham, 73, 76, 77 ; his discoveries, 76, 77 ; on hydrogen, 76, 79 ; on composition of water, 80–85 ; and Priestley, 138, 139 ; death of, 217
Cavendish, Sir John, 71
Cellier, 178
Charcot, 101
Chemistry, history of, 42 et seq. ; state of, in 1772, 48
Chenier, André, 119
Chesterton, G. K., 55
Clark, Mr., 36
Cobbett, William, 212
Coffinhal, Pierre-André, 182–189, 195
Cole, William, 5
College Mazarin, 2–4
Combustion, 49, 51
Condé, Prince de, 158
Conservatoire des Arts et Métiers, 88
Cook, Captain James, 56

d'Alembert, 105
d'Amerval, 19
Damiens, 28
Danton, 143, 171
Darwin, Erasmus, 128
Daventry Academy, 36
David, 20, 21, 152
Delaage, 184
Delaage de Bellefraye, 185
Delahante, Etienne, 163, 175, 177, 178, 180–186, 192, 194
Delambre, 123, 146–149, 166, 193
Democritus, 43
Dephlogisticated air, 66 et seq.
Descartes, 95
Deslon, 97–99, 159
Deville, 164

223

Universitas BIBLIOTHECA Ottaviensis